Treasures of Tutankhamun
is the most spectacular exhibition the British
Museum has held since the first showing of the
Elgin marbles.

On display at the British Museum for six months
from April 1972, the 50 priceless items – never
before seen in this country – are covered by a
British Government estimate-indemnity for
several million pounds. They were flown from
Egypt to the United Kingdom by the R.A.F.
and a series of specially chartered jet flights
under a strict and very elaborate arrangement of
security precautions.

The treasure has been lent by the Arab
republic of Egypt to mark the 50th Anniversary
of the discovery of Tutankhamun's tomb in
the Valley of the Kings by archaeologists
Howard Carter and Lord Carnarvon.

"A discovery which exceeds our wildest dreams"

Otto Neubert, seafaring traveller, archaeologist, scholar and popular author, was present at the opening of Tutankhamun's tomb.

The teenage monarch and his treasure – his several tons-worth of scarab-encrusted coffin, his chariots, weapons, lavish folding beds, ostrich-feather fans, ivory toys, even wine, all ablaze with electron and pearls and a green stone and orange gold unknown today – had lain dormant for nearly 4,000 years in a dust-stuffed catacomb of demotic curses and long-dead Egyptians. Son of a concubine, seeded by the visionary husband of the lovely Queen Nefertiti, he was king of an elitist society possessed with overcoming the darkness of both life and death. He ruled in the land of the architect Imhotep's great Pyramids, which until the Eiffel Tower were the tallest structures the world had ever seen, and whose final passageways and entrances were a secret which died with the abandoned and hyena-chewed slaves who made them. Within a necropolis of Tutankhamun's time lingered the mummified corpses of families, volunteer sacrifices, dwarfs, cats and crocodiles, stillborn foetuses, and very young girls whose dead bodies were at the mercy of abusive embalmers before being immortalised in *Mûm*, and whose payments for the privilege of this process were made from immoral earnings.

To bring Tutankhamun to life for modern readers, the author tells the whole incredible story of ancient Egypt and its magical cities of Thebes, Luxor and Memphis, and includes lively, playful quotes from the temperamental historian Herodotus. His unique book, written, he has said, "for the common man who feels a need to review his life", has already been translated into 16 languages.

*Published by Mayflower Books
simultaneously with this volume*

NEFERTITI by Nicole Vidal

Tutankhamun
and the Valley of the Kings

Otto Neubert

Mayflower

Granada Publishing Limited
Published in 1972 by Mayflower Books Ltd
4 Upper James Street, London W1R 4BP
Reprinted 1972

First published in Great Britain by
John Hale Ltd 1957
Copyright © Otto Neubert 1954
Translation copyright © John Hale Ltd 1957
Made and printed in Great Britain by
C. Nicholls & Company Ltd
The Philips Park Press, Manchester
Set in Monotype Times

This book is sold subject to the condition that it shall
not, by way of trade or otherwise, be lent, re-sold, hired
out or otherwise circulated without the publisher's prior
consent in any form of binding or cover other than that
in which it is published and without a similar condition
including this condition being imposed on the
subsequent purchaser.
This book is published at a net price and is supplied
subject to the Publishers Association Standard
Conditions of Sale registered under the Restrictive
Trade Practices Act, 1956.

To All Friends of
World Peace
I Dedicate This Book
        O.N.

A word about the spelling: Transliterations of Egyptian sounds vary not only between one country and another but within individual languages. Although the least popular English spelling of *Tutankhamun* is here used, and *Amun* has been accepted as the regular spelling of the word for "Egypt", *Akhenaton* is popularly known as *Akhenaten*, literally "Yech-en-yeten" meaning "Spirit of the Sun", and the cult of *Aton* as *Aten*.

A pharaoh represented as the god Amun. In his right hand a sword and in his left the staff, *was*, symbol of royal origin. On his head a crown with conventional feathers as an attribute of divine power. Behind him three tributary nations, symbolically fettered.

Contents

1 Egypt is the Nile   11
2 Seven Thousand Years Ago   16
3 Pyramids and Mummies   40
4 Sanctuaries, Thieves and Harem Nights   79
5 Slave, Work or Die!   103
6 Gods, Idols, Demons   128
7 Nefertiti   151
8 The Discovery of Tutankhamun's Tomb   175
9 Tutankhamun's Curse   201
10 The God Sails to the Kingdom of Death   221

Chapter 1

EGYPT IS THE NILE

In the uplands of Uganda in Central Africa, south of the Equator, lies Lake Victoria, a great saucer which collects the equatorial rains. From this lake a river flows northwards. Here is the cradle of the Nile.

The river traverses Lake Kioga and Lake Albert, lying nearly two thousand feet above sea level. But "it knows no peace by day or night" and in its course receives many tributaries and affluents from African mountain regions and passes through wide areas of desert and marsh which abound, and always have abounded, in wild life of every kind.

Reinforced by further tributaries, the river becomes the "White Nile". It flows for hundreds of miles through the Sudan where antelopes, zebras and giraffes, leopards and lions, elephants and buffaloes come down to drink; the insatiable crocodile stalks the dozing cormorant and vulture and the hippopotamus wallows in its mud. The hippopotamus actually gets its German name from the Nile.

From the Abyssinian Alps and Lake Tana, another river, the Blue Nile, fed by many tributaries, comes to join it. But when "Blue" and "White" meet it ceases to be either. It is simply "The Nile".

Many of us have never known, or have forgotten, that the Nile is the second largest river in the world. Its course of four thousand miles is five times as long as the Rhine. A freak of nature has decreed that when it reaches Nubia, and has still seventeen hundred miles to go to reach the Mediterranean, it has nothing but deserts ahead of it; the Nubian desert, the Libyan desert and the Sahara.

The scene has never changed, yet the Nile is a beautiful river. All in all, it is the father and mother of the land we call Egypt. It is barely a hundred years since modern man discovered the source of the Nile and had no real idea of what had happened to the peoples inhabiting its narrow valley for over seven thousand years.

The average width of the river is only five hundred yards.

On both sides is fertile land, in many places but a few miles wide. Here and there the desert comes to the water's edge on one side or the other and the river often flows at the foot of high cliffs.

North of Cairo the picture changes, as the river enters the Nile delta, a most extensive region of high fertility. In areas flooded by the Nile plant life positively luxuriates as if some magician were at work. Here wheat, cotton, sugar cane, oranges and olives flourish, while a few miles away there is nothing but the burning sand of the desert.

Of Egypt's total area of 387,500 square miles only 13,560, *i.e.* 3·5 per cent, are productive. All the rest are desert.

Egypt has no forests. Rain is almost unknown. A poor country, one would think, but Mother Nature is resourceful and "imports" rain to fertilize the soil. Her method is simple.

At the sources of the Nile in Africa's high plateaux the rainy season is from June to September. Torrents of tropical rain descend, often accompanied by tremendous storms and tornadoes. The forests are then smitten as if by some gigantic hand and the green treetops heave as wildly as the waves in a hurricane. A colossal volume of water falls from the clouds. For thousands of years the resulting flood waters have brought down masses of mud which have gradually formed the Egyptian valleys and produced fertile land.

In the development of Egyptian cultures the Nile has always played the part of schoolmaster. The necessity of regulating the Nile flow made a knowledge of surveying essential. The ancient Egyptians calculated the arrival of the inundations by observing the stars and the Nile may thus have initiated them into the study of astronomy. We know that they observed Sirius, that fixed star in the "Dog" which is only ten light years away from us. Its rising on the 19th July was the Egyptian New Year.

The first calendar thereby came into existence.

The rising of the Nile was a regular annual event but it was not always exactly on time. In an effort to fix the vital day the Egyptians picked on Sirius, also known as Sothis. Their astronomers had observed that this star, which rises late in the morning sky, frequently vanished from sight for considerable periods and then reappeared from a certain day. That day, now calculated to be the 19th July, was made New Year's Day.

The year was divided into three periods, inundation, summer and winter. Each period had four months and each month thirty days and there were five intercalary days in addition. This Nile year had 365 days. In course of time it was realized that the Sirius year (like our solar year) was a quarter of a day longer than the Nile year and this discovery complicated the calculations. In 238 B.C., in the reign of Ptolemy III, someone hit on the idea of straightening things out by introducing an intercalary day. In 46 B.C. Julius Cæsar made a further improvement and in 1582 this Julian calendar became official during the papacy of Gregory XIII.

The 19th July of 2769 B.C. can be regarded as the birthday of this calendar which conquered the world.

To the ancients the Nile also meant river transport. The builders of the houses, temples and pyramids of that time had their materials brought by water. On the river moved thousands of commercial ships as well as barges with cabins for the rich. The Nile became the cradle of shipbuilding because there was no real road system.

From that day to this it has been the father and mother of Egypt.

There have been no inundations since 1902. The flow of the water has since been controlled by the dams at Aswan, Esna, Kaluit and Asuit. It is now possible to harvest each year three to four times more than before.

The industrious *fellahin* still plough with the same wooden plough as was used in the time of the Pharaohs. To irrigate their fields they draw water by *shaduf* or waterwheel from the most primitive cisterns. Women and children are the best "beasts of burden" and the *fellah*, who knows nothing of tractors and iron ploughs, seems to be a thousand years behind the times. The poor vegetate in dark and comfortless mud huts, the breeding ground of all sorts of diseases. Such people live hard. They can neither read nor write and no one has troubled to teach them anything about progress, with the result that they are quite satisfied that the only answer to everything is "Kismet" (it is the will of God), "There is no God but Allah and Mohammed is his prophet." All Mohammedans prostrate themselves before their prophet as a sign of submission – or perhaps from habit.

At least five thousand times has the majestic gaze of the Sphinx been fixed on the spectacle of the Nile drowning and

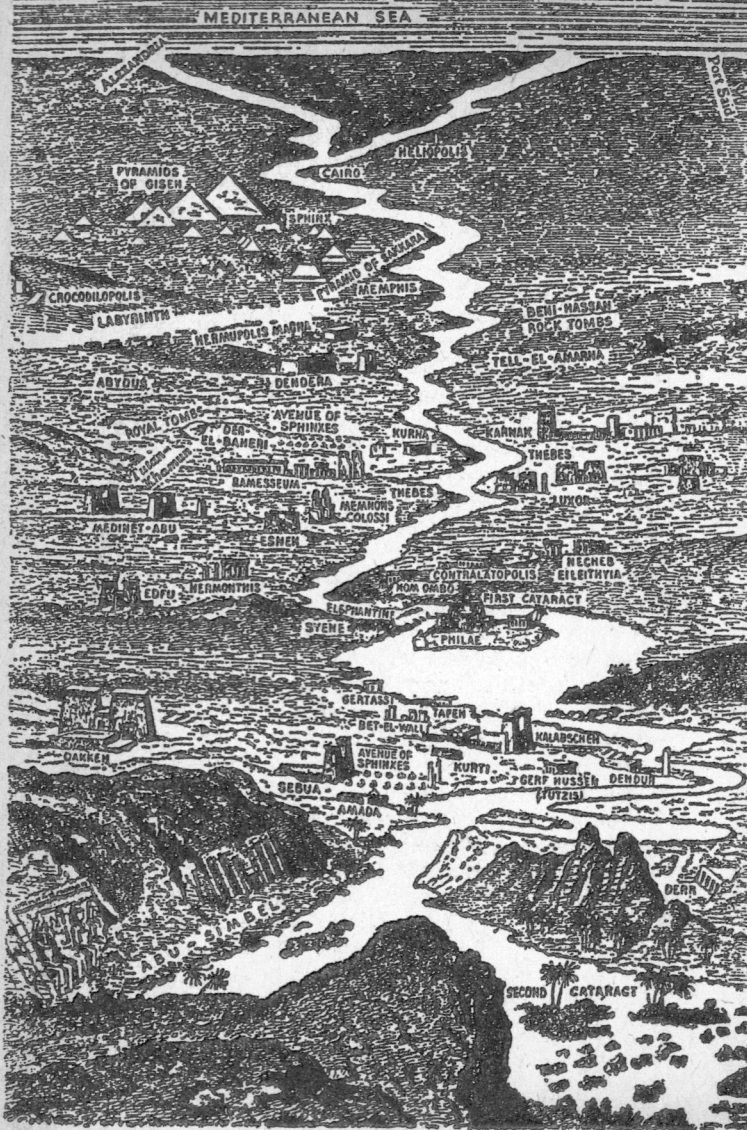

Historic sites on the Nile

fertilizing the fields of Egypt. In 450 B.C. Herodotus, whom Cicero called the Father of History, described the country as "the gift of the Nile".

The sun shines down on good and bad alike, the good being the great majority who have suffered and still suffer silently, the bad the minority who, whether Pharaohs in antiquity or pashas in modern times, have used the sanctions of religion to impose their harsh rule on others.

Egypt has changed her masters many a time but the system has never varied. Under the rule of the Pharaohs, Libyans, Persians, Greeks, Turks, French and English, the peasant has stuck to his patch of Nile mud and led a hard life.

The Nile is an ancient and patient river which has seen much history and even more human suffering. Its waters tirelessly lap round the cement foundations of its great dams and flow past the sites of the activities of the dynasties of Tuthmosis and Rameses, and the ruins associated with the Ptolemies and the caliphs.

The white and brown sails of the clumsy *dhows* swell in the breeze and there are many tourist vessels to enliven the picture, for Egypt is also a favourite tourist and health resort for those with deep purses. The dry, warm climate is beneficial for internal complaints.

Trading vessels flit along the Nile like moths and hundreds of houseboats are moored by its banks. The scene from a boat on a bright moonlight night is a glimpse of a magic world.

But it cannot be said too often that whereas historical events, languages and religions have never lacked for variety, the peasant has remained the unchanging symbol of the land in which he dwells.

Yet the spirit of Egypt produced the mightiest monuments of human achievement. The dry air and the preservative properties of the sand have through five thousand years preserved for us buildings, statues, domestic utensils and writings – and the miracle, and curse, of Tutankhamun.

Chapter 2

SEVEN THOUSAND YEARS AGO ...

Egypt is readily granted the distinction of being the earliest civilization in history. At a time when other nations of antiquity, notably the Greeks and Romans, were still living in darkness the Egyptians had kings as far back as 3000 B.C. and we still have inscriptions and monuments of that period as evidence. A few dynasties later, pyramids were built, those pyramids at the foot of which there are car parks today.

Gravestone of King Djet – carved 2,400 years before Christ

The hoary classical scholars who laughed at Egypt did more to kill history than to write it. Even at the beginning of the twentieth century they believed that history began in 776 B.C. For a long time, it is curious to relate, man imagined that his planet was only a little older than himself. In 1654 Usher, primate of Ireland, declared categorically that his study of the Bible proved that the creation of the world took place at 9 o'clock on the morning of the 25th October, 4004 B.C. Nor was this primate alone in his belief. A century and more later it was heresy to accept an earlier date.

The pyramids and temples of Egypt prove its high antiquity

and justify the veneration in which it is held. Yet at the beginning of our era, when the star appeared above a manger in Bethlehem, the decline of the empire of the Pharaohs was already complete.

This immense span of six thousand and more years must be borne in mind when we are inclined to inflate the significance of a thousand years of modern European or Roman history.

Only 1,230 years separate the foundation of Rome by Romulus in 753 B.C. and its collapse in A.D. 476 in the reign of the last emperor, Romulus Augustus. What a contrast Egypt offers!

Innumerable inscriptions carved in stone or written on papyri prove that the Egyptians were a literate people. In A.D. 643, when Egypt's ancient civilization had passed away, Caliph Oman had masses of papyri collected and burned. No one deplores this piece of fanatical barbarism more than Egyptologists and anyone with any sense of history will share their indignation. Fortunately, many papyri have survived.

The tragedy was repeated in Christian Rome in the sixteenth century. Ancient monuments which girdled the Roman forum were ruthlessly destroyed. Popes had antique marbles torn up to adorn their fountains. The Serapeum was blown up with gunpowder and the usable stone employed as building materials for the stables of Pope Innocent. For centuries the Colosseum was treated simply as a quarry and as late as 1860 Pope Pius IX continued the work of destruction in order to beautify Christian buildings with pagan works of art.

Any visitor to a museum containing Egyptian antiquities will find many objects of stone, wood or linen which are covered with remarkable inscriptions. But the favourite medium was paper – papyrus. The Egyptians had neither ink nor pens. They used a stilus and a wooden palette with cavities containing colouring matter.

The invention of writing, and the use for that purpose of the immense mass of reeds growing in the Nile valley, led to literary activity

As with the devotees of Islam and other religions, the Egyptians left the art of writing in the hands of the priests. Only the children of rich families learned to read and write and they were taught in schools conducted by the priests. It was not easy for them as more than five hundred signs had to be mastered!

For the masses there were professional scribes.

The prime object of all teaching in the various departments of learning was the promotion of religion. Among the Egyptians knowledge was bound up with the belief that the actions of the gods had a paramount influence on the destinies of man. The essential principle was that good would be rewarded, evil punished. If the Egyptians had always observed that principle their nation would not have declined!

From the reports, laws and ordinances recorded on papyri we know something of the life of the ancient Egyptians, their wars, the intervals between their wars and their good and bad times. We know many of their tales and legends which breathe the poetry manifested in their religion. Here are some examples.

A father is worried about his son. He wants him to learn to read and write because he is not suited for manual labour, which in any case is too hard work.

Egyptian scribes (Relief on a monument)

A writer who lived in the reign of the warlike Rameses II, about 1300 B.C., describes the hardships suffered by an Egyptian officer during a campaign, the losses of a peasant through a great drought, mortality among cattle, robberies and extortion by tax officials.

The scribe had a much more pleasant life. His work brought him honour and glory. He did not even pay taxes. But if he did not do his work well he was in for trouble. A scribe criticizes a junior colleague: "What you have written is very silly and full of pompous and meaningless expressions. Your head is stuffed with trivial ideas. Your work is full of mistakes and you put down wrong words as they occur to you and without thinking." And as if that were not enough, he continues: "You are writing in the jargon of Lower Egypt." But the letter ends with sound advice.

When that was written, probably in the time of the Jewish law-giver, Moses, there was a fashion for using Semitic words. Egypt had been involved in many wars in Asia Minor. The resultant intertrading, and the settlement in the Nile valley of Jewish families many of whose members became high officials at the Court of the Pharaohs, fostered the adoption of foreign words. The archæologist Brugsch found in a papyrus an ordinance that Egyptians must avoid foreign words in order to maintain the purity of the language.

There is a tradition that as far back as 2350 B.C. there was a library in Memphis. It was so extensive and valuable that a very high dignitary (his mummy was found at Giza) was appointed as its curator. Unfortunately, out of all its treasures only a few small treatises on moral philosophy have come down to us.

These few examples show that the ancients were men of letters, though their activities, like all others, were subject to the law of evolution. In its earlier stages literature is primitive. Decadence marks the end.

It is noteworthy that hieroglyphs are free from foreign words. The cuneiform writings of the scribes of Babylon cannot be compared with those of the Egyptians. We do not know whether bureaucracy existed at that time, though evil tongues assert that it did.

In the time of her decadence Egypt was occupied by foreign powers, the Greeks among them. Herodotus, the Greek historian who lived from 500 to 424 B.C., has told us a good deal about Egypt, though only in fragments. The few references in the Bible do not throw much light on its history.

If the truth be told, the ancients of the East never knew much about Egypt and the little that was known in the West has been forgotten. To some extent even the monuments themselves were swallowed up by the sand of the desert.

About 33 B.C. Strabo, the Greek, visited Egypt. In 39 he was followed by Diodorus, from Sicily, and in A.D. 50 by the Roman, Pliny. But they have very little to say about the country.

We naturally wonder why the Romans made no investigation and did not take to the spade. Were they unaware of the existence of the treasures awaiting them, or merely afraid of dishonouring the dead? Was it so much easier to despoil the living? No one could have realized what the desert sand was hiding, yet it is certain that they admired all the monuments and even the peculiar signs which they called hieroglyphs. But the idea of giving back a vanished civilization to the world never entered their heads. Egypt remained a mystery.

Rome possessed many papyri, with delicately painted figures of lions, serpents, beetles, fish, geese and hawks, as well as rings, half-rings, dashes, full stops and abbreviations, which obviously formed part of a connected whole.

They were assumed to be sacred symbols, a secret of the priestly art and incomprehensible to the laity. This view is propounded in a little book dating from the time of the Graeco-Roman occupation. In the fourth century A.D. its author, a

Hieroglyphs

Greek named Horapollon, gave a list of hieroglyphs with a transcription in Greek. But these Greek equivalents were just guesswork and the effect of his enterprise was to make everyone equally distrust later interpretations.

In A.D. 320 Constantine had an obelisk brought to Rome. Another obelisk of granite and nearly a hundred feet high, was transported to Constantinople where it can still be admired. A writer of this time records the inscription on the obelisk. It was neither mystic nor mysterious but an adulatory dedication to the Pharaoh who originally erected the monument.

Although it has been subsequently established that this translation was correct, no one had previously believed in its accuracy.

The German Jesuit, Athanasius Kircher, a miracle of learning who lived from 1601–1680, inventor of the Laterna Magica, professor at Würzberg and subsequently member of the Collegium Romanum, published in Rome four volumes of hieroglyphs with translations. Very much later it was proved that not a single line was correct.

A hundred years later de Guignes, a member of the Paris Academy, made comparative studies in hieroglyphics and expressed the view that the Chinese were Egyptian colonists. Some English savants also believed that the Egyptians came from China.

A Parisian savant professed to recognize the 100th Psalm in some hieroglyphs in the temple of Dendera and said that the inscription on the obelisk of Pamphylia dating from about 4000 B.C. contains an account of the "Victory of the Pious over the Evil".

At the end of the eighteenth century Akerblad and Zoega, two Swedish-Danish specialists in arabic, had a better idea about hieroglyphs. Akerblad had copied some in Cairo and believed the signs were parts of an alphabet. Zoega thought that the oval rings contained the names of kings.

Both were right, but these discoveries did not carry the matter much further. Hieroglyphs had not yielded up their secret. Egypt still slumbered.

This general state of ignorance persisted for a very long time. The existence of a number of temples and pyramids was known, but their purpose was shrouded in mystery. What about the spade? It was the whipping-boy of the sciences, of interest only to a few greedy financiers. There were to be many chances and changes before the thirst for knowledge aroused scholars to its uses.

One of the best "chances" was the arrival of Napoleon Bonaparte. When the Corsican returned from a campaign in Italy in 1797 he started to compare himself with Alexander the Great. He wrote: "Paris weighs me down like a mantle of lead. Europe is a molehill, but in Asia, where there are six hundred and fifty million people, great revolutions can be brought about."

Egypt was a gate to the East and a springboard for great enterprises. As is known, in 1798 Napoleon and his army sailed in three hundred and twenty-eight ships to Egypt in order to break England's naval power in the Mediterranean. He took with him eighteen hundred guns and also one hundred and seventy-five experts, astronomers, geographers, geologists, zoologists, botanists and philosophers, as well as painters and poets. The soldiers called them "asses and idiots".

Napoleon's army soon conquered Egypt. The ancient

monuments seen by him and his men filled them with amazement. One day, in the shadow of the mighty pyramids of Giza, Niebuhr's *Arabian Journey* in his hand and surrounded by his scientists, he addressed them thus:

"Soldiers of the pen, soldiers of science! From the tops of these pyramids fifty centuries are looking down upon you. A great task awaits you. The world yearns to know the history of Egypt. Get to work!"

Whatever may be thought of Napoleon and his thirst for conquest, these words make him immortal, if only because he translated them into action. The summons to "get to work", marked the beginning of Egyptology and the inauguration of systematic investigation.

Good things develop slowly, however. Egypt still presented its greatest problem, hieroglyphics. To solve this problem all known sources of information were drawn on, but no one could agree and no progress was made.

As so often happens, when prospects were most unfavourable, an event occurred which caused the greatest excitement. On the 7th August, 1798, the English fleet under Nelson destroyed the French at Aboukir on the coast of Egypt. The French army expected an enemy landing and threw up entrenchments in the Nile delta. Near the village of Rosetta a soldier struck a flat stone with his spade. It was carefully dug out and proved to be of black basalt and about the size of a small table top. One side was polished and covered with inscriptions similar to some which had been seen elsewhere.

The soldier had no idea that he had discovered anything valuable. His name is unknown, though history has unfairly given the credit to his officer, Bouchard.

This stone had three kinds of script on it, fourteen lines of hieroglyphs at the top, thirty-two lines of demotic in the middle and fifty-four of Greek at the bottom. Almost all scholars read Greek. Even one of Napoleon's generals possessed that accomplishment.

The Greek text of the stone recorded that in 196 B.C. priests from all over Egypt were summoned to Memphis to consider what honours should be paid to the young King Ptolemy for the services he had rendered to the temples and the priestly caste. It was decided that a statue of the king should be placed in every temple and that each statue should have an inscription in three languages recording this sacerdotal decree.

As is known, Napoleon's expedition ended in disaster. England won another victory and harvested its fruits, the Rosetta stone among them. General Hutchins brought it with other antiquities to London and George III presented it to the British Museum.

Unfortunately Napoleon's defeat meant a setback for knowledge. For the time being, investigation at the cost of the state came to an end.

One of Napoleon's savants, Dominique Vivant Denon, took

The Rosetta Stone

his work very seriously and breathed new life into the subject. Shortly after his return from Egypt he published a description of the land of the Nile, *Description de l'Egypte*, in twenty-four volumes of text and twenty of plates. A literary monument!

The world paid some attention. Some mocked at his achievement and there were wiseacres to criticize it, perhaps because Denon was primarily a painter and the darling of the Court ladies. But the outside world was interested and Egypt became a fashionable craze.

But what about hieroglyphs?

In actual fact, the philosopher's stone had been found and men of science were convinced that they would soon be reading what had been a secret for so many centuries. Many an expert had broken his teeth on the subject. The antiquarians and archæologists of all nations pored over drawings and copies of the stone and for years pondered deeply, as absorbed as any chess player. De Sacy, an orientalist living in Paris, pronounced that the problem was very involved and scientifically insoluble. It looked as if hieroglyphs were to remain as impenetrable as the Ark of the Covenant.

Akerblad scored a modest success when he isolated some of the demotic signs. A few years later Thomas Young, an English doctor who first propounded the wave theory of light, succeeded in distinguishing some hieroglyphic signs which could stand for the name *Ptolemy*. But he got no further.

Many others tried their hands. Some worked seriously because they were really interested, others with an eye only to the publicity value of success. The interpretation of one scholar was immediately contradicted by another. Disputes were most prolonged and obstinate. As soon as anyone claimed that he had solved the problem someone else pointed out his errors and called him a fraud. To whom would the great prize fall?

At the time when the Rosetta Stone was discovered there was living in Paris a boy named François Champollion. Some would call him an infant prodigy. This gifted child was taught by a priest who lived in his parents' house during the troublous times of the French Revolution. He could read and write well when he was six years old. His elder brother, a philologist, taught him languages and by the time he was eleven he was a genius with good knowledge of Latin, Greek, Hebrew and Syrian.

France was passing through stirring times, in the intellectual as well as the military field. Napoleon had become First Consul and then Emperor. By the age of twelve François had read the Old Testament in the original text and thereby acquired a passion for truth and a firm conviction that the republican form of government could alone guarantee justice as between man and man. The boy soon discovered that he was a revolutionary at heart.

In due course a savant who had taken part in Napoleon's campaign heard of the young genius and took him to a museum exhibiting some Egyptian antiquities. What he saw left men of ripe years quite unmoved but it touched off a spark in the boy's soul. Pointing to some hieroglyphs, he explained: "I'll decipher them some day."

After adding Arabic, Persian, Sanskrit and Chaldaean to his languages he collected everything he could find about Egypt and buried himself in Coptic, the speech of the first Egyptian Christians. Champollion was thus better equipped than the English antiquarian Young, who was never shaken in his belief that hieroglyphs were a script of symbols.

At seventeen, Champollion produced a historical map of Egypt though he had never visited that country. At eighteen, this student of high intellectual powers was an Academician. Shortly afterwards he was made a member of the *Académie des Sciences*. Unfortunately, his health was poor and he had to limit his energies to the problem of deciphering hieroglyphs.

The English had had the Rosetta Stone copied and many scholars in Europe were poring over the three columns. But Champollion's affairs were in a bad way. He had no employment and could not pay his rent. His clothes and shoes were worn out. He caught a cold and his lungs were affected. As a revolutionary he was suspect. To earn his bread he wrote for the press, coached schoolboys and students, corrected manuscripts, worked on hieroglyphics and his Coptic dictionary. When the latter had reached 1069 pages he wrote: "The dictionary gets fatter while I get thinner."

When he recovered he was due to join the armies of Napoleon, who had again plunged Europe into war, but influential savants managed to save him from military service and he forged ahead with his studies like a man possessed.

At that time a certain Count Palin was also absorbed in the problem of hieroglyphics. This stupid but cocksure individual announced one day that he had come round to the doctrines of Pythagoras, the Kabbala and our friend Horapollon and in one night had freed himself from the "systematic errors" to which so many scholars had fallen victim. A week later he crowned his follies by printing his conclusions.

The competition to decipher hieroglyphs was like the rivalry between Captain Scott and Amundsen to reach the South Pole.

One day Champollion had a terrible fright. On his way to the College he met a friend who told him the hieroglyphs had been deciphered. The news had been given in a brochure entitled *Nouvelle Explication*, said to be published by Alexander Lenoir. Champollion was somewhat relieved when he heard that the author was Professor Lenoir as the latter, though a prominent scholar, was no genius.

But he ran to the bookseller, bought the book – on credit – and returned home. He settled in a sofa, read the book from beginning to end and then burst out laughing. His unrestrained and audible hilarity brought his landlady in hot haste up to his room. He told her of the rubbish which the "idiot" Lenoir had written. But it took him some time to get over his fright.

This genius in languages was given a professorship at the age of nineteen. But the honour aroused a lot of jealousy. Older professors intrigued against him and as a result of their efforts he received only a quarter of the emoluments of the post.

He wanted to buy an Egyptian papyrus and needing a thousand francs tried to obtain a loan from some rich countrymen. They would not part with a sou. He wrote to his elder brother: "My destiny is decided. I'm as poor as Diogenes. I'll buy a tub and a sack for my rags and hope that the well-known generosity of rich Athenians will keep me alive."

The young student never deviated from the path he had set before himself. Nor did he ever waver in his fight for truth and justice or his demand that men and knowledge should be free.

When revolution and civil war threatened to engulf France he protested against Napoleon's dictatorship. He wrote revolutionary pamphlets, mounted the barricades and preached resistance.

But when General Latour and his royalists bombarded the centre of Paris he rushed home. He was just in time to extinguish the flames which were about to consume the house in which he had his little room, library and scientific papers.

Unemployed once more, he was charged with high treason and banished for eighteen months.

Prussia had freed herself from the French yoke. The English sent Napoleon to Saint Helena. Peace once more reigned in Europe and better days dawned for science.

Egypt had become a magnet to which many were drawn. Traders, speculators, the curious and the mere sensationalist hastened to the Nile to collect statues, mummies, papyri and other antiques. "Good business" for one and all was the cry, for the museums were good customers.

Champollion was allowed to return and although he had not entirely recovered his health he devoted himself once again to the study of hieroglyphs. He had already deciphered several words and the names of some kings but a final result still seemed far away.

Ill and without employment he returned to Paris in 1821. Yet in that unhappy time the ring was destined to close. He had recently discovered that hieroglyphs could not be symbols of single concepts because the number of signs in the hieroglyphs was three times the number of words in the Greek text. He had also found a clue to the name of Queen Cleopatra in a demotic papyrus.

He traced the name of Queen Cleopatra again in an obelisk with inscriptions in Greek and hieroglyphics which had been brought to England. With a drawing of that obelisk in his hand he was sure that he had been right about the name Cleopatra.

He identified the letters p, t, l, m, i, s, k, e, a, r and a second sign for the t.

From this obelisk and some other objects he realized that the words set in ovals were two royal names, Ptolemy and Cleopatra. All his doubts were at an end. The hieroglyphic signs were letters of an alphabet. He obtained drawings of other monuments with hieroglyph inscriptions and was able to decipher the names of gods and other kings, names such as Rameses, Tuthmosis, Thoth and Isis.

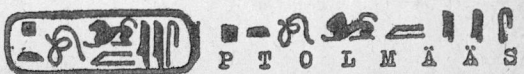

Spurred on by his discovery he continued his work with ferocious energy and crowned twenty years of arduous toil with a triumph which is still one of the wonders of learning.

François Champollion had reached the goal he had set before himself, but his health was broken and he had barely time to yell "I've done it!" to his brother before he collapsed altogether.

In the autumn of 1822 the Paris Academy could be informed that hieroglyphs had really been deciphered. For Champollion, however, the days of misery and want were not yet over. As a result of his sentence for treason no one would give him employment worthy of his abilities. He was charged once more with the same crime. Fortunately he found a patron on this occasion, the Duc de Blaccard, who was deeply interested in antiquity. This friend secured the withdrawal of the charge and made it possible for him to go to Turin where he found more papyri and hieroglyphs and could continue his labours in the great cause.

Then came 1828. Champollion was now twenty-seven. Leaving the world of jealousy and intrigue behind him, at last he could visit Egypt. There a regular triumph awaited him. The *fellahin* swarmed around him. They wanted to see the man who could "read the writing on their old stones". Ceremonial receptions and festivities were organized in his honour and he was treated everywhere like a saint. But that was not what the modest archæologist wanted. He had come to Egypt to find out about a nation which had vanished and to serve the cause of historical research.

Now he could live in a land which had ever been the object of his youthful longings. Apart from the interpretation of hieroglyphics he had been working on a chronology and topography of Egypt and adumbrated a number of theories. He continued his investigations in these subjects and finally obtained confirmation of ideas in which he had always believed, though his views had brought him no reward except the mocking laughter of the so-called "Egyptian Committee" in Paris.

Champollion examined many temples, tombs and pyramids and was intoxicated with the wealth of inscriptions, hitherto a closed book to the world, everywhere to be found on columns and walls, obelisks and pylons.

At Dendera there is a temple which he found had originally

been dedicated to the goddess Hathor, the Egyptian Aphrodite Urania. We know to-day that its construction dates from the Twelfth Dynasty, about 1900 B.C. Tuthmosis III enlarged it in honour of the gods and subsequent additions were made by the Ptolemies, the Roman emperors Augustus, Nerva, Domitian and, finally, Trajan in A.D. 110. It is considered the finest temple in Egypt.

Champollion and his companions spent a considerable time at this marvel of art. They were quite overcome by its beauty. He at once deciphered several of the inscriptions and read the hymns of praise of the gods which thousands of years ago had here been carved in stone.

Although it was late and the moon was down Champollion could hardly tear himself away. Subsequently he recorded what he felt:

"I cannot describe the impression which the portico in particular made upon me. I can give the bald figures for its length and breadth but language can convey no idea of its beauty. Charm and majesty are here associated to perfection. We stayed two hours and, filled with a sense of ecstasy and magic, wandered through great halls. Even by moonlight I could read some of the inscriptions on the outer walls."

His stirring experiences and the world-wide recognition that he had been right made him a happy but not a conceited man. Yet his enthusiastic letters were quite misjudged in Paris by many who did not mean to forget that he had been charged with high treason.

It was the tragedy of the life of this intellectual giant that it ended much too soon. He spent three years, working feverishly, in Egypt. Then his old complaint recurred and he died on the 4th March, 1832.

Immediately after the death of this, the first Egyptologist and etymologist, his rivals who had failed to solve the problem of hieroglyphs themselves again published derogatory criticisms in the press.

It was eight years before Champollion's posthumous works, an Egyptian dictionary and Egyptian grammar, were published.

After his death there was no one in France competent to carry on his work. Fortunately, a successor was supplied from Germany in the shape of Richard Lepsius (1810–1884).

For all his genius in reading hieroglyphs Champollion had

never been absolutely clear as to their exact character. This was the point on which he was open to attack from those who questioned his achievement. It was Lepsius who first comprehended the grammatical construction of the hieroglyphic script and methodically described it.

But it would be wrong to think that other scholars were only waiting to follow up the new discovery. For more than thirty years historians and orientalists adopted a cautious and sceptical attitude. Of course they admitted that the names of a few kings could be read, but they did not believe that the inscriptions could be translated. Their doubts persisted until they had to yield to the evidence of a counterpart of the Rosetta Stone, the "Decree of Canopus", which was discovered in 1869. This stone also had an inscription in three languages, but it was longer and it clinched the matter.

The doubts and hesitations of the previous generation of scholars were not altogether a disadvantage as their successors who now appeared on the scene came to their task without prejudices and with the utmost enthusiasm. In the van were a young French lawyer, Emmanuel de Rouge, and a student. Both specialized in hieroglyphic and hieratic inscriptions. With them were associated Joseph Chabas, a French wine merchant, and an English lawyer, Charles Goodwin. Later they were joined by Rossellini, an Italian, Lermans, a Dutch-

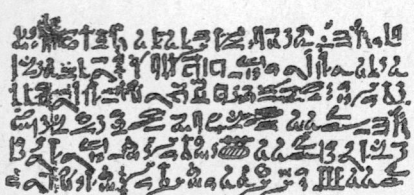

Hieratic script (from the fables in the Westcar papyrus)

man, Flinders Petrie, an Englishman, and Lepsius, a German. These men of different nationalities but with a common purpose continued the work of investigation and achieved amazing successes which gave immense impetus to the science of archæology.

In 1842 King Frederick William IV of Prussia sent an expedition to Egypt at the suggestion of the naturalist, Alexander von Humboldt. Lepsius was put in charge. On his triumphant return the young professor founded a museum in Berlin.

The hieroglyphic script, which was the writing of the upper classes, underwent various transformations. With the object of simplifying it the hieratic script was developed, and out of the latter in turn was evolved the even simpler demotic script of the Egyptian people in general. No one in the era of which we are speaking could read that script. Its elucidation was to come later. Fate again took a hand.

In 1827 Heinrich Brugsch was born in Berlin. He was the son of an officer in the Uhlan Guards. In 1840, while still at school, Heinrich displayed a lively interest in the land of the Pharaohs. When he had mastered hieroglyphics and the grammar he threw himself into the study of the demotic script, which had developed out of the hieratic, and to the astonishment of savants produced a grammar.

Whether from envy or some other motive, the archæologist Lepsius at first criticized it adversely, though the work was acclaimed in Paris.

Alexander von Humboldt was a great patron of Brugsch. Good luck and ability here again joined forces. When he left school, Brugsch went to Cairo and there met the French Egyptologist, Mariette.

After a period of study at Berlin University, Brugsch went to Persia. There followed an interval at Göttingen and then he returned to Egypt as consul. There his passion for archæological investigation gave him no peace and he entered the service of the Egyptian Government.

He explored the antiquities of the country from the necropolis at Memphis to Abu Simbel.

The head and front of his literary achievement is his dictionary of demotic in four volumes, with a three volume supplement. Demotic had been deciphered and Heinrich Brugsch Pasha had become one of the heroes of science.

Here is an extract from Adolf Erman's translation of part of the animal fables in the Egyptian myth known as the "Eye of the Sun". It can be found in the papyrus in demotic script in Leyden:

"There was once a lion. It lived on a mountain and was very strong and a mighty hunter. The other creatures of the mountain feared it. One day it met a panther whose coat had been ripped.

Demotic script. A fable. [Translation below]

" 'How hast thou got thy coat like that?' said the lion.
"The panther replied: 'It was Man.'
" 'Man! What is Man?' asked the lion.
"The panther replied: 'There is nothing more cunning than Man. Mayest thou never fall into his hands.'
"Then the lion raged exceedingly against Man and left the panther to look for him."

The dramatic struggle to decipher the script employed by the ancient dwellers by the Nile was at an end. Scholars can now read what they wrote as easily as their mother tongue. Without that knowledge it would have been impossible to learn anything about Egypt.

Although we are much further in time from the ancients than the Romans, who subsequently conquered Egypt and the world, we know more about them. It is certain that the Romans admired the Egyptian monuments because they brought home columns, obelisks and statues. But they had a very hazy idea of the Egyptian way of life.

Egypt was old when America was not even a dream, and when the surface of Europe was nothing but marsh and primitive forest, the kingdom of the elk and the bear.

"Remember that you are dust. Generations will be born and die. Nations will rise and fall. But we are eternal." That was what the Egyptians thought about themselves before Rome and Athens existed and it is really remarkable what the scientific use of the spade has brought back to life.

It would be futile to claim that the whole field of knowledge of ancient Egypt has been covered. There are gaps. In any event Egypt without its mysteries would be a dull subject. "There is more to come" must be our watchword. Of many kings we know no more than their names, and the sandy wastes still hold many secrets. Egypt will long remain the paradise of the digger.

On the banks of the magical Nile, sweeping from torrid uplands to the cool sea, we must penetrate further into the spirit of a people who, under the influence of a burning sun, allowed a blend of fanaticism, decency and vice to luxuriate in a fashion unknown elsewhere on this planet.

The discovery of clubs, flints and scrapers, the standard implements of prehistoric man, shows that men were living on the banks of the Nile six thousand years before Christ was born. No doubt the first inhabitants were nomads. They may have ultimately settled there because the climate was good and the soil fertile.

They buried their dead in the desert sand immediately beyond the fertile area. Corpses and funeral offerings dating from a period about 5000 B.C. are found today in an excellent state of preservation, a tribute to the dry air and the constituents and properties of the sand which have prevented decomposition. The reader must always keep that point in mind.

Graves of the neolithic period have been found in which the body is in a squatting position, with the face turned to the east. Among funeral gifts such as ceramic pots and vases the most striking objects are cosmetic palettes made of slate with traces of vivid colours.

In Upper Egypt burial in cemeteries was the rule. The corpses, wrapped in goatskins or linen cloths, were also placed in the squatting position but with the face towards the west, i.e. where the sun sinks to rest. Graves have also been found containing several bodies. Perhaps they were the graves of a whole family, or possibly the dead master was surrounded by his slaves. One remarkable feature was that each corpse had a limb missing. Why? There has never been an answer to that question. The prehistoric dwellers by the Nile were certainly not cannibals. Clubs, bows and arrows were found in these tombs.

In Heluan, opposite Sakkara, was found a subterranean cemetery with eight hundred and twenty-five separate graves.

That these dated from the earliest times was proved by the fact that the bodies had not been embalmed and most of them had been placed in wooden coffins or receptacles made of clay. The chambers reserved for articles which the dead would require contained unguent spoons, cosmetic pots, ivory objects and religious symbols in the form of amulets.

There is no certainty as to the original home of the Egyptians. Opinions vary. It has never been proved that they came from Sumeria. The tombs on the Dolmen highway, various mummies found in Egypt, many reliefs, some in bright colours, some wonderful statues of kings and other objects are an indication that the ruling caste came from some type of Nordic man. Perhaps the original negroid Egyptians were conquered and enslaved as the result of massive Atlantic Nordic migrations. Who knows?

Some say that the kings of the Second Dynasty came from the south, their capital was Tis (hence their classification as the "Tinitite Kings") and they invaded the north and founded a new capital at Memphis. Professor Reisner says in his book *The Development of the Egyptian Tomb down to the Reign of Cheops* that their tombs were of brick.

But it is not my object to provide my readers with a guide through the obscure pre-history of Egypt. My aim is to tell the story of Egypt and Tutankhamun as revealed to us by the hieroglyphs, a story which is rich in drama and of the highest interest. My starting point shall be the time when the Egyptians were already living in an organized state ruled by a king.

The first king of whom we know reigned about 3000 B.C. If we add the two thousand years that have passed since the birth of Christ we get a period of five thousand years which our thoughts have to span. It is a long time!

The Egyptians, who knew nothing of continuous chronology, must have found it very difficult to divide time into definite periods. The method they adopted was to parcel it out into periods corresponding to the dynasties of the kings who had reigned over them. In 305 B.C. a priest and scribe named Manetho, who lived during the Greek occupation, made a list of the names and dates of the dynasties. Though only part of his work has survived it is an authority of the greatest importance, even if the figures are not always accurate and he has sometimes gone wrong in the course of his long history.

The chronological table is also based on the "Sakkara List" in the Cairo Museum, the royal names in the temple of Seti I and the Turin papyrus.

When this "Turin" papyrus was found scholars were very inexperienced in handling such fragile material as papyrus rolls or leaves. It dated from the period of the XIXth dynasty and gave a list of the Kings of Egypt. Unfortunately it was almost destroyed through bad handling. We should have been spared a great deal of trouble if this precious papyrus had been treated by modern methods.

It is certain that politically the country was divided into Upper and Lower Egypt. Each sector had its principal deity. We have always been taught that King Menes united the whole country but the distinction between the two parts was preserved. The serpent Buto and the vulture Nechbet were the respective state gods but the emblem of Lower Egypt is the lily and that of Upper Egypt the papyrus.

In the following table, based on one prepared by Scharff and Moortgat, only the names of the most important Kings of Egypt appear. In 1953 Hermann Otto, a member of Hamburg University, published a more extensive list.

Manetho gave the names as written in Greek. He gives Djoser instead of Netery-er-Khet (his Horus name), Cheops instead of Chufru, Chephren instead of Chefré, Mykerinos instead of Menkevré, Phiops instead of Pjopi, Amenophis instead of Amenhotep, and so forth. We will in general follow his example. Incidentally, Pharaoh means "Great House", much as a Turk refers to his government as the "Supreme Porte".

Chronological Table of the reigning Dynasties

		B.C.
Prehistory (Menes?)	................before	2850
The Old Empire	........................from	2850

Dynasties

1–2.	Narmer, Horus	2850–2650
3.	Djoser, Snofru, Sanacht..........about	2650–2600
4.	Cheops, Chefren, Mykerinos, the pyramids of Giza ....about	2600–2480
5.	Sahure, Unas, Userkaf	2480–2350

6–8.	Teti, Merenré, Pepi I and II etc.	2350–2190
9–10.	Herakleopolitan Kings	2190–2052

The Middle Empire......................from 2052

11.	Mentuhotep	2052–1991
12.	Amenemhet	1991–1972
	Sesostris	1971–1930
	Amenemhet II	1929–1898
	Sesostris II	1898–1841
	Amenemhet III	1840–1792
13.	Intermediary period ....about	1778–1610
15–16.	Hyksos period ....about	1670–1570

The New Empire 1610

17.	..............................about	1610–1570
18.	Amosis	1570–1545
	Amenophis I	1545–1524
	Tuthmosis I and II...................	1524–1502
	Hatshepsut	1501–1480
	Tuthmosis III	1502–1448
	(Battle of Megiddo)	1480)
	Amenophis II	1448–1422
	Tuthmosis IV	1422–1413
	Amenophis III	1413–1377
	Amenophis IV	
	(Akhenaton – the El Amarna period)	1377–1358
	TUTANKHAMUN	1358–1349
	Ay................................	1349–1345
19.	..............................about	1345–1200
	Haremhab	1345–1318
	Rameses I	1318–1317
	Seti I	1317–1301
	Rameses II	1301–1234
	(Battle of Kadesh...................	1296)
	Menephtes	1234–1220
	Seti II and the troubles at the end of the XIXth dynasty ....about	1220–1200
20.	..............................about	1200–1085
	Setnat	1200–1197
	Rameses III	1197–1165
	Rameses IV to XI	1165–1085
21.	Separation of Thebes and Tanis........	1085–950

| 22–23. | Libyan Kings (inter alia Sheshonk) | 950–720 |
| 24. | King Bokoris of Saïs | 720–715 |

The Last Empire 715–332
25.	The Nubians (Shabaka and others)	715–663
26.	Psammeticos I to III	
	Necho, Apries, Amasis, Montenhet	633–525
	The battle of Pelusium, conquest of Egypt by Cambyses	525
27.	Persians, particularly Darius I	525–332
28.	Amytaios of Saïs	404–399
29.	Kings from Mendes	398–379
30.	Kings from Sebennytos	378–341
	Alexander conquers Egypt	332
	Egypt under the Greeks	332–31
	Egypt under the Romans	31

A.D.
Egypt under the Arabs ....after 640
Egypt under the English 1885

From the first Pharaoh to the Emperor Augustus in A.D. 1 Egypt must have been ruled by about three hundred and fifty kings. Herodotus speaks of three hundred and fifty kings up to the time of the Greek occupation. We are indebted to the writings of the Egyptians for our knowledge of their names and reigns and of those deeds, good and bad alike, which brought their people sometimes peace and happiness, sometimes war and misery and eventually final disaster.

But there are many gaps in our knowledge of Egyptian history. Perhaps they may never be entirely filled. Certainly very much excavation is required to obtain a complete picture.

The Egyptians speak most clearly from their tombs. It is their funeral furniture and offerings, the wall paintings and inscriptions in their graves which tell us most about them, how they lived and what they regarded as their main purpose in life. The ancient Greeks burned their corpses, but the Egyptians were optimists who firmly believed that life did not end with death. They gave material expression in their cult of the dead to the belief that life continued in the after world.

Skorpion is said to have been the first king of the first dynasty. Nothing is known about him. A little more is known of his successor, Narmer. A cosmetic palette of remarkable workmanship of his time has come down to us. On one side is a picture of four standards being carried before the Pharaoh. Behind these symbols of godlike power he strides, trampling on corpses in his path. Below are shown two fabulous monsters intertwined. On the other side the king is seen smashing the skull of a captive kneeling before him. This is the sort of scene which greets us everywhere in Egyptian history.

A cosmetic palette. On the left the Pharaoh is beating out the brains of a captive

Narmer's tomb tells us how he and his officials mounted a procession to celebrate a victory over the inhabitants of the north. On the king's sceptre it is recorded that he took 120,000 prisoners and his booty amounted to 400,000 oxen and one million goats. War was made to pay even five thousand years ago!

Let us have a glance at the tomb of Hamaka, a courtier and vizir of King Usaphias of the First Dynasty. When the English archæologist Emery discovered this tomb he was very disappointed to find it empty. Thieves had obviously been at work. But when he provided himself with a better light and looked more closely, he found forty-two adjacent chambers which had been walled. All were filled with a bewildering number of miscellaneous objects.

The most remarkable find was a large number of objects like discs, made of stone, metal and ivory. Each disc had a stem and most of them were decorated with conventional designs or figures. The soil of Egypt had never yielded up anything like this before.

What was the purpose of all these discs? Were they pieces in some game which was popular 5,000 years ago? Perhaps they were amulets or some sort of talisman which would bring good luck to the deceased. Or they may have been objects invested with magical properties and of high mystical significance.

Emery also found arrows, some of them tipped with flints. One bundle of these arrows was in a leather quiver. A wooden casket crumbled to dust the moment it was touched. In it were wooden axe handles, wooden sickles with flint teeth and flint knives. There was a large supply of food and the vizir would find two thousand jars of wine in his tomb if he felt thirsty.

Chasechem, a king of the second dynasty, when pyramids were still unknown, had his tomb enlarged into a huge building 208 feet long and 50 feet wide, with fifty-eight small chambers. This tomb had been completely cleared of its contents in antiquity. The walls of these early tombs were gaily painted and covered with inscriptions.

A wonderful discovery such as is only possible in the romantic land of the Pharaohs was made by Emery in the tomb of another vizir of the second dynasty. One chamber was fitted out as a dining hall with a table laid and the food ready. The jars and plates were of slate or alabaster. The fare provided was roast pigeon, fish, vegetables and a whole side of beef, not to mention sauces, fruit, round pastries and triangular pieces of bread. Everything had become completely desiccated in the Egyptian climate but was otherwise well preserved.

Unfortunately the wooden sarcophagus of the deceased had crumbled to dust, but the bones were intact. The jars and vessels, of the most refined workmanship, had not been touched by the hand of time.

Here we must leave the First and Second Dynasties and turn to the Third, the era of the first pyramid.

Chapter 3

PYRAMIDS AND MUMMIES

Camels have played a part in many a historical event though no monument records the fact. They have figured in many battles and often given them the decisive turn. What would the desert be without the camel, the one-humped ship of the desert? The popular idea of Egypt is hardly possible without it.

Though the ancient Egyptians frequently depicted the horse and the ass in their paintings, the camel is conspicuous by its absence. Yet many explorers know its worth, though they also know that no other animal is so stubborn, bad-tempered and cowardly.

Animal experts are at one in thinking that the camel is stupid, but others respect it as clever, willing and devoted. And they are right. It carries its rider an average eighty miles a day under physical conditions which would defeat any horse. It will carry a load of at least 300 pounds in the desert and considerably more on good roads.

Marvellous tales are told about its ability to dispense with the necessities of life. Fourteen days without drinking is not exceptional. The camel is equally economical with food. Its hump – the source of stored energy – enables it to go without for long periods. But the richer its fodder, such as thistle, steppe grasses and thorn, the bigger the hump. Thorn and scrub are the normal food of this creature of modest requirements.

The camel will chew up spines thick enough to penetrate shoe-leather and it will drink more than ten gallons of water at the outset of a desert journey calculated to take weeks.

Camels are nervous creatures. They tremble at the sight of a hare, cry out over a fly, shy in terror at a heap of stones and roar when a mouse startles them. They spend their whole lives shivering over their miserable existence, which seems almost more than they can endure. They are always being frightened or bellowing, and wind and water are objects of terror.

Yet it seems to have no fear when its hour has struck and it lies down for the last time in some remote spot in the desert. A majestic tranquillity seems to descend upon it as, accepting the inevitable (something it has never done before) it awaits death. Next day there is nothing to be seen but a heap of bones. Vultures, jackals and hyenas have done their work.

There are few milestones in the deserts but plenty of skeletons to show the way to other travellers.

Such is the camel, which has contributed more to the creation of Egypt than any other animal. Yet no one has any affection for this "brute". It is the garbage-can and slave of the animal world, exploited and ill-used. Abuse and the stick are its portion in life until it is handed over to the butcher or finds a welcome death in the sandy wastes.

The necropolis of Sakkara and Giza is a stretch of desert, many miles in extent, without tree or bush. It can only be traversed on camel back. It is noteworthy that the ancients refused to waste an inch of fertile ground. They created the great necropolis at Sakkara out of rocky ground in the Libyan desert on the west bank of the Nile near Cairo, opposite their old capital, Memphis. The fertile ground is sharply marked off from the desert where all animal life has vanished and deep silence reigns over a sea of sand which seems to have no horizon.

Did they value the dead no higher than the sand?

It is a silly question to ask because the Egyptians gave up everything for the dead; they lived and worked for the kingdom of the dead.

Many loads of earth had to be moved to prove to a doubting world that the history of Greece began long before 776 B.C., the previous starting point of historians. It is quite otherwise with the history of Egypt. The Egyptians were old, and speaking through their pyramids, long before there were any Hellenes and the pyramids were still telling the world of that age-old race long after ancient Greece had ceased to be. Stones speak when men cannot, and the speech of stones is known only to the excavator, whose work is to find out the secret of how the ancient Egyptians lived and why their civilization perished. Hence every "find" is important. The most trivial object, even a potsherd, can often solve some problem which has defied the learned world for years.

But methodical excavation was unknown at first. Explorers streamed to Egypt like gold-diggers to California. When a tomb was discovered the coffin was broken open, any gold torn away from the mummy or a papyrus snatched from the tomb chamber. Then the "explorer" had no further interest.

The native workers were quick to learn from such men. These "excavations" were no different from the tomb-rifling of ancient days and fostered traffic in sham antiques.

When the Frenchman, Mariette, was residing in Egypt to buy papyri for the Louvre he was amazed at the prevalent vandalism. He could almost hear the piteous appeals of the ancients for rescue. He forgot the Louvre and longed for freedom and the spade. He saw fine sphinxes lying in the gardens of elegant houses and assumed that some depository for sphinxes had been robbed.

At Sakkara he noticed the head of a sphinx in the sand. It was not long before he had laid bare a whole avenue of one hundred and thirty-four sphinxes through which magnificent processions had once passed. Mariette made Egypt his second home and devoted himself wholly to exploration. But he did more than discover tombs. He was a collector and founded a museum in Bulak, thereby doing something to prevent the indiscriminate export of antiques. After a short time he gained the confidence of the Egyptian Government which appointed him Director of Antiquities.

Such were the beginnings of the world-famous Egyptian Museum, which was opened in Cairo in 1902, long after his death, and which became one of the greatest museums in the world. Today all finds are brought here. Nothing can now be taken out of the country. In the forecourt of the Museum is the statue of Auguste Mariette. Subsequently the grateful Egyptians interred his body in a marble sarcophagus. Since that time the director of the Museum is traditionally a Frenchman.

Grébant, de Morgan, Loret and Gaston Maspéro were his successors.

When Flinders Petrie arrived in Egypt twenty years later he was furious that so few explorers followed Mariette's methods. He taught that the archæologists' first task was not to produce a mummy but an Egyptian before he was turned into a mummy. That alone was the proper work of conscientious Egyptology. His idea at length prevailed, particularly as the rich store of written evidence about the ancient Egyptians clearly showed the way.

Egypt had a religious code which made three demands on a moral man. First to honour the gods and make continuous sacrifices to them. In that regard there was no lack of industry on the part of the Egyptians. Secondly, one must respect one's fellow men and help to keep them out of evil ways. This requirement was more neglected than observed. The third and highest obligation was to honour the dead, give them fine tombs, filled with all sorts of splendid gifts, and offer continuous sacrifices in the mortuary temples. The dead needed gifts and sacrifices in the after world and this third requirement was better observed than the others, though they clearly reveal the great differences between rich and poor, even in death.

The soul in the form of a bird

It was part of the recorded beliefs of the Egyptians that death does not separate the soul and spirit from the body. They did not accept the idea that a corpse is a "shell worn out by life". On the contrary, the soul has only departed temporarily and is making its habitation for the time being in a bird. Later it will leave this bird and return to the old body provided that the latter is in a good state of preservation. If the body has been allowed to decay the soul cannot return and dissolves into nothingness. So what must be done to save the dead body from corruption? Haunted by this idea the Egyptians first learned the art of embalming. They rubbed the corpse with precious essences and costly *Mûm*, hence the word "mummy". The embalmers were experts in their art for they were responsible for preserving the corruptible body and creating an incorruptible shell. Apart from a few exceptional practitioners who had to embalm kings and others of the highest rank, their occupation was despised and avoided, however necessary. They belonged to the lowest social classes. Painters, carpenters, jewellers, goldsmiths, sculptors and all stone workers, on the other hand, were highly esteemed because their knowledge and skill were serviceable to the dead. All were under the protection of their own special deity.

Herodotus relates that when anyone died it was the usual practice for many women mourners to assemble together. They smeared their heads and faces with Nile mud and then passed in procession, trembling and wailing, through the streets to the house of the deceased. This custom can still be observed today in the East. Then the body was delivered to the "House of Death" where it was embalmed. The ceremony was particularly impressive. The embalming process usually took thirty days. In the case of circumcised and tattooed Egyptians (i.e. all men of rank from priests upwards) it took longer, and even 70 days for kings. The embalmers were specialists in their particular art. During the process priests offered up prayers if the deceased was of high rank. The main object of all this was to preserve the corpse from decay, keep evil spirits away and help Ka, the soul, in its fight against demons. Ka is the symbol of the eternal in man.

Fashion may also have played a part in the mummification process. Sometimes corpses of both sexes were completely shaved, even to the pubic hair. But even the reverse was quite common. Mummies have been found with the hair elaborately arranged, and that of women meticulously waved and "permed".

The embalmer started by drawing the brain through the nose with a wire. Then the intestines were removed from the stomach, the inside of the body was flushed out with a mixture of wine and herbs and a chemical substance was injected into the blood vessels. Then the corpse was immersed in a salt solution. After a certain time it was ready for the next stage which was the removal of the liquid element. This was not easy because 75% of the human body consists of water. The stomach was then treated with precious fats and oils of cedar and filled with myrrh, cassia, cinnamon, roasted lotus seeds and aromatic essences. The body was then sewn up again.

Meanwhile much had been done to the exterior. The entrails were treated on approved principles and placed in a canopic jar. A sacred amulet occupied the place of the heart. More will be said on that subject in a later chapter. Finally the cosmeticians were set to work, painting the face and colouring the lips, nails, palms of the hands and soles of the feet. A plate of gold and resin was laid over the incision in the stomach. Swabs of fine material were inserted in the nostrils to absorb the trickle of secretions which had formed in the skull during the pickling process.

Then the skilled "undertakers" showed the mourning relatives various models of mummies, the primitive, the plain, the superior or the de luxe model, painted in bright colours by professional artists. From these the family decided, according to its means, upon the "make up" for the corpse.

It was also a question of money whether one or several priests should pray by the body during the embalming. No doubt this custom led to many abuses. There must have been plenty of needy embalmers and low-class priests hanging about in the expectation of presents from the family.

Next the body was swathed in countless yards of the finest linen obtained from the royal looms. Herodotus called it "Bythus cloth". Pads were inserted at the points of pressure to prevent damage through tight wrapping. Dr. Derry found a mummy with a shroud over twenty yards long and about two yards in width which had been folded in eight and used as wadding. The whole body was then coated with a rubber solution. Such is the description given by Herodotus of the most elaborate embalming process.

The financial position of the deceased determined how many jewels and ornaments of gold or precious stones should be inserted or placed in the wrappings. The embalming of kings, high dignitaries and sacred animals was a state act of great importance in which the public played a major part.

What Herodotus has to say about the art of embalming has been largely confirmed by the investigations of archæologists. An interesting light on the subject is thrown by an inscription from the tomb of a high official of the time of Tuthmosis III. Much can be learned from it:

"After the 70 days of embalming have passed thou art laid nobly in thy tomb. Thou art placed on the bier and drawn by oxen who have no blemish. Thy path on the way to thy tomb is washed in milk. Thy children weep from a full heart. Thy mouth is opened by the priests, and the priest of Sem shall purify thee. Horus moves thy lips and opens thine eyes and ears. Thy body is perfect in everything pertaining to thee. Words of praise are spoken and thy virtues are proclaimed. A sacrifice for the dead is made to thee. Thy heart is with thee as in life. Thou art as thou wast on the day thou wast born. Thy courtiers bow before thee. Thou goest to a land which the King has given thee, to the grave of the West. The fitting ceremonial is observed. The funeral dancers come proudly towards thee."

The period of 70 days for embalming is often mentioned. It occurs in the Bible where it is said that the Jews also used oil. Herodotus says this of the second quality process:

"Those who cannot face the high cost must choose the cheaper method. Here the embalmers fill their syringes with cedar oil and fill the body with it. They make no incision and take nothing from the body but insert the syringe in the anus, block up the passage to prevent the oil from seeping and soak the corpse in a natron bath. On the last day they let out the cedar oil which is so potent that it completely dissolves the entrails and draws them out with it. But the soft parts are largely destroyed by the natron and the corpse is nothing but skin and bone. Finally, the embalmers return the corpse."

Mummy (about 2000 B.C.)

Dead slaves and criminals of Egyptian blood were not granted the favour of embalming. Otherwise it was available to all Egyptians, even the poorest. It was a function of the temples to provide it. Even persons of moderate means were handed over to the "Houses of the Dead", of which there were many, graded like society itself. But in the third class there was less emphasis on reverence for the dead and more on the economies of mass burial. The corpses were hung on meat hooks and thrown into a big cauldron for five persons where they lay in salt solution for thirty days. There were thirty days in the Egyptian month. Each establishment had thirty cauldrons, one for each day of the month, as prescribed by the regulations. It is obvious that in such cases only the cheapest preservative was used and the process of mummification, otherwise so costly, must have been very primitive when the relatives could not pay much.

The embalmers were accustomed to the repulsive smell. The profession was held in high regard when it dealt on the royal level but it was otherwise with practitioners for the common herd. It was common knowledge that the latter were drawn from the lowest classes and frequently quite unconscious of the "sacrosanct" character of their work. They set about it in a rough and indecent way, quarrelled among themselves, splashed themselves with putrefying matter and not infrequently abused the corpses of young girls immediately after death. "It is a professional practice," writes Herodotus, "and for that reason the relatives wait three days before handing over the bodies of young women and girls to the embalming establishment!"

Such men were corruptible and quite ready to scrape their precious preservative off one corpse and use it again on another if there was a prospect of a present from the relatives. Slaves were considered unclean and not allowed to work in the "Houses of Death". In the hot climate of Egypt putrefaction set in at once. There was no natural or artificial ice and the sights and smells in these establishments must have been horrible. After the corpse had been embalmed, coated with resin and made aseptic the relatives took it away. If they could not afford a wooden coffin it was wrapped in an ox hide or papyrus inscribed with verses. Those who could not or would not pay the cost of preserving the body in a common vault had to be content with burying it, to the accompaniment of pious wishes, in the desert sand.

Thus it sometimes happened that some dark night, when the guards were asleep, the relatives would steal out with the body to a cemetery earmarked for the great ones of the land and bury it in the vicinity of a royal tomb. This was a service of love to the deceased in the hope that the poor might get something left over from the funerary gifts of the rich. A sad illusion!

Herodotus says elsewhere:

"If an Egyptian or foreigner is found drowned in the river or killed by a crocodile, it is the duty of the inhabitants of the nearest city to embalm and adorn the body and bury it in a sacred place. No one else, neither friend nor relative, may touch it. The Nile priests bury it with their own hands as if it were the corpse of a god."

As to the grave, it was not a hole in the ground. "From earth we come and to earth we shall return." Not at all! A strong, thief-proof tomb of stone was what every man contemplated as his place of interment, provided that "every man" is understood to mean not all Egyptians but only the rich ones. They must have a strong tomb in which the corpse and all the funerary gifts would be safe against marauders and the gnawing tooth of time. But such graves were costly and beyond the means of all but the well-to-do. I will leave to a later chapter a description of the splendours surrounding the deceased on his journey to the next world. Relatives who could not afford one of these tombs de luxe had to be content with renting a space in a mass grave which was kept up by the priests. Here the mummies were stacked like baulks of wood, with a perfunctory, regulation burial service. To buy absolution for the great Beyond was the Egyptian's main object in life.

From all this it is clear that in Egyptian eyes the earthly home was a minor matter, but the "House of Eternity", as it is called on monuments, must be impressive. The result is that archæologists have seldom found remains of what we understand by towns and houses. There are few ruins of what might once have been royal palaces. As the ancients relate, and excavators have confirmed, the palaces – even those of the Pharaohs – were considered as nothing but earthly caravanserais. Such buildings were often constructed of nothing but mud bricks and accordingly have completely disappeared.

This is not to say that these secular buildings were primitive. A palace laid bare at Medinet Habu between 1910 and 1918 showed definite traces of splendour. This "House of Joy" had been given all the decorative treatment current in the highly artistic period in which it was built. Coloured statues, wall decorations, glazed tiles, pavements and paintings had created a cultured and prosperous atmosphere in the rooms. The walls had been hung with tapestries and the tiled floors made vivid with hunting scenes and other pictures drawn from animal life. Some of the walls were encrusted with turquoise and lapis lazuli, the patterns effectively brought out by inlaid gold leaf. In addition there was exquisite furniture. The whole find gave an excellent idea of the taste prevailing at the time and the current standard of luxury in a royal palace. Such palaces often stood in the midst of magnificent gardens.

Temples and tombs, on the other hand, were intended for eternity and therefore built of granite in order to defy time and thieves. Primarily they were for the benefit of royalty but subsequently the higher priesthood, high-ranking officials and officers and rich citizens were also catered for. It is obvious that there was no place for the common herd. The lot of the ordinary man was a cheap sacred amulet as a funerary gift and a blessing from the priest as a prelude to his journey to the heaven of the poor where happiness costs little. The necropolis of Sakkara, where social distinctions had to be observed even in death, was not his last resting-place. Another bit of desert was reserved for him.

Perhaps the oldest Egyptian monument is the royal tomb at Negade in Upper Egypt which de Morgan discovered in 1897. The building was about 50 yards in length. In the centre was a tomb chamber, with side chambers where no doubt the funerary gifts were deposited. It has been attributed to King Menes. Other graves of the earliest times have been found at Abydos.

One explorer was surprised to find that one of the kings had his household with him in his tomb. According to the inscription the Queen, several concubines, some dwarfs (such as were usually found serving in the houses of the great) and a dog were buried in the same tomb. These members of the household had been "sent to join" the dead king. This sounds horrible, but the victims considered it an honour to be with their lord in the next world as well. In later times this custom fell into desuetude.

I have said above that the funerary gifts attracted thieves. Brick buildings were therefore abandoned in favour of those mighty monuments the pyramids, which we regard as the incarnation of Egypt.

Let us have our camels saddled for the morning, but we must start early, if possible at sunrise, to reach the necropolis of Sakkara in good time. When the sun gets high the ride will

Above: the Step Pyramid. Left: the "sham" Pyramid. Right: the Bent Pyramid

be nothing like as pleasant. At first our little caravan threads its way through the fertile Nile valley. We see the hardworking *fellahin* busy in their fields. From time to time we pass one of those primitive water-wheels by which the Nile water is drawn up and distributed among the furrows. As in the time of the Pharaohs, the motive power of these contraptions is supplied by an ox, a camel or a donkey. We see too how the peasant ploughs his fields with the same primitive wooden ploughs as were used in antiquity. The *fellah* has never been able to adapt himself to motors and other modern inventions.

Then we ascend to the higher-lying desert where some of the Sakkara monuments are to be found. The first is the Step Pyramid, built by King Djoser about 2650 B.C. It was a huge building, nearly two hundred feet high, containing one tomb chamber. We know today that originally the Step Pyramid was not in its present form. King Djoser first built a long, low mastaba. He did not like it. He had another added and eventually five were superimposed. In this way the first pyramid came into being. The glory of discovering this monument fell to a German professor, Ludwig Borchardt.

Many achæologists have worked on this pyramid and to all of them it has yielded up secrets. Two alabaster sarcophagi were found. In one of them lay the body of an eight-year-old child. The mummy of the king had been stolen, but there was a detached foot in the tomb. In the other sarcophagus the archæologists Firth and Quivell found the remains of a wooden coffin which had once been gilded. A few fragments of wooden bands were lying about – the first evidence of their use to prevent tampering. In one chamber there were three thousand stone vessels. How many other objects may it have originally contained!

After the burial, the long passage leading to the tomb chamber in the innermost recesses of the pyramid had been closed with granite blocks. No thief could penetrate to the tomb, but neither could the food and drink, needed by the deceased in the other world, be brought in. So a mortuary temple was built just in front of the pyramid. In it was laid everything required for the dead man's welfare. The temple was also a sanctuary where the living could commune in thought with the deceased.

Laid out round the pyramid were graves for the queen, the princes and princesses and high dignitaries. The builder, Imhotep, may not have realized that his pyramid was to be the model for many others.

For a long time the Step Pyramid was the only visible monument – a proud and rather melancholy monument – among the sand dunes at Sakkara. Today the area has been cleared of loose sand and about thirty small pyramids have been discovered as well as a buried town, with houses, temples and tombs. It is an Egyptian Pompeii.

In 1954 Dr. Zakaria Goneim laid bare an unfinished pyramid, a mastaba which had been concealed by driven sand for four thousand five hundred years. When he was clearing out the long passage leading forty yards down to the tomb chamber a heavy stone fell from the roof and killed a labourer. Was the god's curse at work?

In the tomb chamber, which was unaccountably hot, stood a huge sarcophagus made of a single block of alabaster and on it lay a large spray of fennel, the gum of which was used for medicinal purposes. There is no doubt that the body of King Senakt, or Sechem-chet, had originally been buried in it, together with a vast store of treasures.

But when the ceremonial opening of the sarcophagus took place on the 26th June, 1954, an unutterable disappointment was in store. The alabaster sarcophagus was empty! Had the body been stolen? Was the chamber a decoy? Had the dead man, a son of Djoser, been buried elsewhere?

The confusion was worse confounded when a wooden chest was found containing twenty-one bangles, a necklace, some tweezers and a drinking cup, all of pure gold. This drinking-cup, a marvellous piece of filigree work, is the finest specimen of the art of goldsmiths who flourished five thousand years ago.

A similar drinking-cup had previously been found in a tomb in Ur, in Chaldea, and another in the Indus region. How can this similarity be explained, having regard to the great distances involved? When will this problem be solved?

The next Pharaoh to build a pyramid was Snofru, in 2630 B.C. Probably he did not use it as a tomb. Its peculiar construction has caused it to be considered as a "sham" pyramid. Although soundly built of stone the upper part subsequently collapsed and was buried in sand. To-day the pyramid is only a hundred and forty feet high.

Snofru built another pyramid, but it is not known whose tomb it was. Hieroglyphics reveal that both pyramids had been sacked by thieves as early as 1200 B.C.

The "Bent" Pyramid, in contrast to some later brick pyramids, is six hundred feet long at the base and three hundred feet high. It is the first work of true pyramid form.

One discovery followed another. Goneim soon noticed that only the first constructional stage of this pyramid had been completed. The king's cartouche gave the name "Sekhem-khet", a hitherto unknown pharaoh. Was he the successor of Djoser? A year later Goneim found an ivory plaque bearing the name of King Djeserti-ankh. In Manetho's list Djeserti is given as Djoser's successor. Sekhem-khet is the Horus name which was given to the pharaoh after his death. It was customary for him to be given another name for use in the underworld.

Djeserti reigned only a few years, which explains why his pyramid was not completed. Even the underground section, extending 150 feet into the sandstone, is of rough and ready construction. Successors rarely bothered to complete such monuments.

The longest passage below ground is 400 feet. Many stone vessels were found in other passages and 120 small chambers. In one chamber was a pile of bones of sacred animals.

But where was the king's mummy? Why was the exquisite alabaster sarcophagus empty? Was the building only a "decoy", or was it a "ritual" grave for the reception of the canopus jars containing the heart, lungs, liver and intestines? Goneim felt certain that the pyramid was the burial place of the royal placenta, or afterbirth.

In this connection we might remember the so-called "south tomb", discovered with others years ago in the courtyard of the walled enclosure surrounding the adjacent Step Pyramid. The canopic jars of Djoser had been buried in it. Nor must we forget that King Snofru had two pyramids built, one for his mummy and the other for his placenta.

The custom of burying the chief's placenta with honours also flourished among the negroes of Uganda not long ago.

When an heir was born in Egypt the afterbirth was saved and preserved in a sanctuary because it was regarded during the earlier dynasties as a "twin brother", stillborn, of course, but none the less calling for honourable burial. It preserved the king's "life force".

The area surrounding the recently discovered pyramid is as large as two football grounds. The boundary wall exposed by Goneim is 650 yards in length. At a later period the Egyptians used this consecrated ground as a cemetery. A very large number of bodies was found here. Among them, swathed in reed matting, was the body of the Lady Ka-Nefer-Nefer (the twice-beauteous Ka) with a gilded death mask. Sixty-two papyri in demotic script were also among the finds.

The name of the architect, Imhotep, is inscribed in red ochre on the white limestone. Manetho says that he was regarded as a miracle 5000 years ago, and 2000 years later the Greeks compared him with their Aesculapius.

Little was known of Snofru himself. But in 1947 Dr. Salem Hussein discovered inscribed stones in the vicinity of this pyramid. With these as his starting point Dr. Achmed Fakhry explored further and in 1951 unearthed some splendid statues of local gods. Then chamber after chamber came to light and finally the mortuary temple of Snofru. More statues were found, among them a particularly fine one of granite – the figure of King Snofru himself. Another interesting find was a

20-foot stela with inscriptions. Snofru was the father of the great Cheops.

Fakhry then tackled the "Bent" Pyramid. A somewhat steep shaft led him down 300 feet into a huge chamber. Its roof was 90 feet above the floor. It was empty. One inscription revealed the name of King Snofru and there was another which ran: "the gates of Heaven stand wide open for the ascending King." It is the oldest inscription in a pyramid and proves once and for all that this Snofru had built two pyramids. A small pyramid in the vicinity revealed the name Hetaphras. She was his wife. But their mummies were never found.

Cheops took over the government about 2000 B.C. He followed custom in immediately setting about the construction of his tomb. The welfare of his people was of less importance. Every advantage of past experience must be taken to ensure that future tomb-robbers should labour in vain.

The shaft at the end of which the tomb and treasure chambers were placed was driven deeper into the rocky ground. The rock itself made foundations superfluous. The first layer of stones could be placed upon it and the base of the pyramid laid out. Each side was 710 feet long. The roof of the tomb chamber was supported by colossal granite monoliths to take

Hauling a block of stone

the weight of the huge mass of stone. A narrow passage led into the tomb chamber where the stone sarcophagus had been placed.

On the east bank of the Nile, not far from Cairo, are the quarries of Mokattam. Thousands of workers must have toiled here under the burning sun for years to cut and shape those stones, each measuring a cubic yard, which were required for building pyramids.

Transport columns, comprising thousands of unfortunates, hauled the heavy blocks on primitive sledges. Crossing the Nile on frail lighters, the team proceeded to the building-sites and then dragged these monster stones to the top of an inclined plane. The distance from the quarries was about six miles. On that causeway of sweat and misery passed nearly two and a half million blocks. The 450 feet high pyramid remains today the visible symbol of the power of a king who intended his people to realize that *he* was their god.

Is it really possible to speak respectfully of such a monument? It is horrifying to think that hundreds of thousands of slaves suffered torture and semi-starvation for twenty years to build it. Another ten years must be added for the laying of the roads. Two and a half million blocks of stone. How many million blows? Can we not still hear the groans of the slaves, and smell the reek of sweat and onions?

How a pyramids was built

But it was not only slaves who were exploited in this terrible fashion. Every year when the Nile flooded the fields and made agricultural work impossible, the *fellahin*, urged on by the priests, presented themselves in droves to His Majesty the Pharaoh, their king and god, to offer him the work of their hands as a token of reverence. Kings conquered and made their vassals pay for the conquest. Cheops robbed them of strength and vigour and then forced them to acknowledge him as a god.

The king was the incarnation of divinity. To be on the same

footing as the gods he had his person and tomb strictly guarded and was prepared to sacrifice half a nation to that end.

Cheops tyrannized over his people for fifty years. He was succeeded by Chefren who followed his example. They practically prohibited access to the sanctuaries. Then came Mykerinos. Of him Herodotus wrote:

"He disliked the work of his predecessors. He re-opened the temples, freed a nation which had been maddened by oppression and saw that justice was done. Mykerinos was a kindly ruler but a series of misfortunes began with the death of his favourite daughter. Her grief-stricken father had her interred in a quite special fashion. A wooden cow was hollowed out and gilded and then his daughter was buried in it.

"The sacred cow was not only to be found in graves. There was one still standing in my time in the royal palace at Saïs. It was draped in a purple mantle. One could see the gold on the head and neck. All the rest of the body was covered up. It has a solar disc between the horns. The cow is not standing but

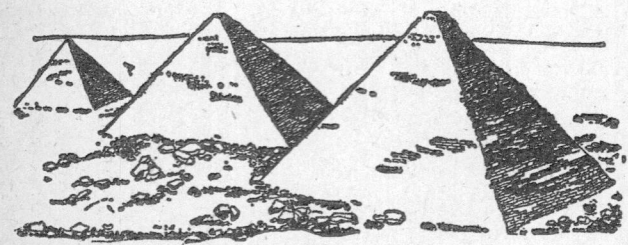

The Pyramids of Giza

kneeling. The Egyptians burn incense before it all day and a lamp is kept burning at night. Once a year the cow is brought out and the Egyptians dance round it, beating their breasts as a sign of mourning. But some say that Mykerinos lusted after his daughter and forced her against her will, and that she hung herself for shame. Her mother cut off the hands of all her maidservants because they had betrayed her whereabouts to her father when he was looking for her."

It may well be that the slaves preferred work on the pyramids. Perhaps they even sang at their work. The knowledge that they were contributing to the erection of a divine monument may have lightened their burdens. It is possible, because the priests stamped on any desire for progress and justice as indicating lack of faith in religion and the gods. Belief in the gods was drummed into the people in the same way that advertising is thrown at their heads to-day.

When the Pharaoh was dead his burial was carried out with great pomp and ceremony and the pyramid was closed for ever. With that end in view the builders cleverly incorporated in the structure a huge block of granite poised over the entrance to the passage leading into the interior. When all the mourners had left the tomb chamber this great stone was allowed to fall into this passage, completely blocking it. A few feet further in, a second block was lowered into position and the whole passage was then filled in and completely camouflaged. The slaves employed in this final operation – who thus knew its secrets – were taken some distance into the desert and slaughtered, or left to starvation and hyenas. No wonder it was thought that those secrets had perished with them. But posterity was to learn that they had not.

Cheops' pyramid was 480 feet high, Chefren's 450, that of Mykerinos 190 and that of Khamet 126. Cheops held the record, his pyramid remaining the world's highest building until Monsieur Eiffel produced a structure twice as high.

These pyramids are remarkable because they are all quite close together at Giza. Khamet's was not discovered until 1933. In its immediate vicinity a wonderful processional avenue, flanked on each side by a row of sphinxes, was disinterred from the sand. Between Giza, Sakkara and Dashur, an area that can easily be inspected in one camel ride, no less than sixty-nine pyramids were successively built.

But there is more than the sixty-nine pyramids. Each had its mortuary temple and an adjacent cemetery with numerous tombs for the royal family and members of the court. Everyone wanted to have a tomb befitting his or her rank as near as possible to the dead master, even if it could not be in the pyramid itself. It must be remembered that these buildings were not only tombs but "safes" for immense quantities of treasure. Altogether one hundred and forty pyramids were built in ancient Egypt.

In 1925 fifteen tombs of members of Cheops' family were discovered, including the three small pyramids of his wives, ten mastabas of sons and daughters and that of the princess

Merasankh who was also married to her royal father. All these tombs had been rifled.

Herodotus records a bit of old scandal about one of the princesses. He says that she met the cost of her tomb out of her immoral earnings. Each of her lovers presented her with a stone. The historian goes on to record that the Pharaoh placed his daughter in an aristocratic brothel in order to earn money.

We know from reliefs that the Egyptian used funeral-ships and models of them have been found in tombs. In 1898–1901 German archæologists found not far from Giza the so-called "Sun Sanctuary" of Abu Gorab, a tomb which King Niuser-Ra had built. It had an outer court with an alabaster altar and at the side a smaller brick building containing a large model funeral-ship, the biggest specimen known. Unfortunately the whole place was in ruins.

Inscriptions showed that there must also be a "southern tomb" with bodies or funeral-ships. In 1954 this tomb was found. Under the direction of the road-builder Kharmal-el-Malakh work was started on a by-pass which would give tourists direct access to the pyramid of Cheops. One day the navvies found a row of sandstone blocks lying close together in the sand. Each stone was 15 feet long, three feet wide and over six feet thick. Were these stones part of the causeway along which the vast stones used in the building of the pyramids had been hauled?

They were not. Malakh had one of the stones tilted sideways and gasped with excitement when he looked into the hole which was revealed. There was a huge tomb-chamber with two funeral-ships, each 162 feet long. These ships had some resemblance to the viking Gokstadt ships in Oslo, but as they were made in the time of Cheops they are thousands of years older.

For his journey in the next world Cheops needed two ships, one to follow the sun-god Ra's course by day, the other his course by night. The Egyptians almost always gave symbols a material form.

The Pharaohs had every part of their funeral-ships built of the finest wood from cedars of Lebanon. Their decks were piled high with treasures of all sorts. Then the ships were walled up underground to await discovery by posterity just like the mummies of the monarchs themselves.

The idea was that the dematerialized soul of the deceased would, like the ships, follow the eternal course of the sun-god and join the company of all good men who have passed into the Beyond. Though the tomb-chambers were hermetically sealed, this precaution has not saved these ships from decay. We must hope that modern chemistry will be able to preserve their hulls, the carved and painted oars, the shrouds and linen clothes, at any rate for a considerable time.

Let us have a closer look at one of the few private tombs which have been discovered, the mastaba of Ti. He was a big landowner with a high position at court and had his "dwelling for eternity" built in the vicinity of the Step Pyramid. His tomb shows that he was very rich. We first enter a porch and pass through a door into a large hall with a wooden roof supported by twelve square columns. This pillared hall was the place of sacrifice and also for quiet communion with the dead. Steps and a passage descending steeply lead through an antechamber to the tomb-chamber with the sarcophagus of the patriarchal Ti. No one will ever know the extent of the treasure buried in the tomb of Ti because thieves got there before the archæologist. Yet it is still a magnificent specimen. The walls of polished granite are covered with reliefs depicting scenes from the life of the deceased.

The lay-out of every tomb with any pretension to consideration provided for as many chambers as there are rooms in a fair-sized house. The tomb of the vizir Merer of the VIth Dynasty had no less than thirty-one!

Most of the scenes in the tomb of Ti deal with life in the country or journeys on the Nile. Workers are seen ploughing, sowing and reaping, threshing and grinding corn, busy with fowls, taking cattle to pasture. There is a relief of an ox being lassoed, slaughtered and cut up and another of peasants bringing fat ducks, geese, fowls and fruits as presents to their lord and master.

Why have time and labour been lavished in decorating the walls of a tomb with scenes like these? What is the significance of this practice? It must be that the accent is on food for the afterworld, and not on agriculture as such. Such pictures are there to remind the relatives of their duty to bring food. Even if they forget that duty, it may be supposed that Ka, the god of the dead, will at any rate derive spiritual nourishment from looking at the pictures.

In the tombs of the Pharaohs, on the other hand, the usual themes are hunting, feats of arms and the slaughter of enemies.

But all tombs of courtiers were not as grand as that of Ti. Many of them were very plain and the mummies of their occupants no more elaborate than the mummies of paupers.

Before we leave the necropolis of Sakkara something must be said about the tombs of sacred animals.

There is a cemetery for cats, dedicated to their patron goddess, Rechet. When a sacred cat died, it was embalmed and its mummy borne to the cemetery in solemn procession. A wall of bricks made from Nile mud guarded the last resting place of these pampered creatures.

In 1882 some peasants were searching for artificial dung in the vicinity of Beni Hassan when they found a very large cemetery with countless mummies of cats; they simply stamped on them and used them as manure.

Mummy of a sacred cat

When a sacred animal died it was mourned as if it had been a favourite child.

Herodotus has a most curious passage about cats:

"Egyptian behaviour is most extraordinary when there is a fire. They surround the burning house but never thinking of entering it to extinguish the flames. If a cat slips through the crowd of spectators and enters the house they all begin to weep and wail. When an ordinary domestic cat dies all the occupants cut off their eyebrows. If a dog dies they shave the whole body. Dead cats are taken to sanctuaries in the city of Bubastis but dogs are buried in sacred coffins in the town where they die.

"To explain why so many animals are sacred would involve me in religious speculation which I usually try to avoid, but I can say that death is the penalty for killing a sacred animal and if it was a beast of burden there is also a fine the amount of which is fixed by the priests."

There were tombs of sacred cats at Bubastis also. At Thebes a tomb for sacred monkeys was discovered. The bodies had been gilded and buried in coffins made from papyrus leaf. Even more important were the tombs of the sacred Apis-bulls, hewn out of the solid rock four hundred yards down.

White bulls with a black patch on their foreheads were classed as sacred. After death the Apis-bull shared the privilege enjoyed by humans of being absorbed in the god Osiris. He himself became a god of the dead and entitled to the appellation "Lord of the West".

Even when the Greeks ruled Greece much later, pilgrimages were still made to Apis-bull shrines. At fixed times on certain days the animal could be admired and worshipped under priestly supervision. An Apis-bull could even be an oracle. Several of its oracular utterances have come down to us.

Its birthday was celebrated annually for seven days. Its death was an occasion for public mourning and it was given a monument on which were recorded its life history, the name of its mother and the village where it was born.

It is very difficult for us to imagine why the death of a sacred bull meant so much and why large quantities of expensive embalming oil were lavished upon it or thousands of yards of linen used in wrapping up its carcase. Its magnificent obse-

Apis, the sacred bull of Memphis. On its head are Ra, the sun, and Uraeus, the serpent

quies, honoured by the presence of the Pharaoh and his court, ended with interment alongside other bulls in a resplendent sarcophagus in the Serapeum.

The final section of the funeral route was an avenue 220 yards long, flanked on each side by 150 sphinxes. Above the Serapeum was a sacrificial temple, a place to which devout pilgrims brought their offerings to the dead bull. As the modern traveller passes through the subterranean passages of this Serapeum he sees on both sides the niches in which the sarcophagi of these sacred bulls were deposited. The sarcophagi themselves are of yellowish quartz or red or dark brown granite. With their surfaces looking as if they had been polished yesterday, it is not easy to believe that they are 4,600 years old. Each is ten feet long, seven feet wide and hewn out of a single block of stone, and the impression produced is remarkable. The visitor has to mount a ladder to see inside them.

Many questions spring to the mind of the modern investigator. How did the ancients fashion these giant blocks out of solid rock without dynamite or drills of the finest steel? How did they master the problems of cutting them into a rectangular shape, polishing them like glass and hollowing them out to fit a bull? Without waggons, lorries, cranes and cables how did they move them hundreds of miles from the quarries in Upper Egypt to Lower Egypt and then over the soft desert sand to the subterranean cemetery in the solid rock?

When a monument is set up today an inscription explains its purpose but no one bothers to enlighten us about the technique of its erection. The minds of the Egyptians must have run on the same lines. The processes they employed were well known and considered obvious. No papyrus has anything to say about them. This silence has provided the archæologist with his opportunity and he has made considerable use of it. In the tomb of Tuthotep was found a drawing showing how a small statue was moved. It was placed on a sort of sledge which was drawn by 1,700 men. The feat looks easy put that way, but in practice it must have been quite otherwise. One thing is certain; that in Egypt nothing could be accomplished save by brawn, skill, patience, perseverance, blood and sweat. The rest remains a matter of guesswork.

On the walls of a tomb at Thebes there are some coloured frescoes showing overseers brandishing sticks. An inscription, as translated by Brugsch runs as follows:

Mummy of a sacred bull

"The overseer speaks to the workmen. Put your backs into it or you will feel my stick."

In the Old Testament we find something similar. "Ye are idle, ye are idle!" The unhappy Israelites cried unto Pharaoh, saying, "Wherefore dealest thou thus with thy servants?" The stick may well be the explanation of the mighty achievements of ancient Egypt. It still rules the world. Even today there is an Egyptian-Arabic saying that the stick is a gift from Heaven. An odd gift, hoary with age and yet eternally young!

No sarcophagus has yet revealed an undamaged mummy of a bull. All have been torn apart and yielded rich booty to the thieves – gold, beryls, chalcedony and lapis lazuli. There is no record of how many objects of gold or precious stones, or amulets against the powers of darkness, were hidden in the wrappings of these mummies. Only the thieves know the secret. To the thieves the sacred bull was no deity but just a common animal. But there is one fortunate exception. When Mariette discovered the bull necropolis in 1851 he wrote:

"I was deeply moved when I entered the Apis Chamber where no human foot had trodden for thousands of years.... What a bit of luck was in store! A few days later I found a niche which had been walled up and missed by the robbers. That niche had, according to an inscription, been walled up by Rameses II in 1270 B.C. The finger marks of the Egyptian who placed the last stone in the wall were visible in the chalk and also his footprints in a pile of sand. Nothing was missing from this mortuary chamber in which an embalmed bull had lain for four thousand seven hundred years."

South of Sakkara lies the fertile Fayum. The ancient Greeks called its chief city Crocodilopolis because, in the XIIth

Dynasty, about 2000 B.C. there was a town on the Nile known as Shedet. It was the centre of worship of the crocodile-headed water-god, Sucho, the protector of the fertile Fayum area. Here in antiquity there was a lake swarming with sacred crocodiles and a temple near by. When a crocodile died its skin was not used to provide expensive handbags for Egyptian maidens. On the contrary, religious law required that it should receive the most sumptuous funeral. It was embalmed and mummified like royalty and then borne with full honours to the tomb set aside for its kind. Long after its death humble folk continued to bring gifts to place in the tomb.

All this may seem incredible, but at Asuit, further south near Komombo, and particularly in a tomb at Monfabut, there are some red sandstone mortuary chapels containing mummies of crocodiles. The ruins of Crocodilopolis in the Fayum remind us of the so-called "Labyrinth". Herodotus saw it and wrote:

"Its size and splendour defy description and it was even larger than the pyramids. It had twelve covered courts. Fifteen hundred rooms were below ground and another fifteen hundred above. The priests would not let me visit the subterranean rooms because they contained tombs of kings and sacred crocodiles. What the Egyptians have built here is indeed a

Mummy of a sacred crocodile

marvel. Huge columns and pillared halls are painted in bright colours and there are wall paintings everywhere. The place is surrounded by a vast wall. There is a pyramid close to where the labyrinth ends. But the greatest marvel is the adjacent Lake Moeris which was excavated by human hand. Its area is 3,600 stadion and its depth 50 fathoms. This Egyptian feat is much greater than all Greek sanctuaries put together."

The ibis (Ibidae), of the stork family, was the symbol of Thoth, the god of wisdom. When one of these birds died it was embalmed and buried with solemn ceremonies.

The sanctuary of Thoth, the "Lord of Shmun" is very

ancient and was subsequently called Hermopolis by the Greeks. It had temples, parks and ponds in which ibis were kept and tended as if in a zoological garden. Their burial-place, however, was deep underground. It was the archæologist Sami Cabra who discovered it. A monumental flight of steps, 120 in number, descends through rocky ground into a large chamber where the embalming took place. Alongside are various rooms in which the priests performed their rites and stored the gifts and money which they received for their services.

These rooms lead into a labyrinth of many passages, several as much as 400 feet in length. In the walls are a great number of niches in which the sarcophagi of the sacred ibis were placed. Long years of excavation have disclosed innumerable urns with ibis mummies brought here from all parts of Egypt.

In a room with an altar a squatting baboon and two ibis of gilded wood gaze at a door behind which is the tomb of the High Priest, Anch-Hor. The stone sarcophagus of the priest has a lid of silver gilt. Alabaster vases with three hundred and sixty-five statuettes of gleaming faience were part of the funeral impedimenta. Ancient custom decreed that these figures should serve as substitutes for the deceased in the work he would have to perform in the next world. Four million ibis and a hermit priest 100 feet below ground!

The Egyptians probably believed that the soul travelled and that all these birds were "aircraft carriers" for the immortal souls of dead Egyptians. Such beliefs and rites seem primitive to us and yet many of the myths have a noble and near-to-nature element which explains why a particular creature was considered a deity. Religion also is highly complicated in many ways. How and when, for instance, could men have thought that the soul returned to the human body, seeing that the latter, though embalmed, was practically destroyed? Equally incomprehensible is the Egyptian idea of eternity. Man himself, coffins and funeral gifts, all perishable, but none the less prepared for eternity!

The rat (ichneumon), the mouse, the toad and the dung beetle, to name but a few others, were also considered sacred. Their remains were preserved in small bronze coffins, fitted with handles, which were hung in consecrated places or inhabited houses. All sacred animals were preserved from ill-treatment and woe betide anyone who injured one. Hawks, snakes and other creatures, were also considered sacred and regarded as gods. They played a great part in ordinary life as well as in the next world.

Apart from the tombs of royalties, high priests and officials, the necropolis of Sakkara and its counterpart at Giza abound in subterranean passages containing mass graves of mummies of the lower classes. After lying desiccated for four thousand years in these dry and warm surroundings they were to experience a very peculiar resurrection. In the first half of the last century travellers used to return from Egypt with wonderful tales about the country and some even had mummies among their luggage. Since many people in Europe still believed in magicians and witches, an ingenious chemist bethought himself of the idea of making a medical preparation out of mummies. A doctor wrote:

"The mummy must first be reduced to powder. This powder is then mixed with vegetable oil to the consistency of paste. This ointment is most beneficial in the treatment of fractured limbs or ribs and inflammation of the lungs."

The French doctor Savary added:

"Only mummies which are quite black and have a pleasant odour must be used."

It is hard to believe that this macabre use of mummies for medical purposes gave rise to an active trade in them, a trade of value to the Egyptians because it helped to fill their empty coffers. When the *fellahin* could not till their fields during the inundations they took to the spade and burrowed for graves containing mummies. There were plenty of them. But when the stock of mummies seemed likely to give out some Jews from Alexandria set about manufacturing fakes. They procured corpses of slaves who had just died, dressed them up as mummies and left them to dry in the hot desert sand for two or three years. At the end of that period they were ready for sale.

It was, however, the thousands of real mummies which gave the "necropolis of Sakkara" its name. It must also be remembered that this was the time when all the museums of Europe were competing for mummies. In one of his novels Théophile Gautier makes Cleopatra say:

"I must confess, Charmian, that I am haunted by an idea which scares me. In other countries men bury their dead so that their dust and the earth may become one. But here in

Egypt you might say that their sole occupation is preserving their dead from decay. Under the ground which these people tread lie other peoples. Every town is built on tombs and memorials and each generation that passes leaves its mummies in a world of darkness."

The dominating feature of the necropolis of Giza is the pyramid of that name. America's sky-scrapers may be higher because the latest architectural technique has been employed in their construction but the mass of material in them does not approach it in bulk.

When we remember that it was built about 2600 B.C., which means four thousand, six hundred years ago, we cannot restrain our admiration for such a feat despite all the cruelties associated with it. This monument of eternity seems to give us a cold and indifferent stare. It was already an antiquity when humanity first heard of Christ and his teaching. The pyramid of Cheops remains unchallenged as the first of the "Seven Wonders of the World", even though the engineers of that age had no modern equipment at their disposal.

If the figure given by Herodotus is to be accepted, the mere cost of feeding the army of workers amounted to the equivalent of many millions of pounds at the present day. But what Herodotus says is not always reliable. It has a considerable quota of contradictions and fairy stories.

The technical lay-out of this pyramid is a triumph of skill even though we know that the architects went wrong at times. Up to a point the construction shows the greatest care in the original plans to achieve accurate calculation, but subsequently mistakes were made. It can also be assumed that many miscalculations have come to light in the case of later pyramids. Error is as old as man himself.

The pyramid of Cheops and the Great Wall of China, two mighty human achievements, are placed at the edge of a desert. They have been exposed to the action of dust which in the course of thousands of years has worn away a very considerable part.

The "Seven Wonders of the World" existed in antiquity. The first was the pyramid of Cheops. It was not till about two thousand years later that the rest made their appearance, the Hanging Gardens of Semiramis in Babylon, the Temple of Artemis at Ephesus, the pillars of the temple of Zeus at Olympia (the work of Phidias), the tomb of Mausolus at

Harlicarnassos, the Colossus of Rhodes and the lighthouse on the island of Pharos near Alexandria.

The eighth "Wonder" could have been the Chinese Wall but it was unknown to the western world at that time. China was too far away. The first and eighth Wonders are still with us but the others have vanished.

According to the archæologists Smith, Moreaux and Piazza, and the engineers Eyth and Taylor, the architects and engineers of Cheops' time must have had an astounding knowledge of their subject. They have poured their knowledge of geometry into stone and given it permanent form over an area of 60,000 square yards.

The following statements are not accepted by all scholars but certain figures and remarkable facts should not be withheld from the reader. They will make him think! The length of each of the four sides of the pyramid is 755 feet. The top has been worn away by several yards in the course of the centuries, but the original height can be calculated from the angle of inclination and the area of the sides.

By dividing the length of the side by half the height we get the figure $Pi = 3.14159$, accurate to five points of decimals. This is amazing because two thousand years later Archimedes, the great Greek mathematician, could get no nearer than 3 1/7. It was not until the XVIIth Century that the figure was given as accurately as the pyramid builders had worked it out.

Moreover the ground plan of the pyramid shows a square the sides of which are aligned exactly north-south and east-west.

The geographical position of this pyramid is equally remarkable, for the degrees of latitude and longitude which cross the site intersect more land than any others. Was it by chance or design that this point was fixed as the centre of the earth's surface? If it was by design, and Cheops really knew Egypt's geographical position, it can be accepted that the Egyptians of five thousand years ago were better geographers than any existing at the time of Columbus!

The Rhind papyrus in London, dating from about 2000 B.C., can be regarded as an Egyptian arithmetic book, with examples of addition, multiplication and division, and the Moscow mathematical papyrus reveals wondrous knowledge. One small example was the calculation of the cubic contents of a square truncated pyramid from its height and the length of the edges with the help of the formula $V = \frac{h}{3}(a^2 + ab + b^2)$. This discovery was often attributed to the Greek Democrites (*circa* 300 B.C.). Herodotus regarded Egypt as the birthplace of geometry.

The Egyptians were not greatly interested in the natural sciences. They had no use for a knowledge of nature or the world beyond their own ken except insofar as it could serve their own purposes. It never occurred to them to speculate about abstract truth for its own sake. Such inquiry was reserved for the genius of the Greeks.

It is true that even the Egyptians of the Old Kingdom had a stock of practical knowledge of astronomy. They had divided the sky into sections, identified some of the fixed stars and invented certain instruments with which to observe them. Thanks to these instruments some practical conclusions could be drawn from what they saw. But they evolved no theories about the course and movements of the heavenly bodies, or their purpose and meaning.

Their ideas about the earth were exceedingly primitive. Was the earth a globe? No nation of antiquity ever found that out. True knowledge about the universe is the result of the most recent research of modern astronomers.

As has already been said, pyramids were primarily royal tombs. In 1880 Heinrich Brugsch Pasha had certain pyramids opened and carefully examined. It will be realized that it was no easy task to penetrate into the mighty mass of stone enfolding the tomb chamber – a nut in its shell. If the pyramid of Cheops were hollow and made of tin it could easily cover St. Peter's in Rome. If all its blocks were joined end on they would make a wall, a yard high, round the whole of France.

With active help from the Arabs Brugsch went to work. His patience was sorely tried for he could hardly wait for the moment to enter the first pyramid. Actually the passages had been closed up and were inaccessible but as the pyramid was built of brick and the top had been worn down to a considerable extent he decided to make the entry there. A lot of hard work brought the excavators to the tomb chambers.

Terrible disappointment was in store. Thieves had got there first and thoroughly looted the whole place. But there was one consolation. On the walls and the sides of the empty sarcophagus Brugsch found inscriptions out of the "Book of the Dead". He continued his operations. His next "burglary" was to open the pyramid of Phiops, a king of the seventh dynasty after Cheops. Unfortunately his previous experience was repeated. The tomb had been looted and the mummy unwrapped, searched for jewels and then smashed up. All that was left was some linen of such fine texture that his Arab assistants thought it was silk. In this pyramid were a large number of inscriptions, all in green lettering. It can be imagined with what ardour Brugsch threw himself into the task of deciphering them.

Many years ago the archæologist Engelbach discovered a tomb not far from the pyramid of Medun. An inscription in the antechamber ran: "The spirit of the deceased will wring the tomb-robber's neck like a chicken." The promise had been translated into performance, for there were two dead men in the tomb and one of them was the thief. At the very moment when he was about to strip the mummy for its jewels a heavy stone fell from the roof and crushed him. The arm of justice had struck a telling blow. The criminal's family had a long time – all their lives in fact – to wait for his return. Vanished, snuffed out, none could say what had happened to him. Now, four thousand years later, his fate is known.

Thieves had also been at work in another pyramid which Brugsch opened. He found the mummy unwrapped, robbed of all its treasures and contemptuously thrown on a heap of stones. The wrappings were lying near by. The mummy was of a strong young man with a remarkable growth of hair. It was well preserved and subsequently removed to the museum in Cairo.

The archæologist Petrie fared no better. He found a pyramid which had not been entered in modern times. The entrance itself was unknown. Believing that he was exploring "virgin ground" Petrie started out with high hopes and began to open up the north side. After weeks of hard work the entrance had not been found. Then he tried his luck on the east side, but with no greater success. Mountains of sand and rubbish were shifted. After reconsidering his problem, Petrie decided to abandon the search for the entrance and dig a tunnel through the middle.

This proved a heavier task than he had anticipated. After working for weeks to get half-way he found himself with a thick rampart of bricks behind him and the wall of a chamber in front. Beside himself with excitement, he drove his tunnel through this wall and found – a nasty shock. In the floor of this chamber was a hole, made by thieves, who had got there first and done their vile work.

Looking into that hole, Petrie did not stop to consider what the thieves could have taken. He meant to find out, though the hole was very small and it was quite dark beyond. A good tip procured the services of an Arab boy who descended into the cavity, holding a candle, by a step-ladder. All he could report was the smell of corruption, eighteen inches of water and two empty sarcophagi.

It was a meagre result!

Petrie enlarged the hole and went down himself. The water came up to his thighs. The two sarcophagi were there. But what had they contained and whose pyramid was this? He came out to fill his lungs, then dived in again but recovered nothing except some pottery fragments and small vessels. But these were inscribed with the name of Amenemhat III. At least he now knew which Pharaoh had raised this pyramid to his own glory and that of the gods.

But the presence of a second sarcophagus was still unexplained. The tomb chamber soon provided the answer. When it was cleared the searchers found a very beautiful sacrificial altar of alabaster embellished with about one hundred figurines which were all dedicated to Ptahneferu, the king's daughter. She must have died before the king and because he loved her so dearly he obviously wanted her to share his tomb with him.

This must have been another case of marriage between a pharaoh and his daughter; she would not otherwise have been buried in his tomb. I shall have something to say later about marriages between fathers and daughters and brothers and sisters.

Petrie considered the situation like any detective for he was determined to ascertain how the thieves had got in. First he found the original passage. It was filled with mud. On his hands and knees he removed the smelly mess and reached the upper part, which was dry. Although the passage wandered in all directions he was able to identify the point on the south side at which he had entered it. After toiling for several weeks he finally found the original entrance and was able to satisfy himself that the pyramid had been broken into about a thousand years before.

This pyramid revealed the skill of the architects in laying out a system of genuine passages and culs de sac. The entrance on the south side was certainly unusual. If the usual practice had been followed it would have been on the north.

Let us imagine ourselves following Petrie in the tracks of the thieves. After a few yards down the passage he found a steep stairway leading down in total darkness to a chamber which seemed to have no exit. Was it there to fool the uninvited? He passed through this door into another passage, but it was filled with stones. After all his efforts, he was in a cul de sac. He retraced his steps to the main entrance and there found another passage, camouflaged, branching off towards another empty chamber. After considerable search he discovered another trapdoor. Passing through both, he was in a third passage which again ended in an empty chamber.

It was as if the architects had been cunning psychologists and arranged that the chambers should whisper: "There was nothing here. You are wasting your time."

Petrie returned to his starting-point again and found yet another passage which led to yet another chamber. But this time there was something new – two depressions in the floor. He felt that these must mark the real entrance to the tomb chamber. A lot of masonry was duly pulled away and then it transpired that the whole thing was a blind and the entrance must be somewhere else. This discovery had not baffled the thieves.

After further search Petrie found a suspicious spot in the floor of the passage which he had traversed so often. Under this spot was a trench. This trench really led to the tomb chamber. But here he was faced with the greatest of all his difficulties – a chamber with granite walls of enormous thickness and no door. The only opening was in the roof and it was covered by a block of stone weighing fifty tons. It was impossible to lift it. The only solution was a toilsome boring through one of the walls.

The task had not proved beyond the capacity of the thieves and they had been richly rewarded. All Petrie found was remains of diorite, settings of lapis lazuli and a few small vessels. Everything else of value had been removed.

Even the chamber itself was an enigma out of the *Arabian Nights Entertainment*. It was not constructed of stones but scooped out of a single block of quartz, 23 feet in length and breadth and 13 feet high. This enormous block, weighing at least one hundred tons, had been quarried and shaped by the ancients.

Even after it had been hollowed out it weighed two thousand two hundred zentner, a figure which corresponds to the tare of eleven railway waggons. How was it fashioned and transported?

It was in fact a giant sarcophagus in which the two smaller sarcophagi of the King and his little daughter were placed.

Yet all the immense labours of the ancient Egyptians were in vain, and their pathetic belief in the inviolability of the after life proved a delusion. The pyramids were too big and too conspicuous to achieve the object for which they were built. Everyone knew that they housed untold treasures, which must be an irresistible temptation to thieves.

But no one should think that such a robbery could be carried out in one moonless night. It was a big affair, arranged and executed by organized bands with the complicity of some of the priests – priests who were guardians of such sacred places and betrayed the trust reposed in them. Such is the story of many a great Pharaoh, born in the purple, laid to rest as a god, and found thousands of years later in no better state than if he had received a pauper funeral!

In a papyrus we find these words:

"They build tombs of granite and great halls in the pyramids and fill them with marvels of beauty but their altars are as empty as those of the tired wretches who die unregarded on the river bank and have no one to mourn them. . . ."

There speaks a pessimist who has lost his faith in the efficacy of the ancient rites.

Petrie's disappointments only incited him to further efforts. A few months later he opened the tomb of the noble Horuta. Once again the tomb chamber was under water. The sarcophagus, buried in mud, had a lid weighing considerably more than a ton. As there was no room to lift this lid it had to be broken up, a task taking six weeks and carried out by candle-light and in great heat. A second lid presented an equally formidable problem, but eventually the great moment came when the mummy of Horuta was unwrapped and the eyes of the patient and indefatigable archæologist were rewarded by the sight of beryl and cornelian amulets, a golden ring on a finger of the mummy, golden birds inlaid with precious stones and statuettes of lapis lazuli.

Petrie said that no archæologist had seen such wonders before. Little did he know that Horuta was a trifle compared with what was to be discovered later.

The results of the investigation of other pyramids were also disappointing and the searchers had to content themselves with what they could learn from the numerous inscriptions which they found. It was far from unimpressive.

The "Book of the Dead" which has been mentioned proved a most valuable source of historical information. It gave the names of the builders, the dates of their reigns and their methods. The hieroglyphics gave facts about earlier royal houses and in some cases reported that they had been hated and despised because they built such huge pyramids and gave the hordes who actually did the work so little to eat.

Of great importance are the inscriptions referring to life in this world and the next. They record that man's life on earth is comparable to the course of the sun. The soul is the emanation of divine light, represented in material form as the sun. The sun's rays enter the human body at birth and at death return to the eternal deity who is the source of light. The human life cycle is essentially part of the solar system. Man, like the sun, is born in the east and ends in the west. After his death and dissolution the human light-bearer must follow the sun in its nightly course to arrive at the starting-point in the east, there to unite with the divinity and enter the region of eternal light.

Such is the theme, the fundamental proposition, with which these inscriptions are concerned but they also elaborate the picture of life after death. Names are given to the stars whose function is to guide the deceased on his journey from east to west and there are descriptions of subterranean regions and the inhabitants of this heavenly hereafter.

The reason is now clear why the Egyptians built their pyramids, tombs and temples of the dead on the west bank of the Nile. The sun sets in the west and the west was the Kingdom of the dead.

Other inscriptions tell us of a law which governs the order in time of the building of the pyramids and their geographical position. According to this law, the first Pharaoh was bound to build his pyramid in the extreme north and each successor must select a site south of the last pyramid built.

The sequence indicated by this law is of great importance to the Egyptologist. It is a fact that throughout Egypt's history the centre of interest progressively shifted southwards. Memphis, near Cairo, was the first capital. Then the focus of activity was transferred south to Thebes. The monuments in the south are always associated with the most recent events, The latest of all, the pyramids of Meroë in Ethiopia, represent a final fling of Egyptian culture in a remote region.

But wherever and whenever the pyramids were built they were always both tombs and manifestations of religious beliefs. Just as our Christian cathedrals were the meeting places of the faithful, the pyramid region was a "Holy Land" where believers assembled to offer sacrifices for the souls of the departed. It had a special local government consisting of a High Priest with a large staff of priestly subordinates.

It is often asked where the Egyptians originally came from. We do not know. But we do know what happened to them. Through wars and human error they eventually went the way of all flesh. No law of predestination but their own failings determined their fate.

The Sakkara necropolis with its innumerable graves – graves without worms, ghosts or the smell of corruption – was created for eternity and yet was in ruin before the first moment of eternity had passed. Today the lecturer haunts the monuments, telling bored globe-trotters about "Wonders of Egypt" which he probably does not really appreciate himself.

The sphinx of Giza, the very symbol of Egypt, has remained substantially untouched by the hand of time, though partly covered, and slightly worn away, by the sand of its native desert. Hewn out of the living rock it has the body of a lion with the head of a King. Without any scientific knowledge to help him man turned nature into a deity. A monument on the sun's parade-ground at the foot of the pyramids is both a warning and a mystery to all mankind.

In Goethe's *Faust* the sphinx says to Mephistopheles:

> "We of Egypt have long been wont
> To bend the world to our will.
> Guarding the pyramids,
> We sit in judgment on the nations.
> Inundations, war and peace,
> Mean less than nothing to us."

No one knows what Egyptian Michelangelo hewed this lump of rock, or for whom. Is this colossus to be looked upon purely as a work of art or must mystic significance be assigned to it? Some light on the mystery was thrown quite recently. In 1943 some excavators found a box dating from about 900 B.C. It was filled with marabou feathers collected by the cruel architect Ephara. An even more important find in the box was a papyrus which referred to "six secret slave-sphinxes". For ten years scholars worked on the problem. Where were these sphinxes and what did they mean? No one could solve the puzzle.

Chance came to their aid. In 1952 a trading caravan led by Omar El Hawari was passing a group of dunes in the Libyan desert seeking shelter in a fierce sandstorm. Taking refuge behind some hillocks they suddenly noticed a human hand, carved in stone, rising from the sand scattered by the storm. The Arabs approached and soon found themselves standing at the foot of a sphinx of red sandstone. It was about 65 feet high. The body, that of a lion, was over 250 feet long. Here the caravan found shelter.

On his return Hawari notified the Egyptologists. Professor Taminaruk and a band of workers hastened to the scene. Using a ladder, the Professor reached an opening, 48 feet above ground. Descending a ruined stairway he found himself in the interior of the monument. A terrible sight met his eyes. From the vaulted roof of a large chamber leather straps, undamaged by the passage of thousands of years, were hanging. Each strap ended in a noose and from each noose hung a skeleton upside down. Hundreds of skulls and bones strewed the floor.

Were these the remains of slaves who had built the monument and then been slaughtered to preserve some secret, or were they victims of some punitive expedition? (Every archæologist knows of the war crimes which were committed, probably during the confused dynastic struggles of the Egyptian-Lybian period.) Or had they been simply human sacrifices?

Since that discovery five more sphinxes of the same species have been found, thus confirming the information given in the Epharas papyrus.

A sphinx always represents some king. Hence the fact that

the serpent Uraeus and a vulture's head are found on the forehead. The sphinx of Giza is 180 feet long and 65 feet high. It may owe its existence to Cheops, but there is no certainty. A temple was built in the rocky ground under this sphinx but no one knows whether this was the sanctuary for the whole necropolis at Giza or a mortuary temple for Cheops himself.

The Sphinx of Giza

Sphinxes did not always take the form of a lion's body with a human head. Many have been found with the head of a ram. All were certainly regarded as the mystical guardians of temples and cemeteries. The face of the sphinx at Giza has been damaged. It is stated, but not proved, that in the Middle Ages the Mamelukes, who hated heathen antiquity, fired their cannon at it.

We regard the sphinx as male, but it is wrong to do so. The word "sphinx" only dates from the time of the Greek occupation. They gave that name to these particular monuments and regarded it as applying to any fabulous beast which was mysterious to man. There are sphinxes in Egypt which have heads other than men's heads, women's heads or ram's heads. Sphinx is the genus of which these are the species and as the word was female in Greek, we should consider sphinxes female too.

The Egyptians had two kinds of temple, the temple of the gods and the mortuary temple. Huge temples were built for gods of higher ranks, the largest of all, the Temple of Amun, for the god of that name. The mortuary temples were built in the vicinity of the tombs of grandees. In these temples prayers were said for the departed and various gifts accumulated, in particular food which they would need in the other world. In these temples priests, priestesses and temple servants performed their allotted functions. The temples in the Old Kingdom are in a very ruined state but those in the Middle and New Kingdoms are well preserved.

Chapter 4

SANCTUARIES, THIEVES AND HAREM NIGHTS

The Old Kingdom had perished by 2000 B.C. Attacks from without and internal disorder may well have brought about its fall. It was followed by the Middle Kingdom. There was a gradual transfer of state activity to Thebes in Upper Egypt and temples were erected, some of them to new gods, in a new centre of religious life round Karnak, Luxor and Dendera. The god Amun and his wife remained the principal deities and it was still a matter of prestige and duty to erect magnificent temples, such as that at Karnak, in their honour. To these others were subsidiary. A number of temples were built at Luxor, some of which were not completed for centuries.

The Ramesseum

We can still obtain an excellent idea of their magnificence in their great days. The Ramesseum, built by Rameses II, is a vast hall supported by huge columns. It had three high naves and six transepts. There is a central block of granite columns each seventy-eight feet high and long colonnades of one hundred and thirty-four columns arranged in pairs – a striking memento of past pomp and power.

In 1889 eleven of these columns suddenly collapsed. When the Egyptologist Legrain re-erected them he discovered more than one thousand statuettes in vaults under the temple. A few years later 779 stone and 1,700 bronze statuettes of gods came to light. These had originally been given to the temple and placed on altars, but after a time the priests had removed them to the vaults.

But in addition to the temple itself there are pylons, obelisks, statues and avenues of sphinxes. The first pylon is a piece of solid masonry 370 feet long, 160 high and 49 thick. The giant entrance was formed by several of such pylons. In front of these pylons obelisks were placed in pairs. The average height of an obelisk was 70 feet and each was usually fashioned out of a single block of pink granite. Up soared these needle-like structures, which were capped with a tiny pyramid, the so-called "pyramidions", frequently of gold but sometimes of copper.

Brugsch says that a secondary purpose of obelisks was to serve as lightning-conductors.

In front of the temple at Edfu there is a pair of obelisks, each 160 feet high. Their surfaces are polished like mirrors and covered with inscriptions recording that they were begun and finished within seven months. The statues are on the same grand scale. There are dozens of huge statues of Rameses, 45 feet high, placed between the columns.

The approach to many such temples is by a long avenue flanked on both sides by sphinxes in the form of rams. Gods taking unto themselves the likeness of sheep!

The Egyptian could not imagine a temple too large for the majesty of the gods. At Komombo there is a temple built out of the solid rock. The dimensions of one hall are 160 feet square and against each side wall giant statues were placed. One can only stand amazed at the skill of the ancients.

The temple of Dendera is another mighty witness to the power and glory of its age. Its columns are detached but the sanctuary has been dug in the solid rock. Its builder was Queen Hatshepsut who was married to her brother, Tuthmosis III. This marriage ended in bitter loathing on both sides. I shall have something to say later on about Tuthmosis, Egypt's mightiest ruler.

The tombs of the kings were also among the greatest monuments. Pyramids, the greatest centre of attraction of all to the common man, could no longer be built because the west side of Thebes, where it was intended to establish the new necropolis, was hemmed in by rocky hills. In places these hills come down to the very banks of the Nile.

Taught by experience that pyramids were too conspicuous and therefore tempting to thieves, the Egyptians bethought themselves of another form of burial place, the rock tomb, for their distinguished dead. The "Valley of the Kings" at Thebes is a hilly desert region a few miles wide, with many clefts and gullies which are highly suitable for tombs.

In accordance with custom, as soon as a Pharaoh began his reign he set about the construction of his tomb. The first step was to drive a long tunnel into a hill. It descended steeply for twenty yards and more and then opened out into a number of large chambers, comprising storehouses for food, a treasure chamber and the tomb chamber itself. The lay-out of a royal tomb would provide for between six and eight chambers.

Tuthmosis I (XVIIIth Dynasty) broke with the ancient custom of having the tomb and the mortuary temple close together. His architect, Ineni, built the temple in a very conspicuous place and tucked away the tomb itself in a hillside a mile and a half away. Inscriptions from Ineni's own tomb record his achievement in his own words:

"I and I alone supervised the building of a tomb for His Majesty. No one else knew where it was or ever heard about it."

Some 150 slaves were employed in the work, for it was desired to keep the number of those in the know as low as possible. These poor creatures were kept isolated from their fellows for years and killed when the task had been completed. The same system was followed in the building of almost all the tombs of kings, queens, princes and court dignitaries, priests and priestesses in the "Valley of the Kings". Each time large numbers of men were murdered lest the whereabouts of the corpse should leak out.

When a king died the chambers were filled with works of art, utensils, statues, statuettes, gold and silver ornaments, clothes, weapons and a very large number of jars containing food of all kinds. The monarch must have in his tomb everything he liked and valued when he was alive. The burial took place in the greatest secrecy. When the ceremony was over each of the chambers was walled up and the royal seal was impressed while the mortar was still wet. Then the entrance and all the passages were filled up with earth and care was taken to ensure that the ground should look as if it had never been disturbed.

When the unfortunate workers who knew the truth had been dispatched the king could sleep his eternal sleep in peace, secure in the knowledge that his burial place was unknown. Of course the public ceremonies to mark the passing of a monarch were held at the palace or in a temple, not at the tomb itself.

Despite all these elaborate precautions, when twenty-seven tombs were opened in 1875 they were found rifled from top to bottom. We know from hieroglyphs that thieves had found them even in antiquity. There were plenty of reverent and pious folk in those days, but their work was undone by cunning and greed. There was no trace of the stolen treasure.

When the thieves were caught they were brought to trial. A papyrus in the Ambrase collection in Vienna shows that sentences were very heavy. On the other hand, the report of another trial indicates that the criminals were handled very lightly and that the proceedings terminated to avoid a scandal. Persons in high position had been in collusion with the thieves and other officials had been lax in guarding the tomb.

Brugsch found in this papyrus the names of the persons who were involved in this case. In addition to some priests they were Peser, prefect of the eastern section of Thebes, Pevero, administrator of the necropolis on the western bank, and Kamwese, vizir of both sections. The last not only knew of the crime and remained silent but had lent his name to the corruption and robberies. A few years later five men were caught in the act. They were the carpenter, Tramun, the stonecutter Hapi, the water-carrier Kemwese, Amenheb a peasant and Ehenufer, a slave. They were thrown into prison and left without food or water. In addition they were lashed so ruthlessly that the palms of their hands and the soles of their feet were reduced to pulp. They were thus ripe for a written confession in these terms:

"We opened the coffins and found the revered mummies of His Majesty and his wife. We found a large number of amulets and gold ornaments. His Majesty's face was covered with a golden mask. We took all the gold from the mummies of the God and the queen and divided it in five parts."

The Court condemned them to death.

There were many similar cases of robbery and corruption under the XXth and XXIst Dynasties. Clearly they were symptoms of a civilization on the wane. The Abbott and Amherst papyri describe a criminal trial in some detail. The accused was a coppersmith, Peichert. He was blindfolded and taken to the tomb of King Sechmere. There the bandage was removed and he was forced to say how he had carried out the crime, what he had stolen and where he had hidden his booty. The papyrus goes on to relate that he was rigorously questioned, flogged, tied to a post and threatened that his nose and ears would be cut off if he did not tell the truth. He made a full confession and gave the names of the other members of his gang who were promptly arrested and brought to trial.

It is an old natural law that every action contains within itself the seeds of reaction, so it might be expected that this wholesale cult of the dead, this phenomenon of life completely absorbed in the contemplation of death, would provoke – as it did – a powerful reaction.

Gold underground could not ensure eternal rest. The gold in the tombs of the rich was not in bars but took the form of ornaments, small figurines of gods and sacred amulets. Caskets have been found filled to the top with such amulets. The figurines were important to the dead in the nether world, and therefore became a commercial article, placed on the market by manufacturers of funerary impedimenta. For the lower classes they were made of plaster, earthenware or stone and sold at all prices.

Amulets of gold or inlaid with precious stones, especially if consecrated by priests of the higher ranks, were far less common and their religious efficacy was much greater. This was well known to thieves who also knew that there was a great demand for such articles in the black market.

The Greek writer Strabo tells us that when he visited Egypt forty royal tombs were open and had already been rifled. Subsequently only twenty-seven were accessible so thirteen must have been closed up again and forgotten. Or did Strabo intentionally exaggerate?

Of the predecessors and successors of Rameses II and the celebrated Sesostris, father of Moses by adoption, little is known beyond their names. But we must suppose that their remains are lying somewhere even to-day.

In 1880 some archæologists on a visit to Thebes either came across certain antiquities or heard that they were for sale in an antiquarian's place of business. The objects in question were some statuettes and a sarcophagus containing a mummy. It was impossible to ascertain where they had been found. The subsequent history of the affair is as follows:

In July 1881, an American named Baton was living in Egypt. He was not an Egyptologist but as a collector of antiquities he knew quite a lot about the subject. One day he bought – of course in the black market – an exceptionally fine papyrus. Disregarding police and customs regulations, he hid it in his luggage and left the country. When he got home he consulted an expert, and was advised that he had secured a very valuable antiquity and that his papyrus threw new light on certain points in Egyptology.

This expert wrote to Professor Gaston Maspéro, director of the museum at Cairo, to tell him of Mr. Baton's find. Professor Maspéro was very perturbed because the museum had recently lost another important specimen. For years valuable antique trinkets, obtained no one knew where, had mysteriously found their way into the black market. Investigation had led nowhere.

Maspéro was also worried because Mr. Baton's papyrus, of which the expert had sent him a translation, had come from a royal tomb of the XXIst Dynasty, a period of which little or nothing was known. Other objects which must have come from the same tomb were being offered on the black market. Archæologists were anxiously inquiring who had discovered the tomb and where it was. Were modern tomb-robbers at work? The mystery must be cleared up. The Egyptian police were unsuccessful so Maspéro decided to act on his own account.

He sent an assistant to Thebes. This young man said nothing about his archæological qualifications but posed as a rich tourist. He took up his quarters in a fashionable hotel, bought several antique pieces in various shops, paid good prices and was lavish with tips. He was soon the talk of the town and ardently chased by dealers with antiquities to offer.

One day a dealer offered him a statue. He realized its value and that it was 3000 years old, but though the inscription upon it showed that it came from the tomb of the XXIst Dynasty, he controlled his feelings, affected not to be interested and turned the offer down. He then appeared to change his mind and after considerable haggling and hesitation not only bought the statue but intimated that he was in the market for more important pieces. The very same day the dealer put him in touch with a rich Arab, Adb-el-Rasul, who immediately showed the foreigner a number of rather minor antiquities. A few days later, when confidence was established, the Arab produced some more important pieces, among them a genuine mummy of the XXIst Dynasty.

The necessary proof had been obtained and the Arab was arrested.

Director Maspéro and the Assistant-Director Emil Brugsch questioned Mohammed Rasul, but in vain. Despite the evidence given against him by tourists, he denied that he had ever been engaged in such illegal activities as secret digging, the unauthorized purchase of antiquities or breaking open sarcophagi which were the property of the State. Friendly advice, threats and offers of money were thrown away on him. But he was still suspected of having robbed tombs and accordingly handed over to the authorities for "grilling".

The *mudir* of Thebes was famed for his severity. He spent two months in cross-examining and even torturing Rasul, but both the prisoner and the witnesses he produced in his defence kept the stream of lies flowing. For lack of evidence Rasul had to be released, but for a long time weals and scars on his body showed how roughly he had been handled.

Professor Maspéro's assistant was in a very difficult position for he had telegraphed to his chief that the tomb-robbers had been arrested and the case had been freely reported in the press. But he was convinced of Rasul's guilt and made further representations to the *mudir*. The latter shrugged his shoulders and advised him to wait and see. He waited in vain for several weeks and then took to his bed with fever. Then the affair took an unexpected turn.

The penalty for tomb-robbing was very severe. Rasul's conscience pricked him and he went to the *mudir* and made a partial confession. The criminal inquiry was resumed and it transpired that all the inhabitants of Kurna, Rasul's native village, were enthusiastic tomb-robbers, the secrets of that occupation being handed down from father to son. The whole community was prosperous, making a steady income out of the sale of antiquities obtained from a source unknown to anyone save Rasul and a few cronies from whom an oath of silence was extracted. The secret was to remain a secret no longer. Rasul was promised a pardon and a large sum of money if, for the benefit of science, he would reveal the whereabouts of the famous tomb.

Maspéro's assistant was unfortunately still on the sick list, so Brugsch was sent to Thebes. The worried and suspicious Rasul handed him a parcel containing four canopic jars of Queen Ahmes Nefertari and three papyrus rolls from the tombs of other queens. This was a good start and Rasul followed it up by taking Brugsch on a day of blazing heat to Deir el Bahri where he pointed out the burial place. The great secret was out.

The sequel was quite sensational. In a remote corner of one of the many rocky gullies Brugsch found a shaft descending almost vertically for nearly 40 feet. From it branched a passage leading after about 200 feet into a chamber 9 yards square which gave access to another passage 250 feet in length. The layout was curious and the excavation work somewhat rough and ready. By whom, for whom and when had the task been undertaken?

When Brugsch and his companion threaded their way by candle light through the dark catacomb he could hardly restrain his excitement. In one passage he found one coffin after another. The floor of one chamber was strewn with small chests filled with figurines, canopic jars and vases. Then he had the greatest surprise of his life and could hardly trust his eyes. There was a chamber full of antiquities such as coffins, mummies and gravestones. He had a fleeting glimpse of inscriptions bearing the names of Amenophis I, Tuthmosis II, Amosis I, Tuthmosis III, Seti I and Egypt's greatest ruler, Rameses II.

Brugsch thought he was dreaming. What stroke of fate had brought him into this distinguished company at a time when little more than their names were known to the learned world? He spent more than two hours in the tomb, so delighted with his find that he hardly noticed the hot, stifling air. He engaged three hundred Arab labourers and, under a strong guard, the tomb was cleared in the next few days. The job was anything but pleasant in the fearful heat but the reward was good – thirty-two coffins containing mummies of kings, queens, great court functionaries and high priests. In addition there were many mummies without coffins, chests full of statues, receptacles for unguents, porcelain vases, baskets of fruit, embalmed pieces of beef, brightly painted glass vessels, jugs,

Brugsch, candle in hand, makes his great discovery

rolls of swathing material and much else. In a chest lay a mummified gazelle, the pet of some long dead princess. Many of the coffins were so heavy that it took four men to carry them. When they were opened it was found that they were double. But there was not a single sarcophagus.

Professor Brugsch divided the antiquities he had found into two groups. The coffins and mummies dated from the XVIIth, XVIIIth and XIXth Dynasties.

In addition to these coffins and mummies there were mummies of high officials and various objects dating from the same period.

The coffins and mummies in the second group dated from the XXth and XXIst Dynasties and included some of the "Priest Kings", contemporaries of David and Solomon of biblical times.

Mohammed Rasul was paid the agreed sum of £500 for the information leading to the discovery. When Brugsch boarded a Nile steamer to take all his treasures to Cairo a crowd of peasant women ran along the bank tearing their hair and shrieking. An antique custom come to life! They made him feel that he was no better than a tomb-robber himself. He had disturbed these mummies in their eternal sleep and ruthlessly dragged them into the light of day.

Many of the royal mummies were found quite desiccated and very brittle. Some were practically destroyed. All ornaments had been removed. Tuthmosis was in pieces and the wrappings round his chest had been torn open in the search for gold or valuables.

Other mummies showed evidence of surgical treatment in

life. The face of Rameses I was covered with marks showing that he had died of smallpox. King Spitah had a club foot. The mummy of King Senken-Ra indicated that he had died a violent death. (It is known that he was killed fighting against the Hyksos.) Special attention had been devoted to the wrapping of the male phallus.

It is said that appendicitis is a disease of modern civilization, but the mummy of an Egyptian princess bore all the signs that she had died of it.

It was now made clear that all these mummies had originally been placed in the tomb which Strabo had found empty on his visit. There was written evidence how the coffins and mummies had been removed and hidden elsewhere. In the XXth Dynasty, somewhere about 1150 B.C., the decadence of Egypt was in full swing. Little was left of her ancient greatness and poverty and distress were increasing fast. It is under such conditions that the authority of the state is relaxed and thieves and rogues get their chance.

Under the last pharaohs of Rameses' line, the so-called Ramessides, wholesale robbery assumed alarming dimensions. Organized bands scoured the country, looted the tombs they found and had no respect whatever even for the sacred dead. Mummies were broken and torn open in the greedy scramble for any gold or jewellery they might contain. There is no doubt that tomb-robbing flourished in the days of the Priest-Kings.

We know from certain inscriptions that from time to time royal commissions were appointed to investigate, and as far as possible restore, the rifled tombs. But it was ultimately found that the only possible course was to clear these tombs, especially the more distant, and remove their coffins and mummies to some inconspicuous family tomb elsewhere.

The mummy of Rameses II, for instance, was transferred to the tomb of his father, Seti I. When the latter was broken into both mummies were removed to the grave of a Queen Inihapu. Ultimately all these mummies, with others rescued from many quarters, found refuge in the tomb of Amenophis I.

This story is conscientiously related by some worthy priests in inscriptions found on the mummies themselves.

This game of hide-and-seek did not defeat the thieves but it went out of fashion in the reign of the Pharaoh Herihor when what was left of the mummies was hidden away in a place destined to be thief-proof.

In the vicinity of the Temple of Deir-el-Bahri the local stone is very soft and this locality was selected for a new tomb layout comprising the shaft, vaults, tunnels and chambers which have previously been described. At dead of night, and without any ceremony, the transfer of the mummies was carried out by a band of faithful priests. Herihor and his successors put an end to the tradition of sumptuous graves. They were buried quietly in this remote "hide". Three thousand years were to pass before they were to be discovered and would accompany their royal predecessors on a journey by Nile steamer to Cairo.

In 1898 the French Egyptologist François Loret discovered another "hide". He was excavating in the well-known tomb of the warlike Amenophis II when he came across a walled-up chamber. It contained a whole series of mummies of kings of the XVIIIth and XIXth dynasties, among them Tuthmosis IV and his famous son Amenophis III, whose reign lasted from 1413 to 1377 B.C. and covered a prosperous period in the history of Egypt when its frontiers extended from the Euphrates to the negro region of Rari, away in Ethiopia.

Amenophis II was the only pharaoh found (in 1898) in his original tomb and his remains were left undisturbed. On the breast of the mummy were withered flowers laid there by loving hands 3400 years ago. Everything else in the way of ornament had been stolen. The tomb was sealed off with an iron gate and left in charge of watchmen.

For two years all went well and then one day the watchmen reported that an armed band had set upon them and forced their way into the tomb. Young Howard Carter, the Inspector of Antiquities for the district of Thebes, lost no time in seeing for himself. He found that the king had been pulled out of the sarcophagus and left lying on the floor. The wrappings had been opened without damaging the mummy.

Such a feat could only have been the work of experts. But if they expected to find any valuables they must have been disappointed. Their confrères in antiquity had left them nothing but a small model of a boat in the antechamber. They helped themselves to it.

Carter examined the locks. They were open but did not appear to be damaged. Everything indicated that the watchmen were in collusion with the thieves. He measured the footprints and a police dog traced them to the house in Kurna where Rasul had been living for twenty years. The measurements agreed with those of Rasul, but nothing could be proved against him.

Ten years passed. Our Rasul's grandchildren followed his example and took to tomb-robbing. Gangs were formed. One day one of the gangs discovered a tomb tucked away in the side of a hill. When another gang heard of their find they assembled on the spot armed with rifles and drove the "discoverers" away. The archæologist Carter heard of this incident which might have come out of a Wild West film. He relates how he caught the thieves redhanded in the tomb and gave them the option of immediate flight or being left in the tomb for ever. They chose the former and he spent the night there.

Carter's courage is to be commended.

The tomb which had been discovered contained nothing noteworthy except a porphyry sarcophagus, no doubt originally intended for Queen Hatshepsut, whose splendid mortuary temple is still the great "sight" on the other side of the hill. There was evidence that it was once intended to drive a tunnel through the hill to connect the temple with the tomb.

The village of Kurna, which is in the centre of the Thebes necropolis, was in existence in antiquity. It is likely that the embalmers, handworkers and guardians of this city of the dead had their quarters there. The *fellahin* who occupy it now proudly claim descent from the original inhabitants but indignantly deny that Kurna was the fountainhead of tomb-robbing.

Although followers of the Prophet they betray many associations with earlier religions. Christianity, it is true, seems to have left no trace of any effect on them and their faith sits lightly upon them. On Yusuf el Haggah's Day (he is the local saint) there is a procession in which the men carry a model funeral ship on their shoulders and priests, soldiers, musicians, singers and dancers follow behind, exactly as if the times of the God Amun had been revived. At every funeral the women shriek wildly and tear their hair, just as the women of old had done in the days of the Pharaohs.

The manufacture of fakes is an extensive and thriving business. Some of the products are so good that even experts are deceived.

I remember once riding near Sakkara. I dismounted to ease my limbs with a stroll and left the two camels in charge of my dragoman. I was loitering by the entrance to the catacomb of the Apis bulls when a *fellah* sidled up and to the accompaniment of mysterious gestures offered to sell me a scarab. H swore by Allah and his prophets that it was perfectly genuine and scattered flattering titles such as "Herr Professor, Herr Doktor, Herr Baron, Herr Graf, Herr Direktor", to convince me of his honesty. When I told him his "antika" was a fake he cursed me heartily and left me flourishing a handful of similar antiques in my face.

But is it fair to call such Egyptians fraudulent knaves and thieves? The modern world has no hesitation in describing them as such, but are we not forgetting that their methods are a product of civilization and that from the earliest times cunning and deception were regarded as fair weapons in the fight for existence. Efficiency was in fact considered as a compound of both. Among the Babylonians, cunning, with a sprinkling of prevarication, was an honoured attribute of the gods. Nor should the story of Jacob and Rachel in the Bible be forgotten.

Lamer, in his *Wörterbuch der Antike*, points out that mosaic law did not peremptorily forbid a lie. He says: "In the ethics of Greek philosophy conduct which we consider dishonourable had a place."

Cunning also figures in the stories of Edda and the Nibelungenlied. The wiles of Ulysses, which bordered on downright dishonesty, were much applauded by the ancients. He deceives Athena and then the swineherds of Eumenias and tells everyone a different story. Do we not find the Greeks boasting of their slippery god Hermes, protector of swindlers, thieves and merchants?

But to resume our story. The mummy of Amenophis III, grandfather of Tutankhamun, was also among the discoveries. He must have been a brave man. Inscriptions record that, using his soldiers as beaters, he himself killed seventy-five wild bulls out of a herd of one hundred and seventy, not to mention hundreds of lions, crocodiles and hippopotami, all with the primitive weapons of those times!

What is more important is that this king was the father of the heretic king Akhenaton who abandoned the Amun religion in favour of that of Aton.

The mummy of Amenophis III was found with two others in a sarcophagus of later times which bore the names of three kings, so it must regretfully be admitted that the body of that great king has not been identified with certainty.

From the religious point of view the concealment of mummies was a tragic necessity. Every right-minded Egyptian was horrified at the idea. For thousands of years men believed that there was no salvation unless they offered sacrifices at the tombs of their departed. To fail in that duty was a grave sin, and much more so in the case of their kings, those half-men, half gods who sat on the "throne of Horus". When the new practice made those pious observances no longer possible it was regarded as a humiliating sign of the decay and impotence of authority.

The discovery of these two secret burial-places was a sort of resurrection without the "Last Judgment". But it was a great stroke of luck for archæology because the mummies were a find of the first importance and of absorbing interest to all scholars.

Yet when we turn from the mummies to the living men they once were it is hardly possible to have much respect for kings like Tuthmosis III, Rameses the Great and Sesostris, whose great political achievements are a record of murder and tyranny.

In the presence of mummies, which we can see and touch, it seems fantastic to believe that more than three thousand five hundred years have passed since the hearts ceased to beat. Egypt supplies an eloquent lesson even to modern rulers of the impermanence of power and glory. In these tombs the gigantic efforts to defy eternity have left something only fit to be an exhibit in a museum.

The prowess of Amenophis in slaying wild beasts is duly celebrated but there is a great silence about the fate of all the virgins he received in his bed. Even his eunuchs did not know how many became victims of his passions.

His wife also knew all that was to be known about that side of life. If the chatter of the taverns and brothels of Thebes is to be believed, she must have been a fit model for Catherine of Russia. No one knows where she came from. Some say that she was a princess from Mitani, others that her original occupation was catching birds in the reeds by the river banks, and that it was while she was so engaged that she met the Pharaoh who was out hunting. Whether that be true or not, she was beautiful, wide awake and knew what she wanted. She became his wife. But she had other intimates, among them a High Priest and other priests with whom she used to go bathing by moonlight. Her maidens could have told us a lot about her.

The passion of society women and prostitutes for "making-up" is a constantly recurring phenomenon. In ancient Egypt the process began with massaging the body all over with pomades and oils. Then paint was smeared on the face, red for the lips, yellow for the cheeks and pale green under the eyes. Another tint was used for the finger and toe nails.

The purpose of cosmetics was to preserve fleeting beauty. The Egyptians knew and used white lead, cinnabar, and antimony and burned sulphate of lead and coal. They were familiar with the properties of verdigris and resin. Cosmetic jars and powder boxes have been found, not mere articles of commerce but *objets d'art* of the first order, which reveal a great deal. Red, a favourite colour, was obtained from a dwarf variety of henna grown in the fields.

Clad in a thin chemise of the finest silk which left none of her charms to the imagination, the Egyptian maiden sought love and laughter under whispering palms by the Nile.

A completely bald head was considered very distinguished for a long time in smart circles. But there was an opposite school of thought which decreed that the bald head must be covered with a luxurious wig. Wig-making was a flourishing trade.

A story is told of one queen that she used to haunt the prostitutes' quarters in the city but always escaped detection by constantly changing her wig. She was on intimate terms with harlots and tavern tipplers and shared their way of life to the full.

For the rich, life was pleasant. Money bought slaves, male and female labour and children and girls for pleasure. The poorest had to earn their bread with the sweat of their brows. Anyone who robbed a rich man was hanged if caught. Such was the will of the gods and harsh laws were the mere expression of that will.

The rod was the instrument by which these divine laws were enforced. From the earliest times it was the symbol of supreme power. The Egyptians, and the Romans after them, could not imagine their gods except armed with whips. Cicero once dreamed that Jupiter gave young Octavius, afterwards the Emperor Augustus, a whip as a symbol of world conquest.

Flogging hurts, and whips were used because of their

physical effect. Lashing slaves is a very ancient custom and the fearsome implement may well have been invented for their benefit. The Egyptian whip consisted of five leather strips with small metal balls sewn up in them. The first stroke drew blood.

The ranks of the slaves were recruited from prisoners of war and persons who had sold their freedom. They were either branded on the forehead or their noses and ears were slit. A black powder was rubbed into the burn to make it indelible.

Constant beating made a slave's life worse than a dog's. It was not only for some offence or indifferent work that his master had him whipped. He was often whipped merely because his master or mistress felt like it.

As to the punishment itself, the wretched creature was stripped naked and then lashed until he (or she) fainted or the bloodlust of his sadistic owner was sated. Even well-bred women of the highest society entirely approved of this revolting practice. If the lady of the house had had a bad night, or been neglected by her husband, or discovered marks of age upon her delicate cheek, she took it out of her women slaves. The shrieks of the victims filled the house. Nor was it misfortune only which produced the feelings that could only be relieved in this way. When the guests at a party had been made really cheerful with drink they usually called for a naked slave to be lashed for their entertainment.

Yet it must not be forgotten that many of those who enjoyed seeing others whipped got considerable satisfaction out of being whipped themselves. It is a curious fact that from the earliest times there have been plenty of fanatics who believe that they honour the gods most by suffering pain themselves. Egypt has produced much evidence of this phenomenon. Herodotus in the fortieth chapter of his second volume writes:

"When they have fasted in honour of their goddess Isis they sacrifice some animal to her and while the sacrifice is burning they beat each other with whips and when they have beaten each other they make a meal of what is left of the sacrifice."

In chapter 61 he writes:

"When the festival of Isis was being celebrated in the city of Bubastis men and women lashed each other while the sacrifice was being offered. But it would be a sin for me to say why they did so, for the shameful secret was betrayed to me by a priest in strict confidence. The Carians who live in Egypt are even worse. They slash each other with sharp knives."

The Syrians also practised self-mutilation in honour of their gods. We are told that:

"the priests cut their arms to ribbons. One of them seems to lose his reason and sighs and groans. He rushes about like a maniac, yelling out that he is filled with the spirit. Nor does he cease screeching until he falls in a fit. But whether he really believes in his theatrical antics I cannot say."

Beating female slaves

But even if flogging provoked desire and self-satisfaction in the few, to the masses it was merely a cruel and hateful stimulus to greater effort. Yet it must be admitted that without her fanatical belief in the gods, her slaves and her flogging ancient Egypt would be something very different from what the archæologists have shown her to be. No pharaoh could rule without his sceptre as the symbol of religion and his whip as the symbol of power.

Under such conditions the poor became poorer, the rich richer, the powerful even more powerful. Happiest of all was the lot of the well-fed priests. The position of the priests defies logic, but they were none the less the stable element in the state and the permanent obstacle to any challenge to the power and glory of the throne. With their immense retinue of retainers and servants they commanded and obtained the submissive obedience of the masses.

The kings themselves were even more favoured. The services of all their subjects were at their disposal. Any sort of physical exertion was not required of them. Their passions were gambling, sport, hunting and music. They lived in palaces set in beautiful parks. A life of luxury was a universally acknowledged right. They had all the money they required and everything needed to make the time pass pleasantly. No wonder they enjoyed being alive!

Their palaces were usually on the banks of the Nile. A prominent feature of the grounds was an ornamental lake glorious with lotus and exotic flowers.

Every rich man had a harem. Of course the largest and most resplendent was the king's. It was known as the "Women's House" and its occupants frequently numbered two hundred and more. There were rooms with wonderful baths, halls with fountains and all the apparatus of luxury. Apartments were set aside as maternity quarters and children's nurseries. There was a hospital department and special rooms for music, games and dancing.

Many of the rooms were decorated with erotic wall-paintings such as are usually associated with bawdy houses and can still be seen at Pompeii.

The harem meant a free and easy life for the girls of every race, young and not so young, but all virgins when they first arrived, whose sole function was to satisfy the desires of their lord and master. Clad in the finest silks, decked out with superb jewellery, nourished on the best of food and wine, they spent their time practising singing and dancing in the nude for the hour when he would summon them to his presence.

The supervision of these women was entrusted to eunuchs, men usually of many-sided talents whose function was to see that nothing was lacking for their welfare.

Training for the profession of eunuch began at a very early age. Hundreds of boys were selected and handed over to the priests to bring up. Their education included instruction in the arts. Not infrequently they became involved in palace scandal and intrigues culminating in serious disorders.

When a girl became pregnant by the Pharaoh she was usually fobbed off on someone else. Even girls of whom he had got tired were generally dismissed and left the palace. There were plenty of rich citizens only too anxious to take over the cast-off mistresses of royalty.

Pimps, and more respectable agents often dressed up as priests, scoured the slave-market and other likely places for virgins suitable for the royal harem. Parents even brought their daughters to the temples in the hope that they would be singled out as promising candidates for the king's bed. To give herself to the Pharaoh, even for a night, was the prayer of many a maiden and as the parents were very well paid, opposition from them was most unlikely.

The area of choice was very wide so that any maiden chosen had to pass the most rigorous tests before she reached the "House of the Women". She must be not more than ten years old, very narrow in the hips and all her other measurements must be perfect.

In the "preparatory" department of the harem she was "groomed" for her duties by experts. Every day she bathed and was then massaged with the rarest cosmetics. Manicure, pedicure, rubbing with various creams, the application of paint and "make-up" followed. Her hair was braided and other hair removed with depilatories. She was given the choicest foods, and aphrodisiacs of various kinds stimulated desire and prepared her for the great day of the royal embraces.

If she found favour in his sight he would welcome further meetings. She might even find herself raised to the rank of official concubine.

Of course there were frequent "scenes" due to the rivalry and jealousy of such women. It was then the duty of the eunuchs to restore order. Young children were sometimes involved in horrible scandals. Society saw nothing immoral in all this. Pharaoh was a god. All he did was godlike. He could do nothing wrong. In fact there were no such things as good and evil. If an act was successful it was good, if a failure, bad.

The culminating point of a royal feast was reached when the assembled company trooped into the women's quarters and feasted their eyes on the sight of naked maidens.

The "House of the Women" also had its quota of wet nurses. Their function was to rear the newborn babies until the latter were handed over to rich families.

Poor families sometimes got rid of their new babies by putting them into a wickerwork boat on the Nile and letting it drift. Their destinies were then decided by hunger, the heat of the sun, the crocodile and the vulture. According to the Bible story Moses would have suffered the same fate if he had not had the luck to be found by Pharaoh's daughter bathing among the reeds.

Many children, even children born in brothels, were handed over to the temples. There they were brought up as minor temple servants and some of the boys became eunuchs. Pretty girls were either attached to the temples and taught singing and dancing, or sold into harems. If a marriage proved childless the wife often went to the priests. They would make good the deficiency. A multitude of children was a religious desideratum. All these customs were regarded as in no sense immoral. No one thought of questioning them. Polygamy was permitted even to the poorest and most men had several wives, if only for their value as labour. Amongst the lowest classes women were regarded as nothing but beasts of burden and child-bearing machines.

Daughters were preferred to sons because they were articles of commerce and their parents could make money out of them. When a man went to war he took a woman with him. A general or superior officer was accompanied by a whole squad of women. Priests and officials were corruptible – and the boss knew less than the beggar. In the eyes of the gods right was whatever the rich wanted and wrong the modest requirements of the poor.

Socially-minded readers of this book will have gathered that there were seamy sides to the life of ancient Egypt and will be wondering whether there was ever any popular reaction or whether lethargy always triumphed over instinct.

Erman's historical researches have disclosed two stories which are eloquent on this subject, the "Warning of a Prophet" and "The Pessimist's Struggle with his own Soul". Both come from a papyrus which speaks of a "Dark Age". When the VIth Dynasty came to an end about 2300 B.C. there was a great revolution. Temple services ceased. The fashion of immortalizing noble kings and athletic men in stone gave place to a very different sort of art. Egypt passed through a period to which the sorely-tried nations of modern Europe are no stranger.

Kings ceased to be regarded as deities. Their statues were destroyed and temples thrown down. Veneration was turned into hate. To the much admired social stability succeeded internal chaos. The "Golden Age" was over. But it was not an external foe, and his occupation of their country and subjection of their brothers, that the "Prophet" and the "Pessimist" denounced. The catastrophe was the fruits of social disintegration. It was the work of the foe within.

The revolution was not directed against a particular social class, but against property owners everywhere. Its object was not merely the abolition of "privileges" but the abolition of law itself. The courts ceased to function. Robbery and violence were universal. It was the turn of the rich to beg and the poor to sit on silken cushions. Brother fought with brother, father with son. Foreigners infested the land and all was chaos. Murder was no crime and the Nile ran red with blood.

Many inscriptions refer to this catastrophe and there are silent witnesses in the shape of ruined temples and battered statues.

One of the kings of the VIth Dynasty was Phiops I. At the advanced age of ninety-three he was worn out in mind and body and indifferent to the world around him. One day the wise man Ipu-wer appeared before him and told him the truth about what was going on in the country. Here are his words, according to the papyrus:

"This is the position. The Nile has risen but no fields are ploughed because everyone is saying there is no future for the country. Laughter has ceased and mourning stalks through the land."

These words indicate the violent protest of the people against the hordes of useless officials. The slaves revolted and freed themselves. The guardians of the corn stores were driven off and everyone helped himself. The decrees of the courts were torn up and scattered in the streets. Judges, tax-collectors and scribes were beaten.

The papyrus goes on:

"The nobles bewail their lot but the humble rejoice and say: 'We will chase the nobles from our midst. They shall hunger and work at the mill. We will not recognize their sons and they shall all go about wishing they were dead. Their children shall be flung against the wall and their babes cast out into the desert.'"

In another passage we read:

"and now it is the turn of the women slaves. They wear the clothes of their mistresses who walk about in rags, begging, starving and snatching the swill from the pigs. Strangers swarm into the land to rob and murder. Cities are destroyed. The tombs are broken open and the mummies of the well-to-do flung out and torn apart. Would that the world could end before another babe could be born!"

The warnings of the Ipu-wers were not heeded. The rage of the mob had turned against the king and senseless revolutionaries ruled in his stead:

"Look how the poor have grown rich and the nobles have nothing left. He who once had nothing to eat now owns a barn. Everything in it once belonged to a rich man. He who once had no oil with which to anoint his bald head now possesses jars full of myrrh. The poor have become the rich and it is they who now offer incense to the gods. The rich are helpless and even lack for a bed. But the worst has not yet been said. He who once had nothing now has treasures. The prince fawns upon him and even the counsellors bow down before the new rich. The women are barren. Women who have never seen their faces unless reflected in water now use the bronze mirrors of the rich. The necks of handmaidens are bedecked with gold, silver and malachite while their mistresses beg for bread. The great are filled with grief while the lowly leap for joy."

Some great social revolution must have occasioned this lament. But it should be said that it is followed by hopes of better times and an indication that men may be returning to their belief in the gods.

At this point the story comes to an end because the papyrus has been torn.

The revolution had been caused by war. It is known that Phiops I led five expeditions against Syria and Babylon.

In that handbook of social philosophy, the so-called Leyden papyrus No. 344 the "Sayings of Ipos the Noble", it is stated that the exploitation of the poor was not the only cause of the revolution. It mentions in particular a universal degeneration of morals and puts forward a point of view which must have been unusual four thousand two hundred years ago:

"The sanctifying force of the old faith was that it inspired man to make the most of his life on earth because there is nothing in the hereafter."

Blind harpists sing ribald songs about death and what lies beyond: "Wreathe thy locks in myrtle while thou livest, clothe thy limbs in fine linen while life is still in thee, live joyously and tire not on earth. None has ever returned from the dead to tell thee aught of the Hereafter! Of that Hereafter thou Knowest nothing!"

This peculiar "Literature of Critical Analysis" bewails the decay of political and economic solidity and social order. The very doubts about God and the future life bring up the problem of theodicy. As the second papyrus, "The Pessimist's Struggle with his own Soul," shows, the serious question is raised which still tortures so many of us: "If man is so imperfect and bad, his creator must be equally imperfect and responsible for many errors."

The dispute with God continues: "If he had realized his failure with his first men he would have put his curse upon them. If he had annihilated them and their posterity and created good men in their stead, envy and hatred, cruelty and oppression would have vanished from the earth."

The Hermitage papyrus preserved in Leningrad contains a "speech" of Nefr-rehu which also refers to a social and religious revolution, and there exists a story of the Egyptian citizen Sinuhe which contains his reflections on the miserable fate of the oppressed and his conviction that some great revolution will lead to far-reaching reforms.

This revolt against the popular devotion to the idea of the hereafter was broken after thirty-four years by the opposition of the priests, but it lived on and was revived eleven hundred years later by King Akhenaton, "the first social reformer".

Egypt anticipated the West even in its revolutions and their

Catching birds among the papyrus reeds (Relief from a tomb of 1850 B.C.)

developments. The records we have been considering all insist upon the violent reversal of the existing order and the obliteration of the distinction between rich and poor. It seems odd that archæologists and historians should concentrate on "the rule of terrorism", the "enemy within" and "the collapse of social order" and forget to mention the evils which provoke revolutions. A popular revolution always looks like anarchy but its purpose is to bring about a new order and the real revolutionary never forgets it. That is as true of antiquity as it is today.

The indolence of the present-day Egyptian tempts us to think that throughout their long history the inhabitants of the Nile valley were temperamentally averse to extreme courses. But we could be wrong. It is true that the Kingdom survived the catastrophe on which these papyri dilate but it also true that the stage was often set for revolution and disorder. The masses were trained to implicit obedience by the priests but they occasionally threw off their chains and turned on their oppressors.

In addition to social revolutions and civil wars Egypt suffered from religious and moral upheavals.

This particular period is called the "Age of Egyptian Revolution". It was inspired by righteous indignation and a firm resolve to win political and intellectual freedom and social justice. The struggle was long and hard.

The priests again proved victorious over the hopes and passions which animated their enemies in that exciting epoch. It was left to Jewry, then the Greeks and Romans and finally Christianity to raise the banner of liberty again. At times it seems as if the triumph of that cause is still a long way off.

Chapter 5

SLAVE, WORK OR DIE!

Coal and oil are the alpha and omega of the modern world. Stones and slaves were the alpha and omega of the ancient Egyptian world.

The great majority of its inhabitants were employed either in agriculture or in stone quarries. All buildings associated with the worship of the gods, the veneration of the dead and the maintenance of royal power were constructed of stone. Stone, and those who worked it, had their own god.

Granite, basalt, limestone, sandstone, porphyry and alabaster, as well as gold and many precious stones, are found in Egypt. Wilkinson discovered a gold mine with the foundations of thirteen hundred and twenty miners' houses and a temple.

Gold was most highly valued by the Egyptians. Its colour challenged the sun's rays. In Memphis the ancient God Ptah was venerated as the patron of goldsmiths. His sanctuary was called after them and its High Priest received the title of "Master of Works" in the service of the god.

The mountains bordering on the Red Sea and in East Africa have ancient gold deposits and others are found at Koptus, on the Nile, Ombos and Kush in Ethiopia. Diggings in ancient gold mines in Egypt and Nubia have revealed how they were worked. Excavators have found sacred grottoes, sanctuaries, miners' dwellings, cisterns, artesian wells, granite millstones, runnels for washing the crushed ore and much besides. It is obvious that these colonies of mine-workers were recruited mainly from prisoners of war, slaves and criminals. They must have led very unhappy lives, of which the classical historian Diodorus tells us something.

Any deficiency in Egypt's gold and other metals was made good from foreign trade and the tribute forced from dependent nations.

From a stela in a temple we learn that an expedition was sent to a distant land to procure copper. There was an advance party consisting of a High Priest, a staff of officials, officers, soldiers and fifty gendarmes. Brugsch completes the passage:

"500 soldiers, 200 non-commissioned officers, 800 foreign sailors from Aan, 2,000 labourers from the royal demesne." There was also a quota of specialists.

Another expedition of 8,368 men was sent to Sinai. Sailors were required because Sinai lies on the far side of the Red Sea. It will be noticed that the party did not include slaves, perhaps because they might have deserted.

In one of the valleys of Sinai the traveller suddenly finds himself looking at a bas-relief in a rock. It shows an Egyptian king with arm raised to beat in the skull of an Asiatic captive whom he has forced to his knees. It is a symbol of brute force, a demonstration of the "rights of the victor", an announcement to the Asiatics that the Pharaoh of Egypt had come to their countries to seize their copper and turquoise mines.

All quarries were the property of the kings or the temples. The head of the organization was the Prince of Thebes and he had a staff of priests and officials. When a city or provincial governor needed stone for some monument or undertaking the king simply issued an ordinance and 10,000 men were mobilized to the cry of "with God for Pharaoh and Egypt".

Criminals were included in the ranks of the slaves and there were plenty of them because it was fatally easy for any man with a sense of grievance to become a criminal. An insult to a priest or criticism of the established religion meant torture and certain death.

The quarries, now swallowed up by the sands, were situated in remote, arid places where no trees sheltered the workers from the pitiless rays of the sun. The expression "proletariat" was used even in antiquity to describe the lowest classes who had nothing they could call their own, could not read or write and were ripe for exploitation in the service of the gods. Specialists such as masons, drillers, polishers and others were no doubt treated better.

Wells and cisterns were important items in the lay-out of a quarry. But there were many quarries without such amenities and in their absence life was all the harder. Water had to be brought from elsewhere by pack animals and long columns of water carriers. The water brought great distances from the Nile in animal skins in burning heat and unfiltered could have barely been fit for drinking. A small ration, fixed by the overseer, was allotted to each worker. Of course there was no water for washing his body, bathed in sweat and grimy with dust.

The reek of oil, sweat, onions and garlic accompanied him everywhere.

In many cases the Egyptians dug canals to the quarries for the transport of the stone but they were stagnant, a breeding-ground for insects and smelled vile. How many slaves, tortured by thirst, must have drunk canal water, repulsive and dangerous though it was. Egypt's climate differs from that of the Riviera. Its heat is tropical and sweat pours off the body, carrying the grime with it. Death was the sovereign lord of many of these quarries. The slave had the choice of work or death. There was no other alternative.

The number of unfortunates who succumbed to malaria or died of thirst must have been astronomical. Any slave who was taken ill, or whose work fell off, for that or any other reason, was at the mercy of his overseer who alone diagnosed the case, decided whether the man was truthful or malingering and had at his disposal the unfailing cure – the whip. There were no doctors or so-called medicine-men at the quarries. They stayed at home, reserving their services for rich patients.

Perhaps this is a convenient moment to record that Egyptian medicine was based upon a certain amount of sound knowledge which had been gained by serious investigation. The so-called "Medical Papyrus" speaks of forty-eight surgical operations. The doctor author of this papyrus states that the movement of the lower limbs is controlled by the brain. It is only four hundred years since Europe made the same discovery.

Another papyrus refers to appendicitis, anæmia, gallstones, poliomyelitis. No mention is made of syphilis. Dental decay was apparently unknown in the earlier times but is referred to later – an indication of progressive civilization. In the Ebers papyrus a list is given of several hundred medicines.

Yet skilled physicians were few in number and solely at the disposal of the rich. The masses had to be content with "doctors" who were little better than witch-doctors and whose prescriptions were of the most primitive kind. Let one example suffice. Broth made from the hair of a black calf was recommended as the remedy for greying hair.

The obstacle to the progress of medical knowledge was the belief in witchcraft, held as firmly by the doctors as by everyone else. It was taught that the devil had invented nine hundred and ninety-nine diseases.

After amputation, and in the case of suppurating wounds, treatment consisted of the application of red-hot irons. To enable the patient to endure the pain he was anæsthetized with some violent poison. He became unconscious, in many cases for ever. Middle class patients and slaves had to face the knife, red-hot iron and forceps without any anæsthetic. For them there was nothing but herbs and sorcery.

A venerated figure was the brain specialist, the surgeon of antiquity. Many diseases were deemed to be the work of demons which swarmed like ants in the head and had to be driven out. If the sorcerer tried his hand and failed the brain surgeon appeared upon the scene. He opened the skull with some stone instrument, removed something and with it the evil spirits. It was a very lucky patient who survived three days but if he did he was considered cured and the surgeon and the God Amun were rewarded with many splendid gifts.

It was not unusual for people to pay large sums to a doctor to make certain that elderly invalids or relatives whose continued existence was inconvenient should not unduly delay their journey to the realm of Osiris. Doctors helped each other to despatch patients and made money on the side out of the funeral arrangements.

Burdensome invalids of the poorer classes were taken out into the desert by their relatives and left to die. Jackals would see to their burial. The practice was contrary to the decrees of the gods but the dirty work was done at dead of night and there were no witnesses.

The idea of death had no terrors for the doctor. To the poorest and the slaves death was always a merciful release. After death many of them looked far happier than they had looked in life.

When a brain surgeon had to operate on a person of distinction he carried out a preliminary experiment on a slave. The latter was tied up and his head was fixed in a vice to prevent it from moving. Then he was anæsthetized in the manner previously described. When the head had been shaved the surgeon made an incision in the skin and pulled the flaps apart. If hæmorrhage was not stayed by magical formulæ an assistant washed off the blood. The small blood vessels were sealed off with a red-hot wire. When the bony structure was exposed it was opened by the surgeon. If the operation failed or the patient died from the effects of the narcotic – as he usually did – a second experiment followed the first.

The treatment of diseases of the brain was left to the gods. Few doctors knew anything about them. If the gods would not help, any brain operation was unsuccessful.

There were specialists for teeth and ears, confinements, the use of the sacred knife. There were even specialists in the laying on of hands. All were under the protection of the god Imhotep, the patron saint of Memphis.

As I have said, witchcraft played a large part in the practice of medicine. In the University of Leyden in Holland there is a papyrus roll, eleven feet long by ten inches wide, which shows that it was addressed to the Egyptian gnostics. References to divinities such as Osiris, Isis, Horus, Amibis, Seth and many others all point in that direction.

The records contain descriptions of incantations and the magician's formulæ and methods. The magician starts off by giving himself out as a god to compel the demon to do what he is told. He will say, for example: "I am Horus, brother of the goddess Isis, the fair youth beloved of Isis and desired by his father Osiris-Onnofer." It must be assumed that the demon is duly deceived, as otherwise there would be a conflict of authority.

Magical practices had their own tools of trade in the shape of various implements, vases and lamps.

"Bring a clean lamp which is not filled with gum. Pour pure oil into it and hang it on a wall facing east. Place an innocent young boy before it and repeat seven times the magical incantation. Wake him and ask: 'What hast thou seen?' If he replies: 'I have seen the gods round the lamp' they will answer any question you may ask."

We need not follow the papyrus into its further preoccupation with magic, that art in which so many too simple people have firmly believed.

There was one malady which it was beyond the power of any doctor or magician to cure, that chronic disease of poverty, starvation. The stock foods of the masses were bread, rice and onions, but there was never enough, particularly when the Nile floods were inadequate and the harvest failed. The Bible is full of references to famine, e.g. "there was a famine in Egypt and the people cried to Pharaoh for bread".

Foods with high protein content such as meat and milk never came the way of the poorest with the result that the men were living skeletons. The women, piteous to look at with their drooping breasts and swollen bellies, were in no better case. The children were all afflicted with rickets. The bodies of all these poor creatures showed what they had to put up with – worms, diarrhoea, scorbutis, sores and boils.

No one thought of improving the nation's health or reducing mortality. Why worry about casualties when tributary peoples and the slave trade were an inexhaustible source of replacements. Slaves were cheap though worth their weight in gold.

When cholera, smallpox or some other plague raged in a quarry the authorities knew of no alternative to sealing it off. It remained closed until everyone inside was dead. When a few weeks' sunshine had bleached all the skeletons it was considered that the germs had been destroyed.

What measures could the Egyptians take against the ravages of smallpox, tuberculosis, cancer and cholera? Who knew that harmful bacteria lived in stagnant water or that flies which breed in dung or the filth of the streets are the carriers of plagues? The Egyptians knew nothing of hygiene.

Leprosy is one of the most ancient of diseases. It always flourished in the East and is often mentioned in the Bible. The Greeks took it home when they occupied Egypt. Roman legions brought it to Italy. Even today there are three million lepers in the world – and in Asia there are areas where leprosy flourishes and has not been mastered by medical science. No wonder the Egyptians were helpless against it.

Antiquity may have been free from some diseases which afflict the modern world but there is no doubt that they had others of which we know nothing.

When sorcerers, doctors and priests alike failed to cope with a plague the masses went in solemn procession to the temples to implore the intercession of the gods.

There is no record of the number of human beings who came to a miserable end by flogging, hanging, crucifixion or disease in the prison camps of the Pharaohs. The sands of the desert have closed over them long ago.

The gold mines must also have witnessed scenes of horror and misery. Captives, chained together in twos or threes, worked day and night in the dark galleries. With oil lamps strapped to their foreheads and closely watched by overseers the unhappy captives hewed the ore with the most primitive of tools. It was then brought to the surface by boys and handed over to older people and invalids to break up into smaller pieces which were then ground to powder by women and greybeards. The final washing was carried out by slaves who had been carefully selected and could be trusted.

Slaves who defied their masters were crucified, hanged or buried up to the neck. Other slaves were marched past the place of execution to learn "wisdom" from their fate

Many of the slaves went blind and others were deliberately blinded. With such methods there was little fear of revolt, especially as foreign barbarians who could not speak the language were chosen as overseers. The practice of setting slave against slave is as old as the hills.

There must always have been several hundred thousand slaves available for work in Egypt. A man could be a slave from birth or reduced to slavery after being captured in war. If these sources of supply proved inadequate more could be obtained by purchase. Slaves bought in the market were often cheaper than those which had had to be fed and trained from birth. The slave trade flourished mightily everywhere. There are frequent references to it in the Bible. Many slaves were trained as skilled artisans and these may have fared better than their fellows. Slaves could also be hired from private owners who had thousands in their service.

Domestic slaves were much better treated and some of them may have led quite a pleasant life. They were put in charge of the children. Negroes and eunuchs were considered particularly faithful. Cases are known of fashionable women taking slaves for their lovers. Slave-owners could treat their slaves as badly as they liked but they were not allowed to kill them unless authorized by a priest. There is no doubt that generally speaking slaves were handled with ruthless cruelty but Egypt without slavery would not be the historic Egypt we know.

Ruthless too were the means employed to extract the last ounce of effort out of these unfortunates, especially those employed in moving heavy materials. The most casual glance at the granite columns, statues, sarcophagi and huge blocks of stone everywhere visible at once raises the question how such ponderous objects could have been fashioned and transported great distances without modern appliances and methods.

There are quarries at Assuan more informative than any book.

In the reign of Mentuhotep a force of ten thousand men was despatched to the quarry at Hammamat to hew out a sarcophagus for the king. The god Min, the protector of the quarry, favoured the object of the expedition and sent a gazelle to meet it. The gazelle led the way and when they tried to catch it it stopped at a huge block of stone of just the size required. This providential intervention enabled the men to get to work at once. Within twenty-five days they were on their way back.

Many an inscription bears witness to similar feats.

As timber is very scarce in Egypt tree trunks and logs could not be used as foundations for roads. Canals and stone causeways were the only means of transporting heavy materials. There must have been a network of such roads but they have all disappeared under the sand.

To haul one block of granite weighing forty-five tons on massive rollers a force of more than one thousand workmen was required in addition to the overseers. One of the overseers stood on top of the block to keep things moving by beating time. One heave shifted the block a few inches so that the operation took months or years if it had many miles to travel. A big building, and there were many such, involved a whole series of such operations.

Two thousand slaves were employed at least three years in hauling the Saïs monolith, a comparatively small one, from Elephantine. No one knows how many poor wretches were flogged to death during that undertaking. It is hardly surprising that some of the slaves revolted and killed one of the overseers. But they paid a heavy price. A hundred slaves were executed as a reprisal.

One of the punishments for quite minor offences was five to twenty-five lashes on the bare back. The penalties for more serious crimes were mutilation, blinding, branding, imprisonment and death.

A very common punishment was the "palmandara". The slave held out his hand palm upwards and his master lashed it with a palm thong hard enough to lacerate the skin and draw blood. A suppurating wound was the usual consequence.

A governor of the province of Hasen, one of the six into which Egypt was divided, had a granite block weighing sixty tons hauled fifty miles from a quarry at Hatnub. Only the gods know how long that operation took. We are told that the statue fashioned from this block was 23 feet high. According to a bas-relief in Phutihotep's tomb the transport of these colossal blocks was child's play but an inscription shows that the statement was far from the truth.

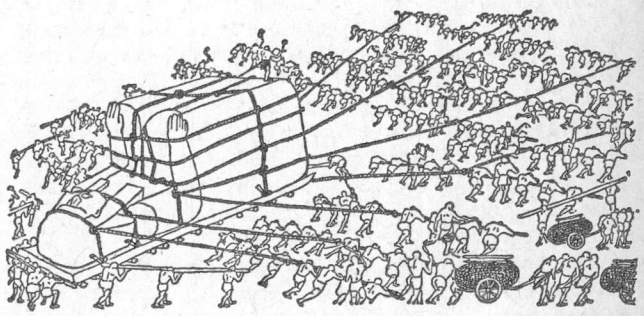

A large obelisk had to be transported to Alexandria from the Nile. The process adopted was as follows. A canal was dug immediately under it, thus making it a sort of bridge. Two boats filled with stones were placed under it. The stones were taken out a few at a time so that the boats gradually rose and lifted the bridge. The idea showed ingenuity and the whole operation must have taken a long time. But time and human lives were matters of no moment.

We are still left wondering how colossal blocks weighing six hundred tons and more were moved from one place to another.

Some quarries at Assuan show that the practice was to pick out the best pieces of granite veined with quartz, red felspar or sparkling mica. Curiously enough it would appear that some violent political upheaval must have put a sudden stop to operations at this site, for several blocks, all ready for carving into statues and sarcophagi, have been left lying about.

Sketch showing the method by which an obelisk was set up. When the base was laid it was surrounded by a wall and the cavity was filled with sand. The obelisk was laid across the sand which was then allowed to run away, thus tilting the obelisk into an upright position

Another problem is how the ancients were able to cut out these blocks. It is known that one method was to bore a series of holes about six inches in depth in a straight line. The implement used was some sort of copper chisel. Wooden wedges were driven into these holes. The wedges were then soaked and the uniform and tremendous pressure produced by their expansion was sufficient to split the rock. It is a possibility, but no more. Much remains unexplained.

Another remarkable "exhibit" is an uncompleted obelisk 136 feet high and 13 feet 6 inches wide at the base. Engineers have calculated its weight to be 1168 tons. It is said to be the largest single block of stone on earth and it may be doubted whether it could be moved very far by modern methods. Yet the Egyptians moved it to Thebes, one hundred and twenty-five miles from the quarry from which it came. But how?

In 1836 the French brought an obelisk from Luxor to France. Their architect Lebas was considered a genius for moving this two hundred and fifty ton monster from Luxor to the bank of the Nile, even with the up-to-date apparatus at his disposal. The obelisk was set up in the Place de la Concorde and bears a tablet describing how the terrible transport problem had been overcome. The Egyptians did not regard their own similar feats as worth commemorating – though they have left some record in stone of everything they considered important.

The living conditions of the Egyptians who were just above the slave class were not very much better. Their mud huts, crowded together and furnished with nothing much beyond a plank bed and a few mats and earthenware vessels, were dark and airless hovels swarming with bacteria and vermin. They were often built against the walls of temples and palaces.

The occupants of the palaces could enjoy the contrast. They had comfort and luxury. The pleasant smell of incense and balm greeted their aristocratic nostrils. Their gardens were gay with palms and flowers. On the other side of the wall the poor had to be content with the odour of dried fish frying in rancid fat over a dung fire, the effluvia from open runnels swarming with filthy flies and the company of dead dogs and cats. In their miserable mud huts were crowded together the old, the sick, the maimed and the blind, many of them old soldiers whose main occupation was exhibiting their suppurating wounds or the stumps of limbs in the hope of extracting from the charitable enough to buy a drink of cheap wine, that drowner of sorrows.

All these poor wretches reeked of their own filth. Flies played havoc with their eyelids and fleas preyed upon them. When some pot-bellied grandee took the air in his litter borne by negro slaves he was literally besieged by a swarm of beggars who had to be clubbed out of the way.

These slums of antiquity were hotbeds of vice and disease and the death-rate must have been very high.

Those Egyptians who were employed on the great landed estates by the Nile lived in less crowded conditions and enjoyed more freedom but they were grossly overworked and wages were low. We know from inscriptions that the poorer classes were often defrauded and exploited by the officials.

The aristocracy of course lived in another world. They

commemorated their achievements in monuments resounding with their praises and recording how many temples this king or that prince had built, and the scale of his offerings to the gods.

But there is a great silence about the horde of nameless outcasts, the dregs of society, who were none the less the pillars of the state and the basis of its economic life. Their value is shown by the fact that many slaves became artisans, artists and architects, and some rose to high position.

Social conditions undoubtedly varied from time to time during Egypt's long history. In certain periods they were more tolerable than in others but generally speaking life must have been very hard for the masses, particularly in war time. The story of Egypt is largely taken up with wars. A long and peaceful reign is a comparative rarity.

To take but one example, Egypt was plunged into anarchy for more than a hundred years during a series of invasions from Asia. Ultimately a provincial governor took over the reins of government. He made Harmonthis the capital. In the vicinity was a provincial town which the Greeks subsequently called Thebes. This is the start of the Middle Kingdom, opening with the XIth Dynasty under King Mentuhotep.

The transfer of the political centre of gravity from north to south was not the affair of a moment. It involved a prolonged struggle in which prince was pitted against prince and one priestly caste against another and the whole country became the scene of devastating civil wars.

Amenophis I moved the capital to the little town of Itjtowe because it gave him better control over the governors of the northern provinces. This king, the founder of the XIIth Dynasty in 1990 B.C., was one of the greatest of his age. In an inscription, translated by Breasted, we find this:

"He restored a country which he found in ruins. He made cities return what they had stolen from other cities and fixed boundary stones to compel them to respect each other's limits. He distributed the waters in accordance with ancient precedent because he loved justice."

The establishment of the Middle Kingdom coincided with the age of feudalism. Kings like Amenemhet I, Sesostris II and III did not rule personally but governed through provincial satraps. It was the duty of the latter to recruit soldiers for "His Majesty's Guard". It was a great age for wars. Sesostris I led an expedition beyond the Second Cataract. Amenemhet II reopened the gold mines in Sinai after a campaign and Sesostris II cleared a passage through the Nile cataract so that his galleys could proceed upstream. He also invaded Syria and opened a period of foreign conquest.

King Kamose fought against the Hyksos. King Ahmose successfully continued his operation. There was an admiral of the same name living at the same time. Here is an extract from the inscription on his tomb:

"My father was an officer in Elkab. I became an officer on a ship called the *Wild Ox*. I was brave and received the gold awarded to the valiant in action. Then I joined the ship *Glory of Memphis* which was with the northern fleet. When I fought at Anaris I brought back the hand of a warrior as trophy and received more gold. Seven times has my bravery been recognized by awards of gold, chains of honour and lions."

In Homer (Iliad XV) the lion is the symbol of bravery in war.

The inscription goes on to record that the war spread to Palestine and Nubia. "Then I became old and now I go to the tomb I have prepared for myself."

This simple summary of an admiral's life-story is a fragment of history. The wars he referred to ushered in the far greater struggles for world power during the XVIIIth Dynasty. The inscriptions tell us that they were fought for the glory of the gods but their real object was gain – gold, slaves and tribute.

It was in this period that Egypt began to build up her colonial empire, using the same methods as were subsequently adopted by the military states of the Christian West. Egypt's trade and shipping flourished mightily and brought her great wealth. Professor Breasted says that the Egyptians were a master-race, the English of the antique world, who conquered many lands and imposed their rule on them.

It was at this time that plans were made for a canal between the Nile and the Red Sea.

Aristotle and Pliny say that it was Sesostris I who first had a canal dug. Then he had an idea that the level of the Red Sea was higher than that of the Nile and work on this canal was stopped for fear that the salt sea water would be injurious to the river water. Ultimately the canal must have been completed, however, for we hear a great deal about Egypt's flourishing water-borne trade with Asia and Africa. Punt, the "land of Incense", is frequently mentioned in this connection.

The ship on the left is oriental, that on the right Egyptian. A very high level of skill in shipbuilding was attained. Inscriptions show that the Lebanon, which was particularly rich in cedars, supplied the timber for temple and shipbuilding. Today it is almost deforested

The canal was certainly in existence in the reign of Rameses II, but it has long since been swallowed up by the sands of the desert.

Diodorus, in his Bibliotheca Historia (1 : 33) and Herodotus (11 : 112) speak of a second canal which was constructed in the reign of Necho:

"It takes four days for a ship to pass through this canal and it is so broad that two boats each with three banks of oars can travel side by side. The channel is much longer because of its many bends. 120,000 Egyptians perished before this great work was completed."

This canal, which had a course of fifty miles, also sanded up. But it was in existence at the time of the Battle of Actium in 31 B.C. Cleopatra's fleet used it to escape into the Red Sea.

The Suez Canal was in course of construction between 1859 and 1869. Twenty-five thousand Arabs were continuously employed and though a daily water ration was brought by sixteen hundred camels there was a high rate of mortality from the effects of the intense heat in the desert. It must have been much higher in antiquity when nothing was known about hygiene.

We know from existing records that Tuthmosis III conducted his seventeenth campaign in the thirty-eighth year of his reign. Nor was this Egyptian Napoleon exceptional. The causes of war may have been much the same then as now. The Egyptians invaded Nubia and Ethiopia for the sake of their gold. On the north their armies entered Palestine and Syria and even reached the banks of the Tigris and Euphrates. They were familiar with Arabia and Libya and there was a prosperous two-way trade with those countries.

Egypt can be accepted as the first and an outstanding example of a colonial power, forcing her colonies to trade with her and exploiting them politically and commercially. Their special products which she coveted streamed to her in an uninterrupted flow for centuries. Nubia for instance, governed by Egyptian Viceroys, furnished gold, negro slaves, cattle, precious stones, ebony, ivory and corn.

There were great rejoicings in Thebes when foreign ships arrived with their varied cargoes. The crowds also turned out in force when the war ships of Tuthmosis anchored off the city and a mob of unhappy Asiatics, most of them chained together, was driven ashore to start life as slaves or furnish fodder for human sacrifices as the gods should decree. The spectators merely mocked at them – and even artists regarded the scene as a fit subject for lively caricatures which can still be seen on the walls of tombs.

All this mass of misery combined with unpitying indifference naturally roused feelings of desperate hatred in the hearts of the captives even though their ultimate fate varied considerably. Some were sent to row in the galleys. Here, chained to their benches, they must have envied the lot of the ordinary draught animals who were at least given some measure of freedom. Others laboured night and day in underground prisons under the supervision of janissaries to make sure that they never relaxed. Vast numbers of chained and starving wretches spent their time in dirty, stinking subterranean vaults from which light and fresh air were excluded. Some learned to suffer in silence. Woe betide those who kicked at the pricks or tried to escape! Their guardians cut off their noses and ears, impaled them on stakes or invented novel methods of torture.

When Tuthmosis III returned from his victorious campaign to the Euphrates he celebrated his triumph in those great obelisks which can now be seen in Istanbul, Rome, London and New York. These mighty monuments were calculated to make the vulgar forget that he who set them up had once been merely a priest of royal blood. There is a whole series of reliefs depicting the enormous mass of booty, human and otherwise, taken in war and the share allocated to the god Amun. The gardens of the temples of Amun were planted with rare and exotic plants from Asia. Ambassadors from north and south frequented the Court at Thebes. Phoenician ships brought the finest products of their country's looms and golden vessels of the most exquisite workmanship. Cyprus and Crete supplied all kinds of *objets d'art*, including ebony chariots, and exported thoroughbred horses and, of course, slaves. Asia's choicest vintages found their way to Egypt.

Enormous quantities of gold and silver were delivered as tribute by defeated enemies. We learn from inscriptions that on one occasion a consignment of 8,943 pounds of the purest gold was deposited in the royal treasury. It was an enormous figure for those days. Nor can that have been an isolated occurrence.

The inscriptions of the time of Amenophis III bear witness to similar feats of conquest and spoliation. Palestine and Syria were turned into Egyptian colonies. Of course the oppressed races sometimes revolted and tried to recover their independence just as India in modern times has struggled against foreign masters. When Amenophis succeeded in quelling one of these "risings" by bloody reprisals and returned home in triumph tradition relates that he made the captive princes with their families and five hundred retainers march ahead of his chariot with all their horses and vehicles. Exhibiting this human booty and 100,000 pounds of copper and 1,660 pounds of gold as a war indemnity, he made a triumphal entry into Thebes. Further to gladden the eyes of the citizens he showed them seven captive kings loaded with chains and had these unfortunate creatures hung up by the feet. Tiring of this spectacle he drew his sword, cried "I will not have them die like that" and cut off their heads.

Here is an extract from a pæon of triumph to be found in the temple of Merneptah:

"Israel has been levelled with the ground and her posterity exterminated."

Incidentally this is the first reference to Israel in an Egyptian inscription.

This Amenophis was also a great warrior and famous for the splendour of his court and the luxurious life he led. He reigned forty-four years – far too long for the subject races.

We get another picture of the ideas prevalent in ancient Egypt in some reliefs in the mortuary temple of King Sahure (about 2500 B.C.) to which the Egyptologist Adolf Erman has drawn attention. They depict gods and goddesses giving life to the king. The goddess Nechbet offers him her breasts. Long columns of subject peoples, headed by their local deities, bring splendid gifts. In another place ships disgorge all kinds of booty including slaves in droves. Another relief refers to a campaign in a country which must have been Libya. We see the king smiting a prince in the presence of deities whom the Egyptians regarded as the gods of Libya. Wailing captives are a prominent feature of the scene.

The fruits of the triumphs of Sahure's armies are enormous – 123,440 head of cattle, 223,400 asses, 232,413 goats and 243,688 sheep. A colossal figure! What the royal commissioners extracted from the defeated nation in the way of money tribute can only be guessed at.

The wars which I have mentioned were the work of a few kings of the XVIIIth and XIXth Dynasties, but no one should jump to the conclusion that the many other pharaohs were pacifists.

It is a sobering thought that these records of wars have been bequeathed to later generations which in that respect are no improvement on ancient Egypt. When future historians describe the downfall of the West their readers will no doubt lay their books aside as relating facts too horrible to be credible.

All the money extracted from defeated enemies flowed into the coffers of the kings and the priests. The common herd had to be content with religious exhortations which neither filled the body nor liberated the mind. The acquisitions were duly recorded in the temple registers under the headings of ships,

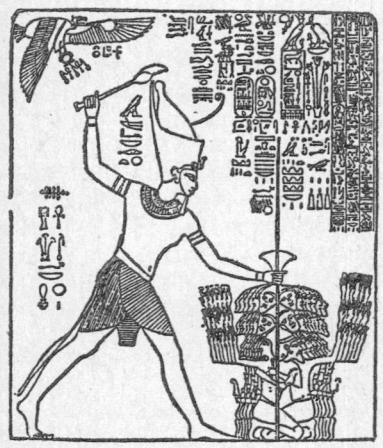

Relief from a temple showing a pharaoh beating in the skulls of captives

dockyards, quarries, landed estates, cattle, gold and slaves. The priests, with their insatiable demands for alms and offerings, led a pleasant life. While others slaved and starved the barns of the gods were never empty. Such conditions clearly called for a reformer.

It is not true that Egypt was always a granary. After an

unsuccessful war – and there were many of them – invading hordes swarmed over the land to steal or requisition anything on which they could lay hands. Egypt suffered foreign occupation on several occasions. These disasters, combined with the effects of internal disintegration, led to the extinction of her ancient civilization.

But it must not be assumed that the nation as a whole was warlike and bloodthirsty. The reverse is nearer the truth. Indeed many Egyptologists maintain that the Egyptians were essentially a peace-loving people. Even in those days wars were the work of the wire-pullers, never of the common man.

It is certain that war in those times was not distinguished by the devastation and mass slaughter which are its characteristics in our "progressive" age. In some ways it was far more genteel. There were no shells or bombs, though plagues and diseases of all kinds decimated the combatants.

Then as now foreign conquests favoured despotism and internal disorder. No ruler was ever so successful in exploitation as Tuthmosis III, the greatest of all the Pharaohs. His glory and achievements were a subject of universal wonder. He was considered the embodiment of restless energy. He led his armies to victory in Asia and simultaneously spread confusion and dismay among corrupt officials. Bribery and corruption were rife throughout officialdom. Even the departmental heads were infected. He proved himself ruthless in extirpating this great public evil. Those proved guilty were hanged out of hand.

He was a consummate statesman and a great administrator whose reign marks an epoch in the history of ancient Egypt. Her frontiers were extended as never before and the resources of the state developed and concentrated to an unprecedented degree. This genius, who started his career as an obscure priest and elevated himself to the purple, was a unique phenomenon. He created the first world empire, every section of which was governed by his regents. Conspiracies and revolts of subjects were suppressed without mercy. For three generations men retained the liveliest memories of his avenging sword. They used his name in taking oaths. It even appears on amulets made hundreds of years later when his world empire had fallen to pieces.

He was responsible for the largest of all obelisks, that

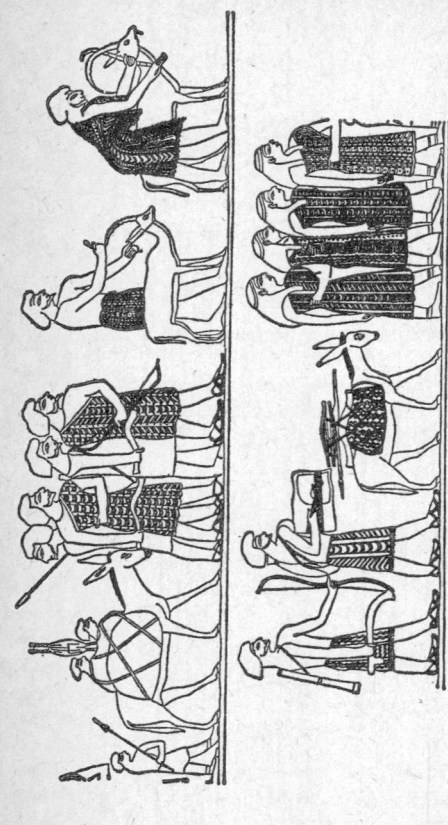

Painting from a tomb of 1898 B.C. at Beni Hasan. Enemhotep, governor of the Antelope province, had it made to show Tbeshah, the chief of a distant desert tribe, and his attendants coming to offer a very precious eye salve as a gift to Sesostris II. There are 36 figures in the train. The painter has been careful to distinguish between the foreigners and the Egyptians. The former have hook noses and pointed beards. The clothes are different. The foreigners wear long, gaily coloured tunics, the Egyptians only a short skirt. The chief leads the procession with an antelope and is followed by servants, male and female, with pack donkeys. The original colouring is excellently preserved mighty monument 110 feet high and weighing 320 tons which to-day stands in front of the Lateran in Rome.

There are some granite reliefs in the seventh pylon of the temple at Karnak which show an enormous Tuthmosis III swinging a censer and then grabbing fettered prisoners by the hair and drawing his sword to strike off their heads – the preliminary to presenting these gruesome trophies as an offering to the gods. The relative inscription reads:

> "The noble King assembles captives from many lands far beyond the frontiers and delivers them up for sacrificial slaughter. Never before has any King trampled so many under his feet. Never will the glory of his conquests fade."

The inscriptions give the names of 359 nations and cities in an area stretching from the Euphrates to the southern border of the Sudan who were conquered by this indefatigable monarch for the glory of Amun. Priests went with the armies as standard bearers. Their function was to exhort the soldiers to even greater efforts.

Before his death a hymn was composed in his honour. It is interesting from both the literary and psychological points of view and shows the great impression his reign had made on the priestly caste.

The hymn begins with his praises and thanks for his achievements and continues with a speech made to him by the god Amun:

"I came and bid thee cast down the princes of Tahi
Among their mountains I flung them at thy feet.
I made them hail thee as the Lord of Light
And see in thy face my own image.

I came and bid thee subjugate the lands of the west.
The peoples of Keft and Cyprus tremble at thy name.
They hail thy majesty as a young bull,
Stout of heart, horned and irresistible.

I came and bid thee smite the people of the Marches.
The country of the Mitani goes in fear of thee:
They hail thy majesty as a crocodile,
The fearsome lord of the waters whom none may approach.

I came and bid thee smite the Islanders
From the depths of the Great Sea they hear thy thunders:

> *They hail thy majesty as the avenger,*
> *Poised to slay the cowering victim.*
>
> *I came and bid thee conquer the peoples of Asia.*
> *Thou hast made captive the chiefs of the Asiatics of Rezenu:*
> *They hail thy majesty in all its glory*
> *When thou mountest thy chariot brandishing thy weapons.*
>
> *I came and bid thee conquer the far places of the earth.*
> *Thou holdest the oceans in the hollow of thy hand.*
> *They hail thy majesty as a mighty falcon*
> *Hovering to swoop when and where it will.*"

The poem continues with similar exhortations to conquer other regions. The call to conquest is the insistent theme of the whole poem. No one was left in doubt that the god Amun summoned the Egyptian nation to wars of conquest, devastation and revenge. The mantle of religion covered all these demonstrations of human ferocity and greed and the determination of one race to lord it over all others.

What was a human life to these great deities? The individual was nothing but a serviceable tool. A small caste of privileged persons wallowed in wealth and luxury among the downtrodden, poverty-stricken, hopeless millions, whose function was to defend that order of society with their lives.

In March of 1448 B.C. Tuthmosis III, having waged seventeen wars, left this world as the god Osiris. The burial of this man-god must have furnished a magnificent spectacle, but his mummy has survived, sufficient proof to us at any rate that this god of mortals was no more than a deified mortal.

His reign is a story of blood, domination and oppression, but it was by no means unique in that respect. Several of his successors were inspired by his example. When King Kamose was warned by his counsellors that the Syrians were a mighty people he burst out: "Wherefore all my power and might? I will seek out this new foe and strew his entrails on the ground." Inscriptions record that when he returned from his successful campaign he boasted: "I overthrew and destroyed their armies. My warriors returned like lions with the spoils – slaves, cattle, fat and honey."

His successor Ahmose continued his work and inflicted further tribulations on mankind.

As I have said, the mantle of religion covered everything. All the wars were waged, all the cruelties committed in its name. Anything was right which redounded to the glory of the gods. Yet in the entrance to a rock temple at Thebes there is a statue of the goddess of Justice, crowned with an ostrich plume. After three thousand years of Egyptian history she is still the goddess of the poor.

History shows that war and slavery were inseparable. While on the subject, it might be mentioned that a poem of the IXth Dynasty records the military achievements of the Pharaohs with truly religious fervour. It is the work of a Theban priest Pentaur.

For hundreds of years the Hyksos Kings ruled over Egypt and this period marks the beginning of that tragic series of wars against the Semites which is treated in the Bible as if it were a minor episode. In reality those wars were a desperate struggle for world power between Aryan Egypt and the Babylonians and other semitic races. During those wars Egypt was occupied for long periods by foreign armies. Hostile occupation is never pleasant.

Some savants maintain that Egyptian history is far less a recital of wars than a record of peaceful progress and that slavery was less repulsive than has been thought. Of course there were kings whose rule was mild and benevolent. In the Sallier papyrus of the XIIth Dynasty there is a passage in the apostrophe to the Nile in which it is said that the Nile god Apis "drinks all tears and gives freely of his bounty to all men. If he withdraws his benevolence they mourn and waste away and the gods in whom they no longer trust are as if they had never been." These lines show that benevolence was not a thing unknown.

But unlike the records of other oriental monarchies the Egyptian inscriptions do not revel in bestial cruelty for its own sake, however much they may be preoccupied with successful wars. No pharaoh followed the example of some Assyrian potentates who personally put out the eyes of captives and had them flayed alive. The semitic lust for vengeance was foreign to Egyptian dignity. Conquered peoples were not exterminated in toto. Captives were settled on the land and employed on building schemes. Public opinion in antiquity regarded such treatment as quite mild, however hard the work. They were usually fed well. Perhaps that is why the Jews hankered after the fleshpots of Egypt.

One of the monarchs of the Middle Kingdom was so well disposed towards his subjects that he instructed his son in the following terms:

Statues of Amenophis III, grandfather of Tutankhamun, called the "Colossi of Memmon". Cut from a single block, each statue is 53 feet in height and weighs 410 tons. Their transport to this site in 1400 B.C. and the method of erection remain a mystery to this day

"Amenemhet to his son Usurtesen – In my reign no man has hungered. Love for my people has inspired all my acts. May it be the same with thee, that there may always be peace between thee and thy people."

Kings who treated their subjects in that way were genuinely regarded as gods. Usurtesen did not reign long but he carried out his father's wishes and his memory was revered for centuries.

Amenemhet III was a true lover of peace and though he built great temples and monuments for the glory of the gods his social reforms must have been revolutionary for those days. His line ruled Egypt for two hundred and thirteen years, a period of peace and prosperity.

It is interludes such as these which alone justify the conclusion that Egypt was a peace-loving power. We must never forget that not a single papyrus or inscription tells us anything about the horror and misery of slavery. The modern historian or archæologist can make good the omission. All history teaches us that despotisms, even the most brilliant of them, have been built up on slavery. One man's glory means another man's suffering. Victory for one side means defeat for the other. The few bask in the sunshine, the many grope in darkness.

Chapter 6

GODS, IDOLS, DEMONS

Mythology shows that all nations and races in the first stage of development have very primitive religious beliefs. Men start by believing in spirits, good and bad, and crediting them with all the characteristics of human beings, including lust, cunning and quick wits. Hence the stories of demons and their activities which the moderns write off as superstition. But when the first phase of credulity is passed and man leaves his spiritual childhood behind him and begins to mature there comes the stage of criticism and reflection. Reflection leads to curiosity about men and things and curiosity leads to comparisons and questioning. Thought takes wing, imagination begins to function and those myths emerge which embody the youthful dreams of the race.

The historian Friedell wrote that the supreme test of a nation is its religion and that it is not the race which produces religion but religion which makes the race. Whether that proposition is true from the biological aspect is quite another question. He added that there were no Arabs before Mahommed, no Israelites before Moses and no Greeks before Homer.

In antiquity the identity of race and religion was not open to question. Its gods were the real masters in every country. If a nation was conquered by another it dethroned its gods. The Jews furnish an excellent example. They were a mixed race and only attained to nationhood through their passionate adhesion to their faith. The Jews who lived in Egypt and called themselves Israelites were far more antisemitic than any other race has ever been because they despised their semitic neighbours and avoided contact with them. Even then they called themselves the "chosen race".

The power of religious beliefs is the first answer to those who wonder how ancient Egypt was capable of such outstanding achievements.

In antiquity men's thoughts and actions were to a very great extent governed by their religion. They looked at the world around them in the light of their faith and it inspired their fears and hopes. Their calendar was based on religious celebrations, and religious customs and usages were the basis of the evolution of their literature, art, science, agriculture and manual labour. Like other ancient peoples the Egyptians regarded their gods as being closely concerned with their daily life. All the natural phenomena around them, the sky above their heads, the earth beneath their feet, were associated in their imagination with some divine myth. In the earliest times the shepherds and peasants thought the sky was an immense cow poised above the earth. Others thought it was part of a female figure bending over the world.

A female harpist. The Egyptians cultivated music as part of their religion. Harps and lyres were their favourite instruments. Musicians enjoyed great prestige and had their own god

Picturesque ideas of this kind were numerous. To the primitive Egyptian the world was the narrow Nile valley and he likened it to a man lying down with plants growing from his back and men and animals living on it. Because he regarded the sky as a vast sea on which the sun and stars travelled westwards every day he assumed that there must be a subterranean Nile by which they returned to their starting point.

No element in his religion was more important than the Under World, that dark corridor traversed by the subterranean river which bore the barque of the sun from west to east. In this under world lived the dead, guarded by the god Osiris and his wife Isis. There are other beliefs of this kind and some of them are less primitive. All religions as they developed have laid stress on the duties of the living to the dead but no nation at any time has attached more importance to such duties than the Egyptians. Their religious beliefs and observances were not, however, organized on any very rigid system. There was a world of difference between popular ideas and the lore of the priests and these differences had some highly complicated features.

The god Seth   The god Sobkh

Like other countries Egypt was divided into regions, provinces and city or village districts. Each province had its guardian deity. The names of many of these local gods are known. Horus was the god of Behdet and other places, Amun of Heliopolis, Thoth of Hermupolis, Month of Thebes, Chnum was the guardian spirit of Herver, Ptah of Memphis, Sukos of the Fayum. In many cases the rôle was filled by goddesses, such as Neith in Saïs and Hathor at Dendera.

Other local deities were called after the cities of which they were guardians. The cat-goddess of the city of Bast, for instance, was generally known as Bastet. From the earliest times there was a cult of the fetish in Egypt. The rites of South Sea aborigines and many African negroes at the present day show that it is by no means extinct. In many places Egyptians worshipped stones engraved with arrows. In later times this cult was associated with the veneration of Osiris and Ra.

The gods Min of Koptos and Ptah of Memphis were often represented as a fetish in human form. The goddess Hathor appeared as a sycamore, the god Nefertem as a lotus flower, the goddess Neith of Saïs as a shield to which two arrows were attached.

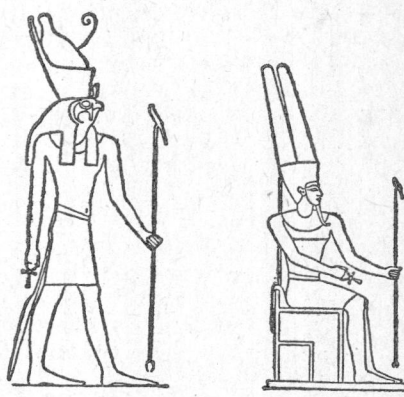

Horus-Ra and Amun of Thebes hold the *ankh*, symbol of life, in the right hand and *was*, the symbol of dominion, in the left

There was a widespread belief that deities revealed themselves in the form of animals such as bulls, cows, rams, apes, goats, crocodiles, cats, mice, lions, frogs, ibis, hawks, vultures and snakes. Certain fishes came into this category and even the dangerous scorpion. The archæologist Lord Carnarvon died from a scorpion sting. Some said that an outraged god was at work and others that the curse of Tutankhamun was proving itself no empty threat.

Chnum took the form of a ram, Horus a hawk, Thoth an ibis, Sukos a crocodile, Neith a vulture and Hathor of Dendera a cow. In addition to these gods and goddesses the Egyptians worshipped various sacred animals which had their special temples and were buried with great pomp. When one of these beasts died its place was taken by another of the same breed, but only if distinguished by certain special markings.

The most famous of these animals was Apis, the sacred bull of Memphis. The tombs of the Apis-bulls are still to be seen at Sakkara. There are cemeteries for crocodiles at Ombos, for cats at Bubastis and for ibis and rams at Elephantine. Other races have also associated animals with their deities. Zeus and the eagle, Athene and the owl and the lion of Cybele come to mind. The "British lion" and the "German eagle" are symbolic relics of antiquity.

Thoth, moon god and god of knowledge. His sacred animal is the ape

At a later stage the god assumed human form and was represented with a human face and limbs and wearing the Egyptian style of dress. He was given the crown which adorns the head of earthly kings. The sceptre and staff symbolized his power. There was an intermediate stage, the half-animal, half-man. Thus Sukos was represented as a man with a crocodile's head, Chnum as a man with a ram's head. Thoth had the head of an ibis, Horus that of a hawk. The same process applied to the goddesses. Mut had a vulture's head and Hathor was given horns to show her association with the cow.

In addition to the gods venerated locally there were gods worshipped by the whole nation, gods such as Geb, god of the earth. Maat was the goddess of truth, Nut the goddess of the heavens, Shu the goddess of the air. The distribution of rain and dew was the affair of Tefnut. Ra was the guardian deity of the sun. Osiris, who was also god of the dead, was the god of vegetation. Among the stars Orion and Sirius were venerated as gods.

Gods who were only associated with the greater manifestations of nature had no temples though they were very real to the mighty and the humble alike. In later times they also assumed human form and certain places were set aside for their worship. Hapi, god of the Nile, became god of decent family life and honest work. His opposite, Seth or Typhon, stood for disorder, the desert, terror and death. A fearsome deity!

The hawk-headed Month became god of war. Min of Koptos concerned himself with fertility and the harvest. Ptah of Memphis was the patron of artists, metal workers and goldsmiths. Hathor, appreciated for her lighter side, was goddess of love and joy. Many local deities became associated with cosmic forces. Thoth was the moon god who established world order. He was also the guardian spirit of hieroglyphics and thus came to be regarded as the patron of scribes and scholars. Horus, in association with the sun, was regarded as the god of the heavens and was given the name of Ra-Harachte, meaning "Ra in both horizons". The cow-goddess Hathor became associated with the sky. Sopdu was the god of the eastern desert; Wen-Nofre the god "whose heart did not beat", i.e. the god of silence. The scarab (dung-beetle) was deified as Cheprure as a manifestation of the sun god. The sacred stone in the temple of Heliopolis was given the name of Benben because it was the first to be touched by the light of the rising sun. Other local gods with particular associations were known and venerated throughout the whole country.

Mention should also be made of the minor gods and the demons and spirits who were beneficial or harmful to man, who was thus concerned to gain their favour. There was Toeris, goddess of birth, who could prolong or hasten labour. Bes, the clown-headed god, protected the nuptial bed. Hecket, the divine toad, assisted at births.

Many gods shared the destinies of humans in having wives and children. In some cases god, goddess and their son shared the same temple. The best known example is Ptah, his wife Sachmet and their son Nefertem. Mut was the wife of Amun. Many gods were also credited with human virtues and passions. There are many spicy tales about the Egyptian deities.

Prevalent ideas about the universe were expressed in the forms of myths. The general notion was that the earth was a great plain surrounded by water and mountains which supported the sky. In antiquity there were diverse views about the sun and moon. For a considerable period men thought that they were the eyes of the god who created the world.

In the temple at Dendera, dedicated to the goddess Hathor, the chamber which is holy of holies is in a perfect state of preservation. It was once the resting-place of the sacred boat in which the statue of the god Amun was carried through the streets. In an adjacent temple dedicated to Osiris, the god of the dead, the visitor may see the famous frieze known as the "animal series of Dendera". Unfortunately it is a plaster cast as the original has been removed to the Bibliothèque Nationale in Paris.

The Egyptians were certainly versed in astrology and made some practical use of their knowledge of the stars.

The god Osiris and the goddess Isis, his wife. On their heads they wear the symbol of their names

Every town and village had its gods, apart from the universal deities. There were even family gods and gods associated with employments such as fishing, ploughing, hunting, handicrafts and the arts. Every human action and movement was deemed to be under the control of some divinity. If railways and submarines had then existed they would have had their special deities. There was no fixed limit to the number of gods!

The Egyptians had about two thousand gods. As has been said, many were drawn from the animal world. The heron, the swallow, the vulture, the goose, the perch, the eel, the lizard, the frog and even the cantharides fly, all had their place in the Egyptian pantheon. Herodotus wrote: "Egypt is surrounded by deserts. The number of animal species is limited, but I know few species which are not considered sacred."

The worship of animals must not be considered remarkable since they were supposed to incorporate the spirits of ancestors and relations. The heads of virile horned animals such as rams, bulls and he-goats were hung over the doors of huts and venerated as local gods. There was a cultural sodomy in Egypt corresponding to the stories of satyrs and centaurs in Greek mythology. Herodotus wrote: "It has been reported in my time that a goat had intercourse with a woman in the presence of many people." We know that women frequented the stall of the sacred Apis-bull. This cult was also known among the Israelites, for Moses called down curses on all having commerce with cattle. In present-day India there are sects associated with the practice.

The people sacrificed to the gods under the watchful eye of the priests. The gifts, which included food, were laid on the altars and after the ceremony the priests disposed of them.

The goddess Maat standing by the scales in the realm of the dead

At certain times the images or statues of the gods were brought out of the temples and solemnly paraded through the streets in a procession led by the priests in their finest robes. The crowd smothered the gods with flowers. These colourful and spectacular ceremonies, with their odour of incense, vessels and robes of finest gold and impressive ritual, were the easiest and surest way to the hearts of the simple and the most effective method of strengthening their faith in the gods.

The Greeks and Romans regarded the Egyptians as the most religious of all nations but could not resist an occasional jibe at their deities. There was no doubt much to laugh at. But are we quite certain that two thousand years hence no one will be poking fun at some of our own religious observances?

In the course of time the accepted hierarchy of the Egyptian gods was often changed. If some ruling house favoured particular gods those gods rose in the national pantheon though Horus never ceased to be the specific patron of the Pharaohs. He was Horus-Ra, god of the sun, god of the Empire. He retained that position even when Egypt was split into two Kingdoms with the vulture-goddess Nechbet supreme in one and the serpent goddess Buto supreme in the other.

The solemn act of coronation was always celebrated in a temple, the climax being reached when the king was received into the circle of the gods and accepted as supreme deity with the title of "Lord of the Sacrifices".

The Egyptian constitution was always monarchic and the divinity of the king was never challenged. In all the temples, even those of Alexandria, the statues of the kings had precedence over those of the gods. Occasionally it was accompanied by statues of his family and in that case the rays of royal divinity fell on the queen also.

Religion entered a new phase when the political centre of gravity was transferred to the south. In Thebes the god Amun of Karnak was considered the sun god and he was promoted as Amun-Ra. There was a popular saying: "Amun is lord of all." It was in his name that wars were waged in Nubia and Asia and temples in his honour were built in the conquered lands. Under the XVIIth and XVIIIth Dynasties he was the national god and became the successful rival of the previous imperial deity, Horus.

To modern eyes this complex of gods and intricate political and religious system seems childish and quite incomprehensible, but it did not prevent the valley of the Nile from being the "Paradise of the Believers".

So many gods required an army of priests to serve them. Every statue had its quota of attendants. The priestly class lived entirely on the sacrifices and took care to ensure that their flock remained acutely conscious of their importance. The state set a good example with imposing sacrificial ceremonies which were national festivals.

On these occasions a swarm of priests crowded round the altar and observed a fixed ritual. They wore white robes and their hands were anointed with oil. The highlight of the proceedings was the sacrifice of a bull which had first to be tied up. Other priests led in the High Priest, a dignitary bearing a diadem on his head and resplendent in a purple robe embroidered with gold. When the assembled worshippers caught sight of him they fell on their knees. The great officers of state bowed to him. The bull was sprinkled with holy water, the chanting ceased and in a tense silence the High Priest proceeded to the supreme act, the slaughter of the beast with his own hand. If he was successful and the blood gushed forth freely a shout of triumph rent the air.

One of the courts of the temple was set aside for the poor. When the priests and temple servants had taken the best parts of the carcase for themselves the rest was distributed to the poor. It can be imagined that with all these famished creatures fighting for scraps there were some unpleasant scenes.

The great national festival was after the harvest when the tenants and peasants had paid their dues in corn into the barns of the temple and the royal treasury. On this great day human sacrifices were required by the god Amun. The rites were celebrated in all the temples and at Thebes the ceremony was on the most sumptuous scale. There the Pharaoh and his wife sat on their thrones, crowned and gorgeous with scarlet robes and flashing jewels. At their side was the High Priest and below them an escort of nobles and high officials. The assembled crowd filled nave, transepts and forecourt.

When the priests had performed the preliminary rites a bell was rung. All sound and movement ceased, except for the apprehensive murmurs of the slaves tightly bound and appointed for death. The king then approached and cut the throat of one of the slaves. His example was followed by the High Priest. The screams of the victims were drowned in a shout of jubilation from the assembled multitudes while the priests twanged their stringed instrument known as the *sistrum*.

The same scene was repeated at the same hour in all the temples, innumerable slaves and captives being immolated in this heartless fashion.

The crowd then trooped in procession past the altars, not only feasting their eyes on the corpses but sometimes dipping their fingers in the blood and dabbing their foreheads with it. On the porches the sacred vultures and other scavengers waited impatiently for the moment when the corpses would be cut up and thrown out.

A stele in the temple at Abydos shows King Seti I offering the god Amun 1,000 loaves, 1,000 jugs of beer, 1,000 pieces of beef and 1,000 boxes of incense. The king holds a censing vessel. Next to him is his son wearing the priestly panther skin and pouring a libation on the altar. There is a wall painting of the king presiding over the dissection of the sacrificial animals. Another shows animals – oxen, antelopes and geese being brought up for slaughter. Four priests are being kept busy. One of them makes a list of the offerings, a second sprinkles them with holy water and the other two slaughter them. Another picture shows priests and soldiers dragging fettered negroes and Asiatics.

These sanguinary rites were not unknown among the Jews for we read in the Bible how Abraham was about to sacrifice his son Isaac when God called to him: "Lay not thine hand on the boy." The scene of that occurrence was the temple in Jerusalem and visitors are still shown a rock in the Mosque of Omar which is the traditional site. Other races are suspected of having practised human sacrifice, notably the Maya of Mexico where "skull chambers", filled with innumerable skulls, can still be seen.

The effigy of Amun was then brought out of the temple by the priests and borne through the streets in procession so that the faithful should see their supreme deity at close quarters.

The largest temples had an annexe called "The House of Song" which was the living quarters of a troop of young women, the beloved of the god Amun. These spoiled darlings lived a very idle life and the competition of the priests for the favours of the reigning beauty often led to serious disorders.

The procession was headed by a troop of these girls, singing

Three priests praying. Facing them, another is burning incense and some priestesses provide ceremonial music

and dancing. Their performance was generally applauded but might be criticized, because the spectators knew something about the arts and had certain standards and their own favourites.

To become a temple dancer was every girl's ambition. Selected girls and boys were brought up in the temple schools from the age of six. They were taught singing, music, games and dancing under the supervision of the priests. One of their functions was to show themselves to the devout at ceremonies in the temple or religious processions and on such occasions their make-up was particularly colourful and they wore their finest jewels. To the roll of drums and the refined strains of the lyre they executed dance movements distinguished by their extraordinary uniformity and rhythm and which sometimes ended in a sort of ecstatic frenzy. Art and discipline combined in honour of the great god Amun.

A shrine, with the god Amun in the form of a ram

The effigy of the god was immediately followed by the High Priest. A superb canopy was held over his head and he was accompanied by his priests chanting in chorus. As the procession passed, the spectators fell to their knees and stretched out their hands in supplication.

At the conclusion of the proceedings the effigy was taken back to the temple where it was ceremoniously washed to remove any dust or dirt. The consecrated water used was then distributed as medicine among the sick and the lame who were also supposed to derive benefit from the sight of priests leaping wildly round the statue. Amun was finally returned to his shrine in the Holy of Holies and the door was closed for another year. Priests of the highest rank only were permitted to enter this most sacred place.

On such days of high festival flags were flown from the tall poles of the temple pylons. Flags and gaily coloured carpets were also hung from the windows of the palaces and the villas of the rich and every house or hut would manage to produce some show of colour because the masses were out to enjoy themselves and forget their miseries for the moment. Jollity reigned in the market-place no less than in the tavern. Priests, neophytes, temple scholars and officials, the religious and their opposites mingled freely with the crowds. All social barriers were down. It occasioned no surprise at such times when a priest exchanged his professional attire for lay clothes to have a taste of ordinary life incognito among friends. A hat covered his bald head, that badge of dedication to the service of the gods. A pleasant hour could be passed in some bawdy house listening to Syrian music and watching naked girls dancing. Prosperous citizens borne along in their litters dispensed liquor to all and sundry. "Wine, Woman and Song" was a refrain to which ancient Egypt was no stranger.

This great sacrificial festival of the god Amun was as much a blend of religious ceremony and public revels as a coronation day. It drew strangers in large numbers, for the temples provided other attractions. The net result was a shower of gold and other gifts, while the pious were notably fortified in their faith.

The spirit of sacrifice was second nature to the Egyptians. If a peasant's wife was roasting a goose she would cut off the tenderest part and lay it on the nearest altar. If she wanted to stand well with the priest there would be a nice tit-bit for him too. The daily life of the masses centred round the idea that constant sacrifice to the gods was a never-ending necessity. Sacrifices for the dead were considered particularly meritorious. Ka, the soul, must not want for anything. The Priests alone could keep it alive with their magic rites and eternal chanting. For such service they required to be paid and payment took the form of suitable gifts from the relatives of the deceased. Nor must the latter neglect their duty to bring food and wine for him to the temple of the dead. No wonder the priests lived on the fat of the land!

An additional exaction was the "tenth", a tax of the tenth part of the product of a man's labour, whether produce of the soil, earnings or war booty. This was a universal form of taxation. It was sanctioned by Moses, as we know from his injunction to his people to set aside their tenth every year.

The priests, who were originally a body of laymen, gradually became a professional caste. They were recruited from the best families. In the seminaries they received a theological education suitable for those intending to become servants of the gods. Of course they had to start at the bottom. A period of apprenticeship passed before their promotion to the ranks of those appointed as regular attendants to the temples of the gods or the mortuary temples. For the highest priestly offices candidates were selected from a very limited circle, mainly sons of priests at the top of the hierarchy or of princely houses. Royal princesses usually married their brothers or became priestesses by marrying a priest of high rank.

The priests serving the various holy places formed a corporate body the head of which was the High Priest of Amun in the national temple at Thebes. In addition each temple had a council of governors, usually with a priest of princely rank at its head. The wife of this dignitary was considered the principal concubine of the god, whose real "wife' was the wife of the reigning Pharaoh.

Priests were often selected to command armies. No one could rise to high position in the state unless he could read and write and those accomplishments could only be acquired by children of the upper classes who had been educated by priests. The professions such as medicine, astronomy, the army and the law were only open to those with theological training, in other words those qualified for the priesthood. Men so trained were the pillars of the state and church but there was also an invisible power behind the throne in the shape of a bureaucracy. Kings and priests die but the bureaucracy goes on for ever.

In such soil intrigue, with jealousy, envy, hatred and revenge to feed it, naturally flourished. In many cases it resulted in palace revolutions and the overthrow of the existing monarch, and perhaps the elevation of a priest to the throne.

The lengths to which the priests were prepared to go to maintain their influence is illustrated by the following story.

The Pharaoh Tuthmosis I had a principal wife (who accordingly was not a member of the harem) and three children, the elder son and heir, a daughter and a younger son. The heir reigned with his father on a secondary throne. The daughter, Princess Hatshepsut, was her parents' favourite child. A temple inscription at Karnak records that she was born in the form of a goddess.

"Amun took the form of the noble King Tuthmosis and found the queen sleeping in her room. When the pleasant odours that proceeded from him announced his presence she woke. He gave her his heart and showed himself in his godlike splendour. When he approached the queen she wept for joy at his strength and beauty and he gave her his love...."

There are wall paintings showing the queen in childbed and the goddess Hathor handing over the divine child to Amun. The inscription continues:

The goddess Isis suckling the god Horus

"Her Majesty grew up to be a lovely and lively young princess" and the royal father is quoted as saying:

"Come to my arms, my glorious daughter, and take the place befitting thee in my palace, that thou mayest have power and subdue the unruly, thou my daughter and heiress, beloved of the goddess Uto...."

Hatshepsut, i.e. "Chief of the Noble Women", answered her father's call, mounted a secondary throne and in practice became reigning queen. This was a very rare occurrence. We suspect something of her pride and ruthless ambitions when we see the mighty buildings she erected in honour of the gods.

Queen Hatshepsut married her younger brother who was not in line for the throne. Incestuous marriages in royal families were quite usual as they preserved the purity of the blood. After all, they had the Isis legend to live up to.

The God Osiris married his sister, Isis, Horus being the fruit of their union. An inscription in a pyramid of the IIIrd dynasty tells us of the related myth of the New Year and how the power to bring death or create life was transferred:

"Quivering with love, thy sister comes to thee and from thy body draws that which is Horus, the mighty creator and will be Sothis."

The phallus was venerated in ancient legend as the symbol of procreation in nature. During the IInd Dynasty it was customary for the embalmers to separate the heart and phallus and bury them in canopic jars. The phallus was even identified with the god Hapi. It figured conspicuously in all forms of nature worship. Nature's unfathomable wisdom decrees that all life is governed by sexual activity. A high degree of such activity spells happiness, a low degree suffering.

The incestuous marriage which produced Hatshepsut was a failure and the parties separated. The husband became a priest and entered the feudal corps of priests of Amun. Hatshepsut reigned in his stead. In her reign there were no wars. She considered that Egypt was strong and secure and needed peace. But her rule was far from uneventful. She often sent trading expeditions by sea to Punt, that "Land of Incense" on what is now the coast of Somali.

There is no doubt that Hatshepsut was not only a handsome and popular queen but also a clever woman, in fact too clever for the priests' liking. The temple and tomb she built for herself among the rocky hills at Der-el-Bahri are impressive monuments, apart from the two obelisks, each nearly one hundred feet high and weighing three hundred and fifty tons.

An inscription records her boast of these great obelisks which were dedicated to the god Amun:

"They who will behold my mighty monuments in years to come will stand in awe of what I have accomplished and say: 'We know not how she got together the mountain of gold wherewith to gild them. Surely she shovelled out gold – more gold than Egypt had ever seen before, as if it were so much corn.' And when these words are heard they will not be idle boasting for men will reply: 'With whom can she be compared? She was worthy of her father Amun.' "

Like other female autocrats in history, Hatshepsut, the Catherine the Great of Egypt, gave her heart to a favourite and placed all her trust in him. Her choice fell on Senmut, who educated her daughter Nefrura. This lover was an architect and she employed him to build her memorial temple. We naturally wonder whether this *liaison* was the cause of the divorce.

However that may be, the prince-priest who had been her husband made a sensational return to the scene in the twentieth year of her reign when all the signs indicated that the lover was about to be promoted to royal consort and might even mount the throne of Horus. A bloody drama unfolded. The queen, her lover, her court and retinue and innocent daughter fell victims to the discarded husband's revenge. Even his brother, Tuthmosis II, a possible rival, was ruthlessly murdered. Nor was honour satisfied until the name and all statues and representations of the queen had been removed from all the monuments.

Shortly afterwards, the priests hatched a plot to turn the situation to their advantage. There were times when their power rivalled that of the king, for only an heir who was recognized as the son of the god Amun had the right to succeed and the Grand Council of the priests could grant or withhold such recognition.

On this occasion the priests had one of the king's sons as their candidate for the throne and he was of their own body. After divine sanction had been given to his candidature in a temple ceremony his selection for the throne by the god himself was staged in a very dramatic manner. While the effigy of the god was being taken from its sanctuary to the temple amid the acclamations of the crowd the royal candidate hid himself in the northern transept. The bearers carrying the god wandered about among the columns as if he were looking for something and then came to an abrupt halt opposite the prince-priest who bowed to the ground. The "god" immediately picked him out and he was led to the spot where the rites required that only the lawful king might stand. The prince was thus raised to the throne while his father was still alive. He received the name of Tuthmosis III. This event took place in May, 1502 B.C.

The feelings of many honest Egyptians must have been outraged by this subterfuge.

In the winter of 1927/28 the eminent American Egyptologist Dr. Herbert Winlock discovered in the vicinity of Der-el-Bahri numerous remains of once beautiful statues and statuettes of Queen Hatshepsut, as well as fragments of pink granite blocks, sculptures, sphinxes and other relics of the outlaw. The scale of the destruction gives us some idea of the strength of feeling against him. In a mortuary temple Winlock discovered the secret tomb of the lover. Though only a commoner the great queen, his royal mistress, was determined that he should have his share of the prayers and the offerings of the faithful. The case was unprecedented.

Subsequently a long subterranean passage was discovered which connected the tomb chambers of the two lovers and also a painting in the inner sanctuary of Senmut praying for his beloved. But though such elaborate preparations had been made for the spiritual welfare of both in the underworld, their intentions were frustrated by fate.

In 1903 Carter found the splendid tomb of the queen in the "Valley of the Kings". It had been plundered. In 1916 the Kurna thieves showed him an unfinished tomb chamber which contained another sarcophagus of the queen. The aforesaid subterranean passage led into this chamber. The mummy, however, was not to be found. No one knows where it is. The only relic was a casket containing the embalmed liver.

Three thousand five hundred years have passed since this political tragedy, as moving now as then, took place. The gifted queen, who looked on war as something contemptible, fell a victim to the intrigues of priests, and her former husband, the warrior Tuthmosis III, who waged seventeen wars, advanced the frontiers of Egypt far into Asia and created the first great empire of world history.

A strong Egypt was in a position to maintain friendly relations with other countries. Records have survived which show that in times of peace her trade with neighbours was in a most flourishing condition. Some 350 tablets with cuneiform inscriptions incorporate correspondence between Babylonian rulers and the Pharaohs. Among other things we are told that a princess from Mitani became the wife of an Egyptian king and that an Egyptian princess married an Asian potentate. Names such as Taduchipa, Tushratta and Shutarna crop up in these records. Princess Giluchipa brought 317 women and female servants as her retinue on her bridal journey.

A pharaoh with his wife and a slave carrying a fan

Mutual trade throve on such arrangements. It is plain that the acquisition of gold was the prime object of commerce, but two other products, frankincense and linen, were in great demand by the Egyptians. Frankincense and other perfumes were obtained from countries bordering on the Indian Ocean. Incense was required for religious purposes. Its odour induced an emotional and devotional frame of mind in the worshipper and its use distinguished religious ceremonies from all others.

The Wise Men from the East brought gold, myrrh and frankincense as a sign of veneration and submission to the infant Christ and these costly products were among the luxuries frequently acquired by King Solomon from his business friend Pharaoh and brought back to Jerusalem, to the disgust of the plain-living Jews.

The main article of export in ancient Egypt was linen. They cultivated flax assiduously and were expert in making it up into cloth. A white linen garment was not only the hallmark of a fine gentleman but the regular ceremonial costume of royalty and priests.

Even less advanced nations such as the Israelites used linen as the proper material for temple vestments. Druids and similar officiating dignitaries in the West always wore linen robes. Linen was also used by the Egyptians in the process of mummification.

Egyptian lady at a feast. (Wall painting of 1450 B.C. from the tomb of Rechmire)

The material was made up in different ways according to the social standing of the wearer, as tattooing had proved an inadequate badge of rank. The importance of social distinctions could best be brought home to men through the evidence of their senses. Display and ceremonial were addressed to their senses.

This chapter may conclude with some extracts from Herodotus on the characteristics and customs of the Egyptians of his day:

"The Egyptians are of all men the most god-fearing. They drink out of bronze vessels which they rinse daily. Their linen garments are always kept perfectly clean. Woollen garments are not permitted in the temples. Piety forbids that a man should be buried in wool.

"They cut their sex organs in the interests of cleanliness. The priests shave their heads and bodies every third day to prevent infection by lice. They bathe three times a day and twice at night. They have other pious usages.

"They derive many benefits from their position. They do

not have to provide for themselves but live on the abundance of gifts of bread, meat, goose flesh and wine. Priests and kings are the first of the seven castes into which society is divided.

"The Egyptians do not cultivate beans. The priests will not accept them. Vegetables are considered unclean.

"There is a multitude of priests for each god. One of them is the High Priest and when he dies his place is taken by his son.

Crowns and ceremonial head-dress of princes. On the right, standards and badges of various regiments, with the insignia of contemporary deities

"There are various ways of removing the hide and entrails of beasts which have been sacrificed. When they sacrifice an ox in some special festival they remove the contents of the stomach and fill it with bread, honey, grapes, figs, frankincense and myrrh. Then they roast it and pour great quantities of oil over it. After a period of fasting and wailing the celebrants feast on the sacrifice. Afterwards they indulge in things of which it is not seemly that I should speak.

"The Greeks calculate with counters from the left to right, the Egyptians from right to left. The Egyptians make a point of doing things differently from everyone else. They relieve themselves indoors but eat out of doors, explaining that what is ugly, however necessary, should be done in secret but what is not ugly should be done openly.

"The women do all the work. The men stay at home and

weave. Sons have no obligation to look after their parents unless they want to do so. That duty falls on the daughters whether they like it or not. The women stand up when they pass water whereas the men sit down. The Egyptians are always different and maintain that they are right.

"The Egyptians consider the pig unclean. If an Egyptian even touches a pig in passing he must wash himself and his clothes. No swineherd, whether an Egyptian or not, may enter a sanctuary. No one will give him his daughter in marriage. A swineherd can only marry into the family of another swineherd. But the Selene sacrifice swine at full moon and eat their flesh. It is not fitting that I should say why.

"The Greeks have introduced sacrifices and the phallus cult from Egypt and many of the names of the gods are of Egyptian origin.

"Almost all Babylonians and Syrians go unwashed into the temple and lie with the women. The men are like animals. Birds couple in the sacred precincts in the presence of the gods. If these things were not pleasing to the gods they would not be done. The Babylonians put forward this assumption as an excuse for doing things of which I strongly disapprove. The Egyptians and Greeks do not commit such iniquities in the temples.

"The Egyptians are the most learned race of which I know.

"Their method of keeping well is to take purgatives and an enema three times a month. They believe that all illnesses are caused by food. After the Libyans the Egyptians are the healthiest nation.

"Many Egyptians rent a rectangular piece of land from the king. When the annual Nile flood washes away part of it officials are sent to measure the area and fix the new rent. I think that the Egyptians invented surveying and the Greeks learned it from them. But the Greeks are indebted to the Babylonians for their knowledge of seasonal changes and the sun clock and the division of the day into twelve parts.

"Egypt is divided into many provinces. Their warriors are styled Kalasiri and Hermotybi. Under the Pharaoh Amasis the army reached its highest figure of 250,000 men. A soldier was not allowed to learn a trade or anything not concerned with his profession. They were all given a piece of land, 100 Egyptian ells in area, rent free. The royal bodyguard consisted of 1,000 men and it was changed every year. The men were taken in rotation and no one could serve twice. The men of the bodyguard received an extra daily ration of five mina of bread, two of meat and four *kotyle* of wine."

Chapter 7

NEFERTITI

All the Egyptians were adherents of polytheism with one exception, Amenophis IV, a pharaoh of the XVIIIth Dynasty, whose wife shared his views. His father had had leanings towards monotheism and Amenophis was determined to carry through the religious revolution he had timidly begun. He proscribed the ancient religion and ordered that instead of the pantheon headed by Amun only one god should be worshipped, Aton, the sun god.

Not that there was anything new in the worship of the sun, which had always been regarded as under the special protection of the god Amun-Re. But now Amun-Re was to be dethroned, the sun god to be worshipped as the sole deity and no other gods were to be recognized The young king meant to put an end to the multiplicity of gods and the resulting confusion in public and private worship.

He composed a hymn in honour of the sun god which has come down to us:

Thou shining orb in the depths of the sky,
O living Aton, first to appear in the world!
When thou risest far away in the east
All the earth is filled with thy beauty.
Thou art great and beautiful high in the sky,
Thy rays embrace all the lands of the earth and all that
 thou hast made.
Thou art Re and hast bewitched them,
Bound them with chains of love.
Though thou art far away thy rays reach down to us,
Though high in the firmament thy steps measure the day.
Thou createst the child in the womb of its mother.
The living seed in the body of its father;
Thou givest life to the son ere he is born
And calmest his fears that he cries not.
Thou, guardian within the mother,
Breathest life into what thou hast created.

When he leaves his mother's womb
Thou givest him the power of speech
And meetest all his needs.

Thou hast created all the seasons to crown thy work,
The Winter to refresh man
And the Summer to make him warm.
Thou makest the depths of the sky thy home
That thou mayest survey the work of thy hands.
There, O Aton, thou dwellest alone,
Now beaming in glory, now veiling thy face,
Now disappearing, now returning.

There is a vein of poetry in all the literature of ancient Egypt and it is often difficult to distinguish between poetry and prose.

This royal poet let his fancy rove. His idea of world domination was that of a creator of nature who was filled with paternal concern for everything he had created. In another place this king referred to Aton as the "Father and Mother of everything he had done". His conception of a loving Heavenly Father reminds the modern world of the heavenly injunction to have regard even for the lilies of the field.

It was this element of paternal concern for all men without distinction which Amenophis IV regarded as the essential characteristic of the sun god He drummed into the proud and exclusive Egyptians the doctrine that Aton was the "Universal Father" so that even the conquered Syrians and Nubians must be reckoned among his children The king's revolutionary opinions must be regarded as most remarkable, considering the age in which he lived.

Instead of leading armies he revelled in philosophical speculation, delighting to find himself in the company of intellectual priests His aims and ideals mark him out as one of the most extraordinary of the pharaohs and among the earliest reformers in history.

It was not merely in the realms of religion and art that Amenophis was a revolutionary. He blazed new trails in every department of human activity. Yet he was not a mere dreamer and fanatic, though there must have been a fiery soul within his frail body. A man who struggled so hard and so long to overthrow the existing religious order was no trifler but a revolutionary social reformer.

He held the army of priests in contempt because he regarded them not only as fetish-mongers trading in magic books and "sacred" beetles but also more as soldiers than theologians. A priest who thought that the will of God meant warfare and bloodshed was the reverse of a holy man. Everything the priests did was inspired by superstition and had become a childish game with misunderstood symbols. He issued a decree demanding a complete *volte-face* and proclaiming that religion stood for truth and love for all men.

No one paid much attention to it, but one day a priest was arrested for a serious violation of its provisions and selling a poor woman a "Book of the Dead" to place in the grave of her deceased husband. The priest, a nephew of the High Priest, Bekanchos, was brought to trial, condemned to death and executed.

This incident fired off the train which led to the explosion.

A scene in Egypt in the year 1370 B.C.

We see the great throne room of the palace crowded to the doors with the grandees and notables of the empire. The Pharaoh and his wife Nefertiti are seated in majesty on their thrones. At their side is Haremheb, the Commander of the Guard. There is a look of suppressed excitement on every face. The High Priest, surrounded by priests, faces the assembled dignitaries. The king rises to his feet and addresses them:

"Egyptians! Since I ascended the throne I have pondered long over what I have found among you. My people is caught in the toils of idolatry and worships a multitude of gods with Amun at their head, Amun whose High Priest is Bekanchos. I solemnly declare to you that there is no god who demands blood and death and empty sacrifices. Turn from your ways. There is only one god and we are under his watchful eye and our destinies are in his hands. Our god is Aton, the god who is in the sun and is himself the sun, the great life-giver. Renounce Amun and his idols and follow my precepts! Let men be equal in life as they are equal in death. I have decreed that the priestly seminaries shall be closed. The priests have never been the servants of God and their teaching is false!

"I am closing all the temples of Amun and putting an end to their easy profits. I am seizing their ships and harbours, their workshops and quarries, their lands, barns and cattle, and all other possessions which have enabled them to despise and dominate their fellow men and form a state within a state. The priests are now answerable to the law and can be brought before the courts. The Semites who have come from Babylon and introduced evil customs into Egypt are banished for ever."

No pharaoh has ever dared to talk in that strain before. The priests glower in silence. Then the Grand Chamberlain steps forward and completes the king's proclamation:

Amun, the national god, in the form of a ram. On its head Re the sun, and Uraeus the serpent. It is protecting a pharaoh. [The figure is of stone and dates from 1900 B.C.]

"The Pharaoh declares that he considers Thebes, the headquarters of idolatry, as unworthy to be his capital. He is building at Amarna a new palace in honour of the god Aton. As a sign of his reverence for Aton the Pharaoh has decided to change his name. Henceforth he will be known as Akhenaton. All who wish to follow the Pharaoh will be welcomed at Amarna and new homes will be found for them."

This announcement led to violent disorders in the great temple of Amun which the priests had to protect at the peril of their lives. The soldiers refused to obey their officers. The mob rioted, got out of hand, looted the wineshops, burst into the harems and violated all the women they could find. But order was soon restored and early next morning the royal family departed in state to the sound of the trumpet. An excited mob swarmed into the temple of the ram-headed Amun and surged through the streets and squares in drunken frenzy. Some maintained that Queen Nefertiti had fainted in her husband's arms as the royal barge started on its journey. Others quarrelled over the king's new name and refused to call the former Amenophis IV Akhenaton, swearing that to do so would be to renounce the god Amun who had made Egypt great and prosperous and to recognize the new sun god Aton in whose name the king had set forth to found a new capital and a new religion.

When the royal fleet had left, with the king's standard flying from his barge, only his mother, Teje, remained in the deserted palace. Her heart was full of grim forebodings. She foresaw her own death and the end of the empire. She knew that her husband Amenophis III had paid little need to the war clouds accumulating in Syria and that the mighty Hittite empire was even then making preparations to descend upon Egypt and destroy it.

The young king remained blind to all these dangers. Absorbed in his vision of a new earth and a new heaven he was lost to all sense of reality. His gaze was fixed on his sun god who tolerated no other luminary in the firmament.

The royal poet was undoubtedly stricken with some incurable disease. His servants often found him wandering about in the countryside lost to the world and reciting verses. Nothing could move him from his purpose to destroy the ancient deities, not even sparing the mother goddess Mut. In a sky swept free of rivals Aton the sun god must reign supreme and alone, Aton the god "rejoicing in the mountain of light" who had entrusted the millions of lives he had created to his earthly son Akhenaton, the leader of his nation.

The turmoil into which Egypt was thrown by this grand attack on the existing order was unparalleled. The whole country was involved. Thanks to the priests no nation on earth was more attached to its ancient forms of religion. They were the very foundations of its being. All the ceremonies and supplications and even the most trivial and commonplace actions of the Egyptians were inspired by their faith. The time-honoured cult was the nerve-centre of the body politic.

And now Akhenaton had set himself to root out accepted theology as outmoded superstition. The path to salvation must be through the solar disk, the simple and straightforward symbol of the new doctrine. Confidence must take the place of fear. Apprehension about the life to come must give way to happiness on earth for Aton is the god of love and peace, the master of destiny, the source of abundance and fertility and he who makes the poor and oppressed to smile and releases them from their chains. He helps the chicken to peck its way out of the egg and the child to leave its mother's womb. When Aton shines, men jump for joy. The birds of the air wing their way aloft and the animals and the fishes turn their faces towards him. Men must learn to love truth and simplicity. The king himself was a simple man who had broken with tradition. He mingled freely with his people, cultivated the society of artists and knew the joy of family life with his wife and little daughters.

There is a poetic monument to the new order in the shape of an immortal hymn to the sun which is also ascribed to Akhenaton. The joy of living inspires every line:

The earth brightens when thou ascendest the shining mountain
When thy rays sparkle, Aton the Day,
The two countries are filled with joy.
They wake, they spring to their feet
Moved by thy power.
They wash and clothe themselves,
Their limbs chant thy splendours.
The whole earth labours at thy bidding.
The cattle rejoice in the pasture,
In the green trees and the cornfields
The birds flutter:
Their wings are a hymn of praise to thee.

The lambs skip,
They are alive because thou hast risen for them.
The ships pass up and down the rivers
The way opens before them because thou shinest.
The fishes in the streams rise to greet thee,
And thy rays penetrate into the depths of the sea.

Akhenaton's rapture animates every line of this three thousand year old poem. The new city and the art of the day also bore witness to his enthusiasms.

Everything was in sharp contrast to what had gone before. Consider this cynical extract from the instructions left by Amenemhet I to his son: "Thou must not love thy brother or call anyone thy friend, for those who have eaten my bread have

Glass vase in many colours, representing a fish. 8 ins. x 10 ins. A product of Amarna about 1370 B.C.

turned against me". The sphinxes with their lions' manes which we see today are the true emblems of his philosophy.

But in Akhenaton's realm the emphasis was on beauty, truth and the love of nature. Some great artist made the superb bust of Nefertiti with its delightfully slender neck and royal head dress. "Naturalism" is the keynote of the reliefs of the royal couple. For the first time plaster masks were made of celebrities, both in life and after death. The drawing of a hand begins to be realistic. A foot is given toes. It is in this period also that the lower rows of tomb reliefs begin to correspond with the upper.

Painters and sculptors gave free rein to their fancy, for priestly inhibitions operated no longer. It was as if the spirit of nature had descended upon the earth to break the old fetters and give man the freedom she enjoyed herself.

It can be conceded that the art of Amarna is the development of a process which was at work before the time of Akhenaton and particularly in the reign of his father. But the transfer from Thebes and the new buildings in the "city of the horizon" show that it was only now that the bud burst into flower.

We get some idea of the beauty of that flower from the remains of the pavements of the royal palace at Amarna. All the poppies, cypress leaves, cornflowers, papyrus leaves, lettuce, palms, convolvulæ, figs, cattle, calves and flying geese are painted true to life in tempera on a bright yellow ground. The general design is conventional and familiar but never before had Egyptian art followed nature so closely. The animals seem to come to life, the colours are bright and fresh and above all the painters frequently use half tones – a practice unknown in the Old and Middle Kingdoms.

Even conservative critics concede that the artists of Amarna were decidedly original. It may be that they were influenced by the Mycenae-Cretan school, though that school had only modified something which Crete had originally imported from Egypt. The outstanding difference was the spiritual background. Cretan art is more sensual, erotic, refined and elegant than the realistic if naïf art of Amarna, which corresponded to the character and temperament of the young king.

Queen Nefertiti. Painted limestone. The bust is 13 ins. in height [Berlin Museum]

The faith which Akhenaton preached is a faith fit for paradise. Even the lion and the snake are not forgotten. They leave their hiding-places only when the sun's disc has dropped below the horizon but, in contrast to their reputation in the Christian paradise, they are regarded as harmless children of nature.

But unlike the saint of Assisi, Akhenaton did not confine himself to preaching. He set about uprooting the ancient faith in a sort of holy rage. In the matter that touched him most closely the lyrical poet revealed himself as a pitiless iconoclast. Repudiation of Amun and his kingdom of gods was not merely theoretical. He sent out his soldiers not to fight against foreign enemies but to strip the temples and tombs of all the statues, symbols and names of the old gods. The new era of Light should have nothing to remind it of the powers of darkness!

It may very well be that in repudiating the goddess Mut

Akhenaton was actually taking vengeance on the gods for refusing Nefertiti the blessing of a son. This queen presented him with six children, but they were all daughters. Perhaps that is why her noble features wear a melancholy expression which assorts ill with her beauty.

Akhenaton employed blind men only as singers in the Temple of Aton. May that have been an act of vengeance on the demon which provoked and presided over his epileptic fits?

Slowly but surely fate made him pay heavily for his own blindness to the world around him and the real needs of his people. When tidings of disaster arrived from provinces in revolt he put all his faith in Aton. Nothing could go wrong under Aton's all-seeing eye! It was useless for threatened cities to appeal for aid. Let them put their trust in Aton and all would be well. He was not to be deflected from his holy crusade against the old gods.

The lovely Nefertiti, the daughter of a priest, was passionately devoted to her husband. No one knew him so well. No one sang with greater fervour his favourite hymn: "Aton, thou art bright, clear and strong. Thy love is mighty and all-embracing."

Nefertiti was as simple and unpretentious as her husband. He would not allow his subjects to kneel before him and she was equally averse to anything savouring of the obsequious. She was, and wished to remain, a child of the people. Though not of royal blood she was greatly loved and revered by him and always remained the light of his life.

The royal couple often took country walks together and sometimes they would climb a hill and she would hang on his words as he gave utterance to his thoughts about the sun. When he crushed her to him and smothered her hair with kisses she thought herself the happiest woman in the world.

Both were strictly monogamous and expected everyone else to be the same. The institution of the harem was abolished.

Their views were not shared by the queen-mother, Teje, who had also come to Amarna. She was the daughter of a priest Jua and his wife Tua whose tomb was discovered at Thebes in 1902 by the American Egyptologist, David. Teje was greatly concerned about the attack on the old gods and their priests and was strongly supported by her adviser, Haremheb.

One day both queens were sitting on the terrace. Nefertiti was gazing at the sunset and it was obvious that she was deeply moved. The queen-mother stretched out her hands and said: "Nefertiti, my son still loves thee as much as when he first met him. Didst thou not see how fondly he kissed the baby Nefernefern yesterday?"

Nefertiti cast down her eyes. She was thinking that she had given her husband daughters only. There was no heir to the throne.

"Despair not, Nefertiti, for he still loves thee. Thou art young and the last fruits of the tree are oft-times the best."

"It may be so, noble Queen and dear mother, but..."

"I speak to thee my daughter as the mother of my son, and also as the mother of this sacred country the welfare of which is ever close to my heart, and I feel that thou art bewitched by thy feelings about Aton."

"How could it be otherwise, my mother. How could I forswear this new knowledge which has brought me purity and happiness?"

"Pay no heed to such learning, Nefertiti. Aton must fall. The nation needs a god it can understand. My son Akhenaton teaches his people something beyond human comprehension, something which exists only in the mind."

"But, my dear mother, surely Aton was revered also by thee and thy royal husband?"

"Naturally. But my son, thy husband Akhenaton, has made this sun god something which is quite incomprehensible to the common people."

"But is not the sun the source of love and the giver of life? Without the sun life would cease to exist. Is it not therefore more worthy of our reverence than all the dead gods? There is no greater happiness than to reflect on the goodness of the sun and all the blessings it bestows."

"True, true, Nefertiti, but our people cannot take all that in. They and their priests must have gods whose power they can see and respect. The gospel of Akhenaton is universal love and peace. It has no room for the sword though all that he has achieved has been by the sword. Peace and goodwill are puny weapons. Akhenaton composes hymns and sings them while others shout their war cries."

"Akhenaton loves his people and loves peace, my mother,

and for that his people love him. Can there be anything more sacred than the love which God gives us through the sun – the eternal gift of life to man, beast and flower, the eternal gift of light to the stars. Hast thou no feeling for the greatness of God, my mother?"

"Naturally I have, Nefertiti, but it means nothing to the people. The people cherish their old gods with whom they have grown up. How can they be expected to adapt themselves to the new teaching?"

"But believe me, my dear mother, the king makes himself one with his people, and they love him and place all their hopes on him. Why should they not be weaned from their old gods and walk in the new paths?"

"No, Nefertiti, that which the king does is evil, not good. He does not know his people. He is not one of them and should not mingle with them. He must be their lord and master in all things and at all times. Any other course is an unrealizable dream and in the long run very dangerous. Akhenaton must mend his ways and return to the old gods. Thou alone canst make him do so...."

"How canst thou ask me to lead him back into the darkness of idolatry? When he came to me he knew not who I was. He would have made me his queen even if I had been the daughter of a nobody. I came from the people. He yearns to be one of them and is it for me to hold him back? It would be to rob him of the love of God and his faith in the One and Only God."*

Meanwhile the sun had set and the stars were shining. In the depths of the sky the tail of a meteor could be seen and Nefertiti regarded it as a good omen for her husband.

But the queen-mother's views were shared by others, whose murmurings had come to the ears of Nefertiti and caused her some anxiety. She knew that her husband was loved by the nation at large but regarded with hostility by the priests and the propertied classes. She knew too that the temples swarmed with soothsayers, fortune-tellers, exorcists and mediums, who had a great hold on the popular imagination.

There was only one man who did not believe in all the paraphernalia of sects, means of grace, cheap miracles, street preaching and soul starvation, and that man was Akhenaton, whose creed was summed up in the words: "There is only one

*This conversation is based on Reinhold Conrad Muschler's charming story "Nefertiti".

God who reveals himself in everything that lives and breathes. All other gods are false gods."

He closed many of the temples, which seemed to him little better than sanctified brothels, and strove to put an end to confusion of thought by an appeal for clarity, reason and hard work. He also abolished the eternal court and church ceremonial because he thought that humanity was being suffocated by formalism. God was worshipped by decent living and not by processions, so he prohibited those gay and noisy demonstrations.

Akhenaton's ambition was to close one era and open another in which all men would be brothers. Belief in truth and justice was not enough. He wanted mankind to have heaven here on earth, a heaven built with human hands. He loved men in God and God in men. His own way of life was modest and economical. He liberated all slaves and exhorted the poor and the down-trodden labourers and servants to fight for Aton, if only because they had nothing to lose. The victory of Amun could only mean the return of slavery, poverty, misery and death. He assured them that they need no longer rely on the ordinances and promises of the priests because they should have laws inspired by a proper sense of justice and the brotherhood of man.

The primitive conditions in which the poor *fellahin* of that time lived certainly beggared description. The women usually produced twelve children of whom less than half survived infancy. Akhenaton advised mothers to limit their family to two. A decent existence with two was better than starvation and misery with twelve.

He insisted that all criminal convictions should be subject to appeal. He himself proved a just judge and many convictions were reversed. He even extended protection and fair treatment to animals. Fish spearing and bird catching were regarded as cruel practices and prohibited. Even the slaughter of animals for food in a manner involving unnecessary suffering was made illegal. Animals employed in mines and quarries had a particularly hard life and he decreed that they should not be used for such work – and that old and worn-out beasts of burden should end their lives in honourable retirement to the best pastures. What Akhenaton wished for himself and his loved ones he wished for all men and all living creatures.

He habitually added to his name the words "He who lives

by the Truth", and every act of his daily life proved that this was no idle boast. He had a strong sense of unity with his fellow-men and his own way of life was as simple and unpretentious as if he had been the lowliest of temple scribes.

He called a halt to luxury building and devoted the resources thus released to the provision of dwellings for the people. It was made illegal for asses and goats to live in human habitations. Every house must have proper cooking apparatus installed. Previously the cooking had been done outside. An internal privy was also made essential and the practice of meeting nature's needs in the streets was prohibited.

The architects had to adapt themselves to the New Order. From a report of the Egyptian Exploration Society we learn that the first working man's settlement known to history was at Amarna.

Akhenaton brought about a bloodless revolution. He dissolved the army and treated soldiers as the lowest order of society. They received no pay and if anyone chose to lead the soldier's idle life he had the choice of starving or earning a livelihood by begging.

Akhenaton's creed was that wars were contrary to the will of God, who would have nothing to do with weapons of war, the instruments of tyrants. God meant harmony and peace, not bloodshed.

The subject nations rose in revolt. Akhenaton announced that the god Aton would not tolerate conquest and thraldom and accordingly proclaimed the dissolution of the empire. The first colony to be liberated was Syria, noted for its exports of vice and prostitutes to Egypt.

Before his time every Egyptian was regarded abroad as an oppressor. A popular catchphrase was that the only good Egyptian was a dead one. The subject races murmured because they had to pay taxes to the Egyptian commissioners and the circumcised Egyptians ravished their daughters. Akhenaton decreed that this scandal should cease. Egypt's honour must be restored. He recalled all the garrisons and governors and even castigated them as locusts and common thieves.

The god Amun had been rich because all fertile land was the property of his temples. Akhenaton confiscated all the great estates and distributed them amongst the tenants and the peasants. The rich also had to surrender all lands not required for their bare necessities and were no longer exempt from taxation. Their former slaves must be decently treated and paid fair wages. All doctors were instructed to offer their services gratis in the most poverty-stricken quarters of the city. In many cases such districts were actually evacuated and their inhabitants billeted on the upper classes and the rich.

But no proceedings were taken against those who desecrated the temples of Amun or stole their golden vessels and fittings.

Elderly people, whose fanaticism or conservatism prevented them from accepting the new ideas and who continued to bring offerings to the temples, were considered objects of ridicule and refused admission. But it was a legal offence to receive or keep a priest in the house, for priests were now to be set to useful work.

Tax-gatherers who extorted more than the legal due were whipped and judges who judged unrighteously or accepted bribes were subject to punishment.

Akhenaton also issued a decree prohibiting the acquisition of wealth without work and took all the gold from the temples so that it could be used for the benefit of the poor. In his view the rich were parasites.

Begging was forbidden and the giving of alms made punishable. Every man was entitled to his meed of the bread of justice and the age of stargazers and their like who professed that they could hear grass grow was at an end. Poverty was regarded as an admission of public inefficiency.

But the idea that men should live in peace and amity and that Aton was a god of love and stood for universal love was incomprehensible to the Egypt of Akhenaton's day. The hitherto down-trodden masses did not know what to make of their new-found freedom. They were without leaders, a sense of unity or a corporate aim. They did not understand that liberty is something to be maintained and defended by constant effort. A decree that they must all learn to read and write was not at all to their taste. They much preferred idleness and imitation of the ways of the rich. The sweets of freedom, and in particular its pleasures and vanities, were more desirable than freedom itself. The women must be as "smart" as their betters and took to cosmetics and make-up in the most approved fashion. They adopted the most outrageous style of dress, the upper part of the body uncovered and nothing but a short knee-length skirt slit provocatively up the side.

Not less hostile were the old conservative elements headed

by the aristocracy and the army of priests. Akhenaton had overthrown their god Amon, and closed his temples. He believed that the other gods would go the same way and the people would hail the advent of Aton as one man. But he was wrong.

The priests began a counter-attack. They were able to interfere with the distribution of corn to the peasants, thereby raising the price and causing a scarcity which led to great discontent.

Akhenaton had put an end to the practice of offering incense to the dead with the result that the ships which brought oil and aromatic substances from Punt were no longer required. Sailors without employment were naturally ripe for trouble, which the priests diligently fomented. That body had also brought prosperity to the commercial classes by encouraging pilgrimages and lavish expenditure on offerings to the temples. This "racket" was not a thing of the past and a further section of the public was alienated. There was no more tribute from Syria or gold from the conquered lands. The paralysation of the "mortuary industry" by the prohibition of mummification and the suppression of gifts to the dead also created widespread discontent. All this was fuel to the priests' fire.

Soothsayers and magicians in the temple service prophesied all sorts of disasters and plagues – fleas, frogs, mice, snails, locusts, poisoned wells and drought – as the result of the insults to Amun.

At length matters came to a head in a revolt which was marked by hard and bloody fighting.

The country was split into two parties. On one side were the adherents of Amun, led by the aristocracy and the priests, and on the other the followers of Aton. The latter were reinforced by all the slaves, labourers and servants who had nothing to lose and realized that their freedom was at stake and oppression, disease and death would again be their lot if the cause of Aton did not prevail.

The priests proclaimed a holy war. They had concealed stores of arms with which they equipped old soldiers and negroes whose services they secured by lavish bribes and promises. They were backed by the propertied and commercial classes, the swarms of eunuchs, temple servants and scribes, the idle and the discontented.

One other element in the situation should be mentioned, the

mob which indiscriminately looted the corn stores and wine vaults and took advantage of the dissolution of the harems to ravish all the women on whom they could lay hands. The mob knew nothing of loyalty or noble aims. Class hatred revived, and hatreds know no limits. Houses were burnt down and corpses left lying in the streets or thrown into the Nile where the crocodiles feasted joyously on fat priests – more tasty fare than emaciated slaves. Negroes dressed as soldiers swarmed unhindered in the streets carrying the heads of slaughtered priests on their spears.

Some welcomed such scenes as marking the end of an evil era but others turned away in disgust. Akhenaton himself was deeply grieved at this civil war and called on all men to return to the paths of amity and reason. At the age of thirty he found himself at the head of an empire in ruins. He could only plead with Aton and bewail the betrayal of his country by the priests and princes.

Mercy and justice were his creed and he has a claim to be regarded as the first pacifist in history. But his goodness was his weakness and brought about the collapse of his great experiment.

Before long some of his most loyal supporters changed sides. Even Nefertiti turned against him. The perfect marriage was broken and then dissolved. She was followed by his father-in-law, the priest Eje. Eje had once forsaken the religion of Amun and embraced the faith of Aton, but now the cause seemed lost and its king doomed. The Court Chamberlain and vizirs followed suit. They had been at his side when exulting crowds acclaimed him and now they deserted him like rats in a sinking ship. One of them, Tutu, made a compact with the dangerous enemy, Asiru. Certain letters in cuneiform characters record that while still protesting his fidelity to the fallen Pharaoh he was committing treason by hatching a plot against the country.

Among the conspirators was the king's personal physician, who crowned his infamy by giving him some medicine containing poison.

The last words of the dying monarch are worth recording:

"The Kingdom of the Eternal has no place on earth. All will return to the old ways. Fear, hatred and injustice will govern the world once more and men will toil and suffer again as they used to do. It were better that I had never been born than that I should live to see the triumph of evil."

Once again the temples of Amun were filled with cheering crowds as the priests proclaimed the victory of their cause. The nobility, priests and soldiers inaugurated a ruthless campaign of retaliation and revenge. There were wholesale executions. The slaves trooped back to the quarries. The nineteen years' reign of Akhenaton was forgotten and nothing was left of his gospel of social justice. In its place the nation was offered the picturesque processions of old, and idolatry and relic-worship resumed their place in the lives of the masses.

Heretics hung by the feet from the wall of death

The priests returned to their old game of oracular utterances and predicting the course of events from the appearance of the stars. The institution of the harem, which Akhenaton had made illegal, was re-established. Once more the priests brought their influence to bear on trade and commerce and the High Priest was restored to his position as commander-in-chief of armies sent forth to conquer other lands. The rich regained their confidence and as of yore stored their gold in the temple vaults, though they carefully concealed any wealth of which they could keep the priests and tax-gatherers in ignorance. The great sun-temple of Aton was transformed into a temple of Amun and a new Pharaoh was re-established as the supreme deity. But many of the poor cursed the day they were born.

The revolution was followed by an inquisition as cruel and ruthless as any in the Christian West. Anyone deviating in the slightest degree from the orthodox line was denounced and punished as a heretic. The priests were in their element. They were prosecutor, judge and executioner in one. Men were crucified, hanged, burned and buried alive, or tied to stakes in the burning sun until they died of thirst. These horrors were perpetrated with great public show and of course in the name of the god Amun. A hysterical mob, swollen by all who wanted to curry favour with the priests, mocked at the victims and outraged the corpses. The sentimental who found themselves unable to repress a feeling of pity ran considerable risk of being denounced and punished as heretics.

The cult of Aton had blossomed mightily but briefly, like all exotic flowers. When the great reformer was dead his memory was effaced. The "heretic" was not even allowed a tomb of his own. He was buried with his father. The priests had shown what they could do with one who tried to rouse the world from its sleep. But Aton still meant something to the unhappy masses who returned to the old life of slavery, drudgery, destitution and sorrows.

Three thousand years later excavators made their way into a dank, dark tomb-chamber and deciphered the inscription on the king's plain sarcophagus which enshrined his creed: "I breathe again the sweet breath from thy mouth. I see thy beauty day by day and long to hear thy soft voice coming through the cold wind from the north."

The phrase "coming through the cold wind from the north" may indicate that Akhenaton's idea of the one and only great god may have had an Indo-Germanic origin. It was as foreign to Egypt as Christ's teaching was to prove to Palestine centuries later.

Incidentally, there are innumerable points of resemblance between the teaching of Christ and that of Akhenaton. Was Fate mistaken? Was this first heretic in history sent into the world prematurely to preach his gospel of light, the creed which can be summed up in the words: "From the sun we come and to the sun we return as generation follows generation into eternity." This great problem can only be touched on here. The fact remains that in the long and apparently disjointed history of Egypt, which returned to the old ways after Akhenaton's fall, there is a short and spring-like interlude when truth and beauty reigned.

Unfortunately the priest-king Akhenaton subordinated the kingly element to the priestly and thereby lost his throne and his life.

Destiny decrees that peace, freedom and truth can only be attained and maintained by unremitting effort and at the cost of precious lives. This iron law has remained valid at all times and in all places. Power cannot exist without idealism nor idealism without power to back it. In the case of Egypt the sands which buried the bright dream 3,350 years ago are there to demonstrate its efficacy and universality. Egypt perished because she thought everything of the might of her arms and nothing of justice as between man and man.

Akhenaton devoted himself to liberating man from the toils of a soul-starving religion, the first step to the triumph of individualism:

> "Hail to thee, mounting to high heaven,
> Setting the horizon aflame!
> Hail to thee, glorious god of peace."

How much better for humanity if it had continued in that path! If men had pursued their enquiries into the structure of the universe and the natural wonders around them they would probably have reached the conclusion not only that there was but one god, but that that god was a god of truth and justice who did not dwell in the clouds but within their own hearts and consciences.

But the idea of one god, omniscient and omnipresent, was anathema to the Egyptian priesthood, and not only to them. It is not so long since, even in the Christian West, the adherents of such a belief paid for their convictions on the scaffold. The scaffold indeed provided the best deterrent to their activities. Heretics have ever proved the most devoted servants of justice. Christ himself was the greatest of them and suffered a cruel death.

This chapter must not end without reference to Akhenaton's renown as a poet. Amenophis Akhenaton (Yech-en-yeten = "Spirit of the Sun") left to posterity a number of poems. Here is one of them:

"Living Sun, rising each morning in all thy glory!
The world thou hast created greeteth thee with its love.
Thou art God! Thou art Ra!

Even when thou art far off thy rays fertilize the earth.
The corn sprouts when thou kissest the ground.

Oh Sun, thou givest us the cool days of winter.
Thou has created the summer, bringing fruit and life,

And the peasant at his plough, so that men may live of thee.
Behold how men raise their hands to thee,
How they pray when thou risest from thy nightly bed!"

One wonders whether this extract from Akehnaton's "Hymn to the Sun" is a precursor of the 104th Psalm 800 years later:

"The trees of the Lord are full of sap . . . where the birds make their nests . . . the high hills are a refuge for the wild goats . . . So is this great and wide sea, wherein are things creeping innumerable. . . ."

Both the Hymn to Aton and this psalm are the glorification of the Almighty. Centuries later St. Francis of Assisi gave the world another apostrophe to the sun and even in a work of quite recent times, Holderlin's elegy, *An den Äther*, close examination seems to show that it was influenced by Akhenaton's poems. It is remarkable that the ideas behind them should not have obtained and maintained a hold on men's minds at the time. The ancient Egyptians always reverenced the sun because it was in antithesis to the idea of death and the death cult imposed upon them by the priests.

Thus disappeared the most striking figure in early oriental history and indeed in the history of the world before the appearance of the Hebrews. To later generations he became known as the "sacrilegious" Akhenaten. But even if he is to be blamed for letting the reins of government slip from his grasp, or severely criticized for carrying fanaticism to the length of destroying existing monuments, the fact remains that with Akhenaton a figure disappeared such as the ancient world had never known.

His was a bold, inquiring spirit which challenged the ancient established beliefs of his day. In the long series of conservative, colourless pharaohs he stands out as a forcible, vivid figure who propagated ideas far above the heads of his contemporaries and barely comprehensible even to-day.

Men like him are frequently met with among the Hebrews eight hundred years later, but as the first idealist in such remote times and under such discouraging conditions he deserves all honour from the modern world. In his own way he was unique.

The story of Amarna is brief and exciting from the political point of view. Once again we have to rely on tomb paintings and inscriptions for our knowledge of it.

We have the tombs of Hudje, Akhenaton's court chamberlain, and of Mahu, at one time Chief of Police. Near them is the tomb of the priest Eje and his wife, Akhenaton's parents. The tombs of the priest Tuto and several other dignitaries have also been found.

Akhenaton's own burial-place was discovered in the cliffs above the *wadi*. It bears an inscription: "I wished to be buried in the hills of the east." Not in the west, be it noted, and contrary to the usual practice. The east was the realm of the rising sun, Aton. Nearby is the tomb of Nefertiti, rich in paintings and inscriptions. One of the latter sings her praises in these terms:

"Heiress to all the blessings, a mistress endowed with all the charms, queen of the North and South, a radiant vision with her beauty and jewels, beloved of Aton, the fountain of love and favourite wife of the king. Nefertiti who lives for ever."

In the tomb of the court scribe, Amohse, there is a prayer to Aton:

"Give the king long life and unbroken peace. Give him all his desires, be they as the sands of the sea, the scales on the fishes or the hairs on the cattle. Let him live on earth until the swan turns black and the raven white and the mountains move. . . . Meanwhile I will continue to serve my king until he lets me enter my tomb."

All these tombs were prepared in the life-time of those for whom they were intended. But they were never used, for the reaction from Aton and the ensuing revolution were too violent. Amarna, the city of the sun, was evacuated in such haste that even the royal dogs were forgotten. Their skeletons were found in their kennels as well as skeletons of cattle which had not been released from their stalls. Fear of demons kept everyone away from the city which had been formally cursed by the priests and became the haunt of beasts of the night. In the course of time it was buried in sand where it remained until modern excavation restored it to history.

Ruins and foundations show that the Temple of the Sun was 800 yards long and 300 yards wide. The whole temple area must have varied from 8 to 17 miles across. On the east and west sides 14 tall, inscribed steles were set up. They were quarried from the limestone cliffs in the neighbourhood. One of these monuments is 25 feet high and covered with well-preserved reliefs. An extract from a long inscription on another stele runs:

"On the 13th day of the 4th month of the 6th year of the reign His Majesty arrived for the first time in the City of Light, whose name is 'Aton is satisfied'. His Majesty dismounted from a chariot of silver gilt, drawn by spirited horses. He hastened to the 'Place of Light' and dedicated the monument to Aton, the God of Brightness. Then he took an oath that he would devote himself to the cause of truth for ever."

Another important discovery was made in Amarna. The Egyptian *fellahin* were in the habit of searching the ruins for the saltpetre in the soil which they used as manure. In 1887 an Arab woman found some curious tablets which looked like burnt cakes. She bundled them up in a sack and took them to a trader in the hope of selling them for a few piastres. Unfortunately most of them were broken by rough handling but it occurred to some bright spirit to send them to Paris for examination. After a few months the answer came back: "Forgeries. Worthless rubbish!"

The Arabs continued their search for saltpetre and damaged a lot more tablets but eventually it was realized that the archives of Akhenaton's Foreign Office had been discovered. The tablets were covered with cuneiform inscriptions and had come from the East. Despite the destructive work of the Arabs three hundred and fifty remained intact.

The first savant to commence the systematic excavation of Amarna was the Englishman Flinders Petrie in 1891. Unfortunately he did not make much progress. In 1907 a German expedition under Professor Ludwig Borchardt began to open up the city. The bust of Nefertiti was discovered. But the work had to be abandoned when the 1914 war broke out. It was subsequently completed by the Egypt Exploration Society.

It has already been said that Nefertiti produced daughters only. Akhenaton realized that this misfortune must give rise to dynastic complications and he married a concubine who presented him with two sons, Smenkaré and Tutankhaton. Smenkaré, a sickly youth, had to marry at the age of fourteen his thirteen-year-old half-sister, Merit-Aton (a daughter of Nefertiti) and mount a secondary throne. The young husband died a few months after the marriage. Either from exaggerated fears about the succession or for other reasons Akhenaton then married one of his daughters. Again the only issue of the marriage was a daughter. When he died the intrigues which he had anticipated materialized. The priests of Amun wanted to place their high priest, Bekanchos, on the throne but Nefertiti and her supporters defeated them and procured the succession of Tutankhaton who married his half-sister Enches-Aton, the third of her daughters. At that time the king was twelve and his wife nine.

The young king took over a heavy burden, for Egypt was shaken to its foundations by political turmoil. The priests of Amun were engrossed in their task of restoring the old ways in the religious, political and economic life of the country but the adherents of Aton were still maintaining a violent resistance. The clash of forces and interests gave Egypt no peace.

After a stubborn struggle the cause of Amun triumphed. The news was announced in a royal decree. In a "concordat" between the Pharaoh and the priests the worship of Amun was proclaimed to be the state religion. Justice was to be dependent upon truth but it was left to the priests to decide what was just and true. As they were deemed to be infallible there was no legal possibility of error. The state took over the preservation and upkeep of the temples and undertook to maintain the priesthood in a style of life appropriate to its dignity and functions and its duty to educate the masses in humility and obedience to authority. Priests and priestesses were no longer subject to the jursidiction of the courts. In that part of the concordat which covered the prerogatives of the crown it was provided that the priests should once again emphasize the divinity of the Pharaoh in all their prayers and services and strengthen his position as a god and head of the state.

The king, having given the priesthood the powers he no longer possessed, was allowed to resume his status as pharaoh. As a ratification of the compact the king and queen changed their names to Tutankhamun and Enchesamun respectively. Now that throne and altar were once more united the event was celebrated in splendid thanksgiving ceremonies in all parts of the country. In Thebes they were made into a state occasion. The ram, symbol of the national god, after many years of humiliation, was once again showed to the people who did not, however, display their former enthusiasm.

Immediate steps were taken to erase from the monuments all

references to the "heretic". Nothing must be left to remind men of the shameful days of insult and outrage to Amun. Those were hard times for the remaining adherents of Aton.

In the temple of Karnak stood a monumental stone which is now in the Museum at Cairo. The inscription dates from the time of Tutankhamun. Here is an extract:

"I found the temple in ruins and the holy places partially destroyed. Weeds flourished in its courts. I restored the sanctuaries and enriched them with costly gifts. I made new images of the gods in gold and adorned them with lapis lazuli and precious stones...."

Tutankhamun died suddenly after reigning for only seven years. His tomb is the best source of our knowledge of the political dramas and sensations of that period. So let us follow the explorers and savants to Thebes where they discovered it.

Hieroglyphs in round cartouches are royal names. The one on the left contains the first name, Neb-chepru-Ra, that on the right his official name and title, Tutankh-Amun, Lord of Egypt. In the centre whip and sceptre. Red, green and blue were sacred colours

Chapter 8

THE DISCOVERY OF TUTANKHAMUN'S TOMB

Four hundred and sixty miles upstream from Cairo lay Thebes, a city of world rank and the greatest of the capitals of the Pharaohs. It was the magnet which attracted all the products of world trade and commerce in ancient days. It is familiar to us today under the modern names of Luxor and Karnak where the visitor may see superb temples and pillared halls, pylons and obelisks on both sides of the Nile.

Though an earthquake in 27 B.C. ravaged the whole area and brought down many of the buildings, much of the splendour of ancient Thebes has survived to the present day. Nowhere else is there such eloquent witness to the constructional skill of the Egyptians and their ability to fit stone to stone without the use of mortar. The inscriptions on the columns and walls of all these buildings tell us a great deal about the religion and history of this ancient people.

In Homer's *Iliad* we find references to the giant city of Thebes and its monuments which so impressed him:

"Thebes, a city of Egypt, has innumerable houses teeming with treasures, and hundreds of gates from each of which issue two hundred armed warriors mounted on horses richly caparisoned."

The classical authors Diodorus, Strabo and Pliny also speak of Thebes as the "great city".

The reader is already aware that the kings of the first nine dynasties ruled in Memphis and Abydos and their principal deity was Horus, the hawk-headed god. Political developments and various revolutions necessitated the transfer of the capital to Thebes in the era of the XIth Dynasty and Amun replaced Horus as the head of the Egyptian pantheon.

Thebes had no rival in the ancient world. Not even Athens could compare with the city on the Nile. It was unique. The influence it had on the Christian world was greater than that of the Greeks. It was Egyptian culture which showed the western nations the way to spiritual life.

The great necropolis, with its complex of tombs and mortuary temples, was laid out in west Thebes, on the left bank of the Nile. Of all the marvels of Egypt it is the exhibits at Thebes which move us the most. The appeal of this city of the dead is both romantic and an intellectual stimulant.

Deir el Bahri means "Valley of the Kings". It was in this region that the Egyptians hid their royal tombs in remote and comparatively inaccessible places. The tombs of their queens are at Biban el Harim. Scattered around are the graves of the priests and officials, and in neighbouring valleys the communal mass graves of the common people and soldiers. Wealth and splendour are the keynote of the aristocratic burial places but the popular catacombs, dug in the earth like fox-holes or rabbit warrens, are as plain and unadorned as death itself. The mummies were just piled on top of each other.

More than three hundred and fifty mortuary chapels have been catalogued. Owls hoot and jackals bark in the sanctuaries which once echoed to the chants of the priests, and the roofs are invisible for bats.

But the reader must remember that this cemetery world was also inhabited by a large number of living persons for whom death provided work and bread. An amazing world, in a setting of rock-strewn hills and rugged, narrow gorges, miles in length. The highest point, the "Horn", which is so like a pyramid, dominates the scene from a height of 1,500 feet.

For thousands of years the sun has blazed down from a cloudless sky and burned the landscape into a desert – though a picturesque desert with its mausoleum of eighty generations. It is worth noting that among the Greeks and Italians Thebes was a popular holiday resort.

There has been much excavating in Egypt and nowhere more than round Thebes. The Greeks opened up the area and found more than forty tombs, all of which were looted. Then this strange world passed into oblivion because the peasants, who knew of the treasures buried under their feet, treated strangers as intruders and murdered them.

It was not before the eighteenth century that Europeans made further attempts to visit Thebes. In 1738, Norden, a Dane, succeeded in catching a fleeting glimpse of some of the temples. He was driven away by bandits. Twenty-five years later a German, Carsten Niebuhr, did some exploratory work but was eventually robbed of everything he had found. The same fate overtook the Englishman, Richard Pococke. We learn from his book, *A Description of the East*, that he discovered fourteen tombs but had a very uncomfortable time. Napoleon's campaign of 1798 brought some activity for a time but Thebes then returned to its isolation.

Rescue arrived at last. An Albanian, Mohammed Ali, distinguished himself in the Turkish resistance to Napoleon. Startling life as a pedlar, he rose from the ranks to become general, pasha and, in 1805, ruler of Egypt. In 1807 he drove out the English with the help of the Mamelukes and in 1811 turned on the latter, a dangerous ally, and got rid of them. He invited four hundred and eighty of their most fanatical leaders to a banquet in the citadel of Cairo. When the festivity was at its height, and they were helpless with food and drink, Mohammed Ali's guards rushed in and murdered them all. The Albanian sovereign finished his work by suppressing a few insurrections staged by fanatical sects. Peace and security were restored to Egypt and archæological activity could be resumed.

It is worth noting that though many Egyptologists took to archæology from choice, some adopted that profession through sheer chance. It is said that Giovanni Belzoni was intended by his parents for the Church. Political troubles intervened. He fled to London, toured with a circus and made his living as a prize-fighter. His travels took him to Egypt and there his business instinct prompted him to try his hand at excavation. He conceived the idea of bringing the Colossi of Memnon to England, but when he saw them he realized that he was suffering from a swollen head. Then he turned to acquiring and dealing in mummies. He recorded his experiments thus:

"The stifling air in the long corridors of the tombs almost made me faint. A fine dust filled the catacombs and penetrated my eyes and ears. My lungs almost burst with the effort of repelling the emanations from the mummies. . . . The corridors descended for 300 metres into the earth. Mummies were lying in heaps – a horrible sight. The half-naked *fellah* who was holding the candle seemed to be a mummy himself. . . . After my efforts in the airless passages I groped for somewhere to sit down. As I lowered myself a mummy collapsed beneath me and I fell into it. Bones, rags and wooden coffins dissolved into a dense cloud of dust so that I could not move for a time. . . . Another passage was so choked that I could not force my way through. I could not help brushing the faces of some long-dead Egyptians, and another mummy broke up, smothering me in a shower of bones . . . most of the mummies were lying one above the other, but many were upright and some upside down. . . ."

In those days it was possible to buy mummies cheaply. No one knows how many Belzoni sold to Europe. He was known as the "collector", but he had no feeling for art or history, and his methods were dubbed "hair-raising" by his successors. He made no bones about smashing the doors of tomb-chambers with a crowbar.

In the tomb of Seti I he found an empty sarcophagus. Fortune smiled on him and with the help of some rich Englishman this sarcophagus and some other finds were brought to England. After he had crowned his exploits by carving his name on the throne of Rameses he returned to England and made a name for himself by arranging an exhibition of his antiquities. Yet it is true that he was the first to awaken interest in archæology. Belzoni believed that there was nothing else to be found in Thebes. He would have been very envious had he known that years later Emil Brugsch would make the haul of thirty-one sarcophagi and mummies which I have previously described.

His successors had the sense to employ more suitable methods in their operations.

François Chabès was a French wine-merchant, Charles Goodwin an English jurist, Gavin Davies a clergyman, Theodore Davis an American lawyer. The latter was very successful. In ten years' digging he unearthed the tombs of Tuthmosis IV, Haremhebs, Spitah, Queen Hatshepsut and finally the priest Jua and his wife Tua. The discovery of this "husband-and-wife" tomb was a sensation because, quite exceptionally, it was intact. The mummies were so well preserved that the deceased might have been lying on their deathbed. The priest's skin and muscles still looked soft. He had a few days' growth of beard on his chin and the nose, mouth and chin had hardly changed. The coffin and tomb furniture were of the finest workmanship.

A further discovery was the tomb of Queen Teje which contained cosmetic jars, a catafalque and other objects. The coffin, painted in bright colours, was a surprise. It had once rested on a wooden stretcher, but in the course of time the latter had decayed and collapsed. The coffin had dropped and the mummy fallen out. The tomb had been violated at some time or other.

James Henry Breasted, another example of self-education, also became an archæologist. The child of poor parents, he was born in America in 1865. Though a chemist by occupation, he was an intellectual and consumed by a burning interest in ancient languages. He taught himself Hebrew so that he could read the Bible in the original text. Then he learned Greek, Latin, Aramaic, Syrian and Arabic and turned his attention to cuneiform writing and hieroglyphics. He completed his self-imposed task with French, Italian and German. He was a second Champollion.

On advice, he gave up his occupation and studied theology, but his teacher was soon saying: "You could make a good priest, but that would not satisfy you. You have a passion for truth and truth in its brightest form is found in Egyptology. We need orientalists. The way is hard, but when all is said and done learning is its own reward."

Breasted studied at Yale University. His first publications amazed his teachers. His studies in philology introduced him to worlds which were old when the Hebrews were still nomads. He soon realized that his life's work was to establish one proposition – that man himself has created the ideas which he attributes to the higher powers. An intellectual achievement which he regarded as miraculous.

Of all the ancient civilizations that of Egypt interested him most. There was no professor of Egyptology in America. The best were in Germany. Berlin was the fountain head of oriental studies. Professor Harper of Chicago advised Breasted to go to Berlin. In 1891 the latter took his advice. As a pupil of Professors Sethe, Erman and Meyer, he passed his examinations *cum laude* after three years. He was offered a chair of Egyptology in America, but had no intention of being a "chairborne" worker and went to the "front". He conducted excavations in Babylon, Syria and Palestine but his happy hunting ground was Egypt. He even made an expedition into the fever-stricken Sudan.

The achievements of this pious and industrious worker were quite extraordinary. He suffered great hardship and was often ill but nothing was allowed to hold up his "hunt" for hieroglyphs. He deciphered thousands of inscriptions. Whether lying on a sick bed or at sea on leave he was always poring over papyri. It was in such intervals that he compiled his Egyptian dictionary and deciphered the medical papyrus. He was the corresponding member of the Prussian Academy of Science, and received his certificate of appointment from the hand of the Emperor William II.

This intellectual giant died in America in 1935. It is impossible to measure our debt to him. His greatest monument is his books and writings which stand up like literary "Colossi of Memnon" in the field of archæology.

To me the professor was not only a revered teacher but a dear friend to whom I am eternally indebted. I shall never forget one morning when he took me with him on one of his hunts for hieroglyphs. What I learned that day of the man and his methods I would not have missed for worlds.

Theodore Davis had a young assistant, Howard Carter, who was employed as draughtsman (his father was an animal painter) in the Egyptian Museum at Cairo. Carter had soon come under the spell of archæology. I have referred to him previously.

Davis and Carter worked together with varying success on several excavations. In 1908 they found some burnt earthenware jars containing linen wrappings and mortuary offerings. The discovery seemed unimportant and would have been forgotten if Herbert Winlock, of the Metropolitan Museum in New York, had not noticed the seal of King Tutankhamun on the lids of the jars, and a porcelain goblet. The king's name also appeared on one of the wrappings.

The insignia of this pharaoh had not been seen on any previous find. Davis and Carter thought it indicated that his tomb must be somewhere in the vicinity and might be intact. Davis believed that the possibilities of the "Valley of the Kings" had been exhausted, but Carter was sure that the tomb could not be far away and was filled with a burning determination to find it.

The events of the next few years are one of the sensations of archæological research.

The scene changes to the Taunus district in Germany. The year is 1909. A motor car on the way to Bad Langenschwalb left the road and fell into a ditch. Its owner, Lord Carnarvon, was on his way to join his wife. He suffered internal injuries and convalesced on the Riviera and afterwards in Egypt.

Egypt is the land of antiquities. The principal buyers are agents sent out to acquire papyri, mummies, vessels of all kinds and scarabs for museums. Rich foreigners are also in the market for such things. Purchases are usually made from reputable dealers but there are black market operators as well. Many fakes are sold as genuine.

A view in the "Valley of the Kings"

Egypt makes "collectors" of us all and Lord Carnarvon was no exception. But he took the next step and decided to go in for excavation himself. As his technical adviser he selected Howard Carter, and together they conducted a series of enterprises which had their ups and downs but which were finally crowned with success – and death.

Carter searched for Tutankhamun's tomb at a certain spot in the middle of the valley, but without success. Mountains of earth had been shifted when the First World War broke out and the operations had to be abandoned. At the end of 1917 they were resumed. Hundreds of *fellahin* spent two years in moving further masses of earth, but nothing was found. In the third year they discovered nothing beyond the foundations of workmen's houses. The fourth year yielded nothing and hopes sank. The experts who maintained that the possibilities of the valley had been exhausted seemed to be justified. The fifth year brought fresh disappointment and funds ran out.

Carter and his employer took counsel together. Should they abandon the enterprise or not? The pros and cons were reconsidered while the pessimists drummed into their ears the words "useless", and "the possibilities of the valley have been exhausted". As a matter of fact, over a long period of years, further tombs had been discovered. There were sixty-two known tombs, not all of which were royal graves, but they had all been looted.

Everything pointed to the futility of continuing the operations. Five year's work with nothing to show for it was a pitiable result. Yet hope triumphed over calculation and Carter decided to carry on for a sixth and last year. The decision, after five fruitless years of privations and discomfort, was a bold one and worthy of a man whose devotion to the cause outweighed all other considerations.

Once again hundreds of labourers, fired by the enthusiasm of their employers, set to work to remove masses of earth and sand. Once again weeks passed without any success. Explorers must be patient and know how to wait until a slice of luck comes their way.

As so often happens in similar situations, when things were at their blackest, Carter had an inspiration. He bethought himself of the workmen's huts, the foundations of which had been discovered. From earliest times such foundations had been found close to tombs. Carter told his foreman to remove the remains of one of these huts because they were in the way. The men did so in their usual leisurely fashion. When Carter visited the site next day no one was at work. What had happened?

Three steps of a stone stairway had been exposed. The *fellahin*, overjoyed, had thrown down their tools and waited to report. Carter's delight at what he saw defies imagination. Was this the beginning of an underground passage?

Hopes revived and Carter waited in a fury of impatience while the men dug and shovelled as madly as if they were rescuing someone buried alive. Ten steps were soon free, ten stone steps of a narrow stairway. The men toiled like ants and after three hours fourteen steps were cleared of rubble. Further progress was barred by a door covered with mortar. What was more remarkable was that in the mortar were the marks of a seal which must have been imposed thousands of years before. There was no room for doubt. This was a sealed underground door. The seal, showing a jackal above nine prisoners, was familiar to Egyptologists. It was known to have been used extensively in the necropolis at Thebes.

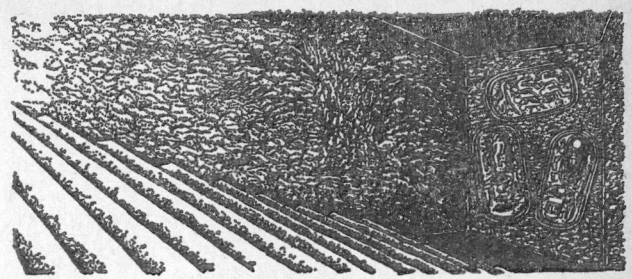

The stone staircase and the first sealed door, with its three seals. A seal was considered to have symbolic and magical significance

What a moment! A sealed doorway after five years of unremitting search! What was behind that door? An unfinished tomb? A store room for the necropolis? A tomb filled with treasures? The High Priest's house? One idea chased another through Carter's head but he never dared to hope that it might be a royal tomb. In fact it could not be a royal tomb because the seal was not a royal seal. But without waiting to solve the mystery, Carter had the stairway covered in and telegraphed to Lord Carvarvon in England:

"Wonderful discovery in the Valley at last. A tomb with undamaged seals. Everything covered in until your arrival. Congratulations."

All work was stopped beyond what was necessary to protect the diggings and watchmen were posted to guard the secret of the site.

Carter left the desert and returned to Cairo where he ordered an iron gate to close the entrance. He was exceedingly busy and spent many a sleepless night wondering what it was he had discovered. The press soon got wind of what was afoot. The papers indulged in guesses about the discovery and exaggerated its importance. Congratulations poured in from all quarters of the world.

With his natural modesty Carter wondered why. Fourteen stone steps and a sealed door were a great discovery. Of course he could easily have solved the problem by breaking down the door and investigating what lay beyond. Why should he not do so? Belzoni would not have hesitated. But it was not Carter's idea of loyal co-operation. He waited weeks until Lord Carnarvon arrived from England. His partner must share the great moment when the mystery would be a mystery no longer. Eventually Lord Carnarvon arrived in Thebes with his daughter.

The stairway was opened up again after an afternoon's work and this time it was discovered that the fourteen steps were really sixteen. Two had been covered by débris. The lower part of the door was now exposed. But the greatest discovery was something Carter had missed in the excitement of his previous inspection. There was a seal of King Tutankhamun.

Two different seals on one door was something new to Egyptology. But there was an explanation. The seal on the lower part showed that the tomb was Tutankhamun's. The necropolis seal in the upper part indicated that at some time or other tomb-robbers had been at work. The authorities had probably discovered what had happened, walled up the tomb again and sealed it afresh. As the royal seal was not available for obvious reasons, they had used the municipal seal.

Thieves in the tomb of Tutankhamun! The thought was enough to make the excavators shiver. To add to their worries, they found a number of pottery fragments with inscriptions mentioning Akhenaton, Sakaré and Tutankhamun, a scarab bearing the name of Tuthmosis I and another fragment that of Amenophis III. What was the significance of all these names?

Carter thought that it was not a royal tomb which he had discovered but a disused storehouse of the necropolis which had been thoroughly sacked by tomb-robbers. He has recorded all this so vividly that his own excitement is communicated to the reader.

Next morning the mysterious door was copied and photographed, after which the excavators broke through it, cleared away the debris and found themselves in a descending passage filled with rubbish, to a height of three feet, which must first be removed. Hidden in the rubbish were fragments of earthenware pots, seals, broken and unbroken alabaster vessels and water pipes. These pipes had probably been used to bring the water required when the broken door was replaced.

The explorers looked at all these things with dismay, for they indicated that the tomb had been broken into. The ancients never left the tombs in such disorder, which would have been considered an affront to the gods.

Carter spent another sleepless night. When the passage had been cleared out progress was resumed, but after some twenty feet the visitors came up against another door, also sealed with two different seals. The previous experience was repeated – a door closed "for ever", then broken down, restored and resealed with the seal of the necropolis. It was impossible to doubt that there had been an organized raid to loot the tomb.

"Yes, I see wonderful things!" The famous antechamber, filled with miscellaneous treasures, including litters, beds, chests, chairs, vases, three biers, three broken chariots and vessels containing food

Carter's nerves were on edge but he was determined to clear up the mystery. He forced an iron spike through the mortar. Once through, there was no further resistance. Not a thing could be seen. The hole was widened and a light test made in case asphyxiating gases were present. But all that came from the other side of the wall was a warm current of air which made the candles flicker. When the hole had been made wide enough, he passed a candle through it and peered into the semi-darkness. He saw strange things, animals, statues, the glint of gold. The few seconds seemed an age to his companions. Lord Carnarvon asked: "Can you see anything?"

Carter's voice quivered with excitement as he replied: "Yes, I see wonderful things."

The hole was rapidly enlarged further, and lamplight revealed a chamber which had lain in darkness for 3,350 years. It was the antechamber, subsequently shown to measure 25 feet by 11 feet. It was filled with gilded litters, life-size statues wearing golden sandals, beautiful caskets, cupboards, beds, chains and cases full of dried flowers. All these objects were crowded together in complete disorder.

What did it all mean?

The hole was closed up again and the party left, after posting the necessary guards.

The sun sank behind the dunes and Carter returned to his quarters. His thoughts were still busy with treasure, sarcophagi and mummies, not to mention the tomb-robbers and their evil handiwork. He tossed restlessly on his bed and sleep evaded him, so great was his excitement over the events of the day.

Of course he could not keep his discovery to himself. The news produced a sensation and aroused the greatest enthusiasm everywhere. The Egyptian Government was extremely interested and promised its assistance.

On the following day electric light was installed and the retaining wall was taken down. Now everything could be seen clearly, and the impression produced on the excavators was overpowering. Objects of all sorts and sizes were piled up to the height of the roof, 13 feet above the floor. Most of them bore the seal of Tutankhamun. It was clear to every member of the party that Carter had discovered a royal tomb.

There was much rejoicing but it was tempered by regret at the obvious depredations of the thieves. One armoire had been broken open and its contents strewn over the floor. The pearls had been torn from a superb corset and thrown in all directions. A pretty casket had been opened and another smashed up and its contents looted. The authorities would have had a terrible job to compile a list of the stolen property.

To the depredations of the robbers time had contributed its quota of destruction. Many of the pearls and articles of clothing and all the woven stuffs crumbled to dust the moment Carter touched them. A life of 3,350 years was too long for such fragile creations, but the articles of metal and stone did not crumble with age. Wooden articles which had not been affected by the warm confined air of the chamber suffered physical and chemical changes when the outside air was admitted, and ominous cracks were quite audible. These were reminders that the life of all things on earth is not unlimited. Many of such exhibits now in museums will not survive more than a few generations.

The great antechamber could now be cleared. In the ordinary way, such an operation, with the usual paraphernalia of three or four big lorries in convoy, would not take more than a day, and within twenty-four hours the finds would be on show in some museum or distributed for sale among the dealers. But Carter was the model savant (another excavator dubbed him "the conscientious salvage-corps") and he had the chamber methodically cleared without haste or furniture-vans.

He sent to Cairo for photographic apparatus, a car, packing cases, timber, thirty rolls of canvas, and a large supply of cotton-wool and wrappings. Then he got together a select body of assistants, a chemist, experts on inscriptions, anatomy and art, a photographer and some skilled mechanics.

In the adjacent tomb of Seti II he established a dark-room, laboratory and thief-proof store rooms for the finds, which were then numbered, photographed, registered, treated with preservatives, carefully packed and dispatched.

The reader may be surprised to learn that it took Carter ten years to clear Tutankhamun's tomb. The figure gives some idea of the magnitude of its contents as well as the meticulous care which distinguished all his work. He spent five years in finding the tomb and ten in emptying it. Fifteen years is a long time, especially when it is remembered that such work can only be done in the winter months. The summer heat puts a stop to the activities of the excavator.

TUTANKHAMUN'S TOMB. A FURNITURE DEPOSITORY

The first objects removed from the antechamber of the tomb were two alabaster vases, followed by a bowl in the form of a lotus flower with buds for handles and inscribed with the words: "to the Lord of the World, the Master of the Heavens" and "Horus, the mighty bull, of noble birth and the giver of noble laws. May thy spirit live for ever."

There was a three-branched lamp which had been made in one piece, representing lotus flowers as the Theban trinity. It had no inscription. These and similar objects were found in great numbers and proved that art in ancient Egypt reached a very high level.

Of the many chests, a specimen in alabaster deserves special mention. It was exquisitely carved and coloured. The handles were of obsidian and bore the names of the king and queen in hieroglyphs. Another wooden chest was inlaid with figures of serpents and solar discs in blue porcelain or gilded stucco. Unfortunately the contents of these chests had been stolen. Other finds were elegant sandals, a tunic sewn with pearls and a robe embellished with three thousand rosettes.

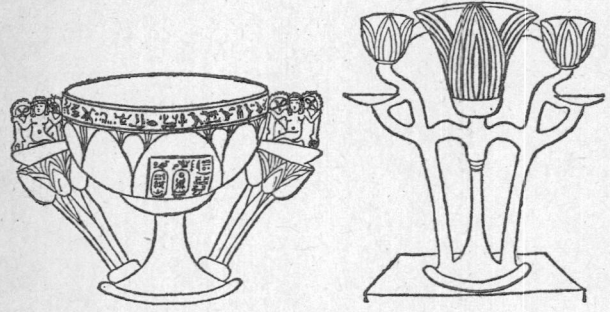

left: Unguent jar 7¼ inches high and 7 inches in diameter. The inscription round the edge means: "Live, O Soul! Live for millions of years, O darling of Thebes, seated with thy face turned towards the north wind and thine eyes filled with love"
right: A three-branched lamp 10¾ inches high and 10½ inches wide

Perhaps the finest chest was one made of wood overlaid with plaster on which superb frescoes had been painted comprising hunting scenes and the king's exploits in battle. The standard of workmanship revealed by this masterpiece was unique. Unfortunately someone had rummaged through its contents and done considerable damage. Thieves again!

Against the west wall stood three great biers. Such objects had not previously been found, though they were familiar to the excavators from wall paintings in other tombs. They were remarkable productions in the form of animals. One had lions' heads, another cows' heads, and the third heads which were half hippopotamus and half crocodile. The wooden framework was plastered over and partly gilded.

Near these biers was a small bedstead of ebony and wicker work with remarkable carving at the foot, and a quiver, bow and arrows. The bow was gilded and delicately engraved.

A small alabaster sacrificial vessel, carved and inlaid with turquoise porcelain and gold, contained a variety of objects, including a priest's robe of leopard skin ornamented with gold and silver stars. There were also a beautiful gold and lapis lazuli scarab, a buckle of golden leaf, a sceptre of massive gold, some pretty wooden necklaces and gold rings. All these things had somehow escaped the attention of the robbers.

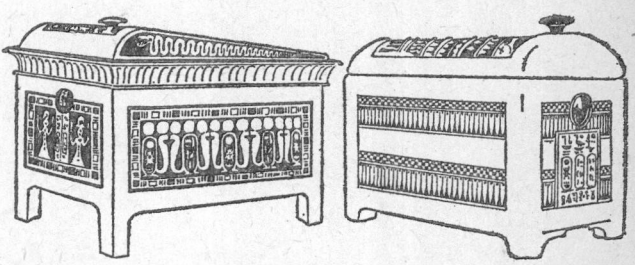

Two chests, approximately 44 ins. long, 24 ins. high and 18 ins. deep

Among the best of the finds were four bronze and gold lamps in a style which is quite fashionable today. One of the original candles was still inact.

In another chest was a collection of royal under-garments.

On the second bier there was a wooden bed frame, painted white, and a rush-bottomed chair. Under the bed lay a round ivory casket inlaid with ebony and a pair of gilded castanets dedicated to Listra, the goddess of joy and dancing.

Many vessels contained food of various kinds and one had a roasted duck in it.

A chest under the third bier was filled with the king's body linen. Nearby was a golden throne inlaid with glass, porcelain and precious stones and a particularly fine chair used by him in childhood.

Another remarkable object was a gilded shrine with folding doors and bearing hieroglyphic inscriptions relating to the king's married life. Inside there was the base of a statue of the king which had been taken away by the thieves, though they had overlooked a chain composed of gold, cornelian and felspathic pearls.

By this shrine stood a large gilt and painted statue of the king, the function of which was to serve as substitute if something untoward happened to the mummy in the afterworld. But perhaps it was only a guardian of the king's wardrobe.

In a corner were carriages, horse trappings and harness and the wheels of four more double-axled carriages. The wood was in good condition but the leather of the harness was so badly shrunk that it was barely recognizable. One of the carriages was surmounted by a splendid canopy of the kind seen in modern Christian churches on special occasions.

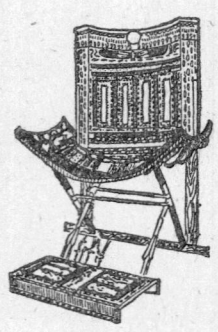

A priest's chair

The objects I have specifically mentioned will give some idea of the artistic achievements of the ancients. There were about six hundred and fifty in all in the antechamber and it would take a volume to describe them in detail. The task of preserving, packing and cataloguing them was enormous.

Another remarkable find was a long piece of cloth lying on the floor. It was probably a scarf worn by the king. In it eight gold rings were wrapped. A detective would offer the explanation that the robbers had been disturbed while at work and must have dropped it as they fled. Other objects of gold left about in the chamber pointed to a precipitous departure.

It seems likely that news of the raid on the tomb came to the ears of the officer commanding the guard of the necropolis. Fears for his own position prompted him to have the unfortunate business hushed up. He had the chamber roughly cleared out and the hole in the door sealed up. As the royal seal was not available he used the seal of the necropolis which was in his custody.

Two ceremonial lamps, that on the left measuring 20 x 11 x 5½ ins. The other is 19 ins. high and 11½ ins. wide

Two of Carter's finds were quite remarkable. Against the west wall of the chamber were five life-size male figures in black wood. Their headdress, with hawks and snakes, and their skirts, bracelets and sandals were of gold. They seemed to be guards. He tapped on the stretch of wall between them and ascertained that there was something behind it, probably another chamber. This wall also bore the seal of the necropolis, which aroused suspicion that the thieves had got even further into the tomb. He would have liked to break through this wall straight away, but patience is the first requirement of the excavator.

The second discovery was another hole in the wall behind the biers. Fragments of stone and mortar indicated that it had been made by thieves. He was in a panic. If the tomb chamber was behind that wall, the probability was that the mummy had been rifled or stolen, for such had been the experience of excavators in all other tombs.

He widened the hole, crept through with an electric torch and found himself in another antechambeer filled with an enormous number of objects, piled together in utter confusion. There were chairs, stools, beds, foot-rests, cushions, fruit-baskets, jugs, caskets, chests, toys, spears, arrows, bows, shields, clothes, dummies, crockery and other things. Many of these articles were lying about smashed or trampled on.

Clearly all this was the work of robbers hunting for gold and precious stones. Robbery and sacrilege of this kind called for the severest penalties in those days and would be condemned by the laws of any civilized community at any time. There is no doubt that the culprits included priests and corrupt officials. It was plain that thieves had got into the second chamber and there had been an orgy of looting and destruction. The terrible disorder in which everything was found made the work of clearance and registration very difficult.

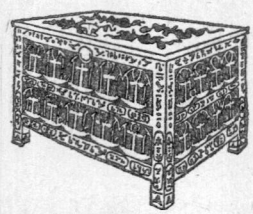

A chest (17 x 19 x 18 ins.)

Carter noticed in particular a beautiful wooden casket inlaid with ivory and carved as exquisitely as a Greek gem. Its main feature, which must have been the work of a great artist, was a representation of the king and his wife in a summer house buried in flowers. One inscription read:

"The beautiful God, Lord of both lands, Nebcheperu-Ra, Tutankhamun, Prince of Heliopolis, who is even as Ra."

Another:

"The Great Queen and Wife, Mistress of both lands, Enches-Amun, who lives there."

Another chest was full of vessels containing frankincense, myrrh, resin, rubber, antimony, gold and silver. Thrown over them was a superb robe of the kind worn by the Pharaohs in processions. It was not unlike the tunic worn by deacons at ordination in the Middle Ages.

"May the Lord clothe thee in the tunic of joy and the robe of rejoicing," says one of the Christian texts. This particular garment was still being worn in Egypt when it was occupied by the Romans after the birth of Christ, and it may well be that the fashion was adopted by the Christians.

The Christian mitre may also have the same origin. This tall headdress was worn by the Pharaohs on ceremonial occasions and something very similar was in vogue among the Babylonians and is still worn by the higher Catholic clergy.

Other chests contained clothes, gloves, linen, embroidered sandals, bracelets, buckles, pearl necklaces and gold chains, and three more were devoted to relics of the king's childhood. One was actually labelled: "Linen chest for His Majesty when he was a child."

A gaming board

There were a number of fans made of ostrich feathers which unfortunately crumbled to dust the moment they were touched. One of these fans had forty-eight quills and its handle was inlaid with gold and ivory. Others resembled the papal flabellum which was used at pontifical processions. Medieval pictures of eucharistic processions showing priests using the flabellum betray its Egyptian origin.

These great fans were borne by chamberlains, walking behind or at the side of the throne, who were officially designated "fan-bearer to the right (or left) of His Majesty".

Two splendid sceptres must also be mentioned. Their golden claws had been broken off by thieves.

Some of the chests contained gaming boards, not unlike chess-boards. Many of them were fitted into miniature tables with long legs. All were of rare woods and painted in bright colours. The dice and pieces used in the games were also of the most delicate workmanship. The finest board was divided into thirty squares and measured 18 by 12 by 6 inches. Other gaming pieces and playthings were stored in a complicated arrangement of drawers. All these articles were placed in the tomb for the amusement of the deceased. Nor were musical instruments lacking. A long silver trumpet was particularly striking.

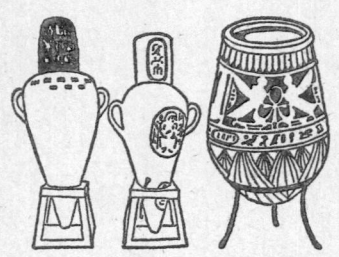

Two wine jars and (right) an unguent jar

Tutankhamun must have been a collector of walking-sticks, judging by the number found in his tomb. They were of all sorts and sizes, with a great variety of handles, and most of them were inalid with gold and mosaics.

Two hat-boxes must not be omitted from this account. They were wooden boxes with a stand in the middle on which the hat was placed. In one of them was a remarkable cap of some materials which crumbled away at the touch.

But it would seem that the bodily needs of the deceased were the prime consideration, judging by the hundred and thirteen baskets in the second chamber which were full of fruit and food of all kinds, including roast fowl. The diameter of these baskets varied from six to twenty inches and they were a triumph of basketmaking. Fourteen wine jars ensured that the deceased should never be thirsty. The wine, however, had dried up, which was a pity because archæologists might have liked to taste wine 3,000 years old!

There were some interesting inscriptions on these jars showing that the wine was the pick of the royal cellars. One of them ran: "Year 9. Wine from the vines of Tutankhamun on the right bank."

The jars were not plain and simple but works of art. A dozen of them were of the Syrian type – further evidence of flourishing international trade. All were sealed and there was plenty of evidence of the care and skill employed in the process of making the wine. Many of the jars were broken.

There was a vast number of weapons – maces, slings, pikes, spears, bows, arrows and swords. The sling, with its stone, is almost certainly the earliest known weapon. Six short and heavy sticks were probably the ancestor of the modern police truncheon. Two curved swords, one fourteen inches and the other two feet in length, were a unique find. The smaller must have been made specially for the king when he was a boy.

The bows and arrows were extremely efficient from the technical angle, although they were most artistic. The bows varied in length between two and four feet. There were several shields (the prime weapon of defence), exquisitely ornamented with heraldic devices, two of which represented the king smiting negroes and Asiatics, the main enemies of Egypt. In one chest was a piece of armour consisting of leather-covered linen, fashioned to form a breastplate. Another find was a large number of catapult stones, probably used for bringing down birds. A particularly elaborate chest was filled with artistic bows. In all there were three hundred weapons in the chamber, in addition to two hundred and seventy-eight arrows of all sizes.

Among the furniture special mention must be made of four superb beds inlaid with gold and ebony. One bed was collapsible and had bronze hinges. There was a good deal of furniture – small tables and chairs – from the king's nursery. The legs of many of the chairs were copied from the legs of cows, lions, dogs and even ducks. The finest piece was a throne which had a leather back on which portraits of the king and queen were stamped. A head-rest was a masterpiece of the art of ivory carving. Its subject was taken from the ancient legend of the creation of the world, according to which the earth and the sky were originally joined together. Then the air got between them and raised the sky.

This piece has two lions couchant, representing Yesterday and To-morrow, and between them the kneeling figure of Shu, the goddess of the air, who is supporting the heavenly vault. Another head-rest was rather like a folding stool. It

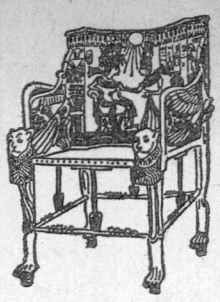

A royal throne

had no symbolic significance but was equally artistic, with its delicate porcelain and lovely lines. A third bore the inscription: "To raise the head of him who lies here."*

A most beautiful but fragile find was a funerary ship. It had a ram's head at the prow and the poop, and a canopy supported by four columns and covering the sarcophagus, in front of which a goddess was seated holding a lotus flower to her breast. This wonderful model, in pure alabaster, is two feet high and just over two feet long and could have been a table ornament.

The ancients knew nothing about matches or phosphorus and produced fire by friction on flints. There were several examples of their primitive implements in the tomb.

There was plenty of evidence that the robbers had visited the tomb twice, the first time to remove all the gold and gold objects and afterwards to collect all the oils and unguents, of which there was an ample supply. The forty-three vessels discovered had contained about eighty gallons of these valuable substances. The jars had been sealed and all were broken by the thieves. Of course they were not ordinary commercial products but superb examples of the ceramic art, on which the modellers and carvers had lavished all their skill. Their height varied from 8 inches to 2 feet 6 inches and two had held at least three gallons. One of these jars had an inscription showing that its contents had been manufactured eighty-five years before the birth of Tutankhamun (unguents were con-

*All the inscriptions in the tomb were deciphered by Sir Alan Gardiner.

sidered to improve with age) and two others bore the name of Tuthmosis III as proof of age. The unguents were a valuable commercial product and no doubt the thieves did good business in the "black market" with them.

A funerary ship

Humidity had added to the damage done by the thieves. This was surprising in view of the hot, dry climate of Egypt. Almost all the clothes and woven materials had all but perished from damp, and sticky substances like lime fell to pieces at the touch. This frustrated the first aim of the archæologist, which is to preserve everything he finds and restore its pristine splendour.

No one obeyed that precept more dutifully than Carter. The explanation for humidity in the tomb is debatable. Perhaps evaporation of the wine and the salt in the chalk accounted for it. The roof and walls had been lime-washed. It is known, moreover, that heavy rain was not unknown in ancient Egypt, and it is possible that at times the Valley of the Kings was flooded as the result of subtropical cloudbursts. Solid rock would not allow water to penetrate but there would be cracks in the limestone through which it could percolate underground.

The tomb had another enemy, woodworm. This destructive insect had been at work on some of the timber before finally perishing for lack of oxygen.

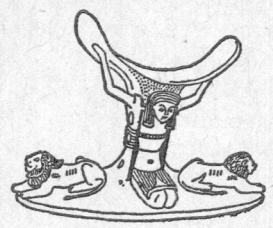

A head-rest (7 x 12 x 4 ins.)

Carter summed up his work to date in a short announcement: "We have made a discovery which exceeds our wildest dreams. We are in the fortunate position of starting on the most important collection ever made." He was in fact more than satisfied with what the two chambers had yielded and had no idea of what still lay before him.

Perhaps he had in mind the papyrus which tells us the story of the Egyptian, Sinuhe. In this document, four thousand years old, there is a passage referring to a burial:

"Thou hast bethought thyself of the day when thou shalt be interred with all thine honours about thee. An evening shall be consecrated to thee. Taït (the goddess of weaving) will weave the wrappings and oil of cedar shall be prepared. At thy burial a crowd of mourners will follow thee to the tomb. The mummy case shall be of gold, its head of lapis lazuli. Thou shalt be laid on a carriage drawn by oxen. The singers shall go before thee. At the door of thy tomb the dances of Muu shall be danced, the prayer of sacrifice offered up and the sacrificial beast slaughtered on the altar stone."

It was unfortunate that serious and unexpected differences arose between Carter and Lord Carnarvon who had financed the excavations.

The Egyptian Goverment's concession had been subject to twelve conditions of which three were as follows:

8. Mummies of a king, prince, high priest or member of the court, together with the sarcophagus and coffin, shall be the property of the Department of Antiquities.
9. Tombs which are discovered intact, as well as their contents, shall be the property of the Museum.
10. In the case of tombs not completely ransacked, the Department of Antiquities shall keep mummies, sarcophagi and all objects of the first importance to history or archæology, and divide the rest with the concession holder.

As it was likely that the majority of the tombs which might be discovered would fall within the terms of paragraph 10, it may be thought that the concession-holder was offered the prospect of reasonable compensation for his trouble and expenditure.

A chariot. Four of them, with leather harness, were found in Tutankhamun's tomb

When the Egyptian Government realized the variety and splendour of the finds in the antechamber it claimed the entire contents as "objects of the first importance". Lord Carnarvon strongly disagreed. He had not embarked on such an enterprise for nothing and wanted to emulate the achievements, a hundred years earlier, of Lord Elgin, who secured celebrated Greek antiquities for the British Museum. Carter demanded that Lord Carnarvon should give way and there was a bitter quarrel. He even told his friend to leave his house and stay away.

The Egyptian Government solved the problem by ordering the contents of the tomb to be transferred to the Cairo Museum. Carter and Carnarvon had to be content with the resumption of their friendship.

Chapter 9

TUTANKHAMUN'S CURSE

The laboratory work seemed endless but at last the two antechambers were cleared and Carter decided to open the wall at the point indicated between the two guardians. I must remind my readers that this wall had been broken down by thieves in antiquity and then set up again and resealed by the supervisor of the necropolis to keep the public in ignorance of what had happened.

Carter had invited guests to be present because he had a premonition that there was nothing less than a sanctuary on the other side of the thin wall, which he gave the order to demolish. When a considerable hole had been made, an electric torch was passed through. It revealed what looked like a great golden wall. The excited spectators peered into a golden room, the burial chamber, measuring 20 feet by 14. He had reached the goal for which all his predecessors had striven in vain!

But relief was tempered by the thought of the thieves, for at the foot of the wall lay a superb diadem and some jewellery which had apparently been thrown away by the criminals in their flight.

When the partition had been removed a gilded shrine (17 feet long, 11 feet wide and 9 feet high) revealed itself to the astonished eyes of the party. It was a magnificent object, with panels of blue porcelain covered with magic signs intended to keep away the powers of evil. The two eyes of Horus on the sides served the same purpose. The sacred serpent figured in the cornice and the winged sun was depicted over the doors.

But, alas, a broken seal bearing the scarab of Tutankhamun lay on the floor. It was obvious that though the excavators had reached the royal tomb chamber thieves had got there first. Once again Carter was forced to consider horrible possibilities. Had the mummy been mangled, destroyed or stolen? He must have passed through some of the worst moments of his life before it was possible to open the doors. But what was his relief when they disclosed a second, inner shrine even finer than the first, and – what was far more important – with an intact seal bearing the sign of Tutankhamun!

All doubts were set at rest. Triumphant cables were despatched all over the world and the front pages of the papers spread the news that Tutankhamun's tomb had been identified by an intact seal, and the excavators were on the threshold of a unique discovery. One man was no longer there to hear the great tidings. A few weeks previously, Lord Carnarvon, who

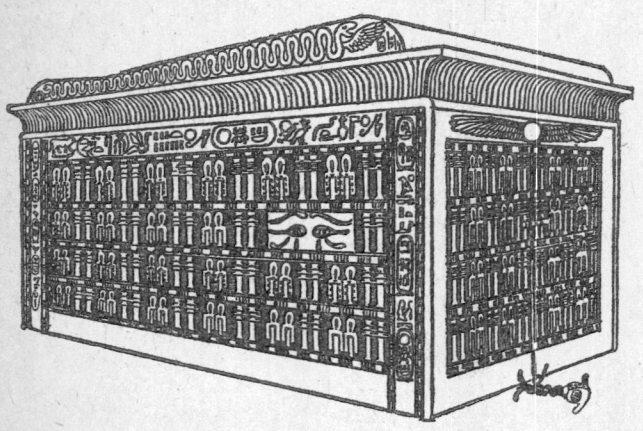

The first shrine, decorated with the emblems of life. In the cornice, the sacred serpent. On the ground at the right, the broken seal

had financed the operations, had been bitten by a mosquito and died. Some wondered whether he had succumbed to a curse pronounced by Osiris, god of the dead, on all who should disturb the dead.

Lord Carnarvon's death was a remarkable occurrence. Anyone living in warm climates is often bitten by mosquitoes and hardly one case in a million has a fatal result. The ordinary and worst consequence is malaria, which is curable these days. Yet Lord Carnarvon died almost at once.

When the tomb was discovered, a peasant uttered a prophecy: "these people are looking for gold but they will find death", and there was no lack of warnings from the superstitious and fanatical.

The experts set to work and opened up the inner shrine. It was no easy task, for the oak boards were two inches thick. The job took a fortnight. The wood, entombed for thousands of years, was dry, but the stucco overlay had stretched and there was great danger of the gold incrustation coming away. Not less tricky was the handling and transport. One side of

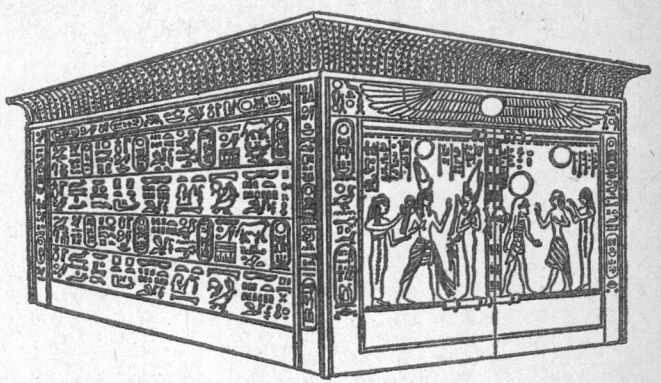

The second shrine, covered with inscriptions from the *Book of Death*. (Height 6 ft. 6 ins., length 12 ft. 6 ins., depth 8 ft. 1 in.)

the shrine weighed more than six hundredweight while its total weight was nearly 1½ tons.

The next step was to remove an enormous pall which had once been draped round the second shrine. It was black and sewn with thousands of small golden stars – surely a tribute to antiquity. Almost dropping to pieces, it had been torn from its attachments by its own weight and most of it was lying on the ground.

The excavators knew their duty to posterity and treated it with a solution of duroprin and xylol which is absorbed by the tissues and helps to hold them together. Incidentally, all the textiles found in the tomb were woven from flax or cotton. Various techniques had been employed, a sure proof of the wide range of the weaver's art in ancient days.

After much effort the second shrine was completely exposed. It was quite as fine as the first and likewise gilded and adorned with blue inlay and protective emblems. The seal too was intact. On one side it bore the king's name, Neb-cheperu-Ra. This seal had once performed its function of preventing thieves from violating the peace of the dead, and once again warning voices were raised all over the world proclaiming that he who would so dishonour the Pharaoh was a thief whom the curse would surely strike down.

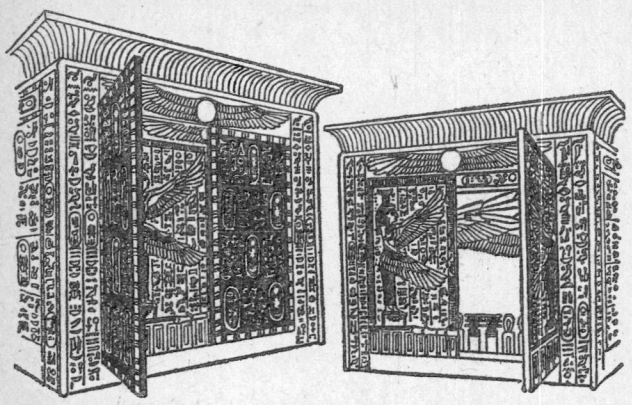

On the left, the third shrine. The open door discloses the outspread wings decorating the fourth shrine. On the right, the open door of the latter reveals the sarcophagus, protected by winged goddesses. The winged sun appears above the doors

Carter and his staff pondered long over the problem. He wondered whether he would not himself earn the title of tomb-robber if he broke the seal. More warning cables arrived, including many from religious sects. "Leave the Pharaoh in peace. Stay thine hand from sacrilege," was the cry. But his scientific pre-occupations and sense of duty to posterity told him that he must solve the mystery. He broke the seal, loosened his ropes which were passed through two metal staples and slowly opened the door.

The sight that greeted his eyes was another shrine, also provided with doors and sealed. What did it mean? Was the seal a further warning? If so, he disregarded its message. He broke it, and opened the doors. For the fourth time a shrine, with sealed doors, met his eyes.

No such spectacle, four magnificent shrines – one within the other – had ever been seen before, and it was an unforgettable moment when Carter broke the last seal and opened one of the doors which disclosed a wonderful sarcophagus of yellow quartz just as it had come from the hand of its makers 3,350 years before. The glitter of the golden shrine and highly polished sarcophagus presented a magic picture.

The first shrine had already been taken apart and it was the work of weeks to remove the three others. The fourth was the finest of all. Its sides were covered with religious inscriptions and reliefs of goddesses protecting the dead. The men who created this masterpeice must have been artists of the first order.

In addition to these outstanding finds a number of funerary gifts, lovely vases, a fan of ostrich feathers, gilded bows and arrows, vessels and statuettes, were discovered in the interstices between the shrines.

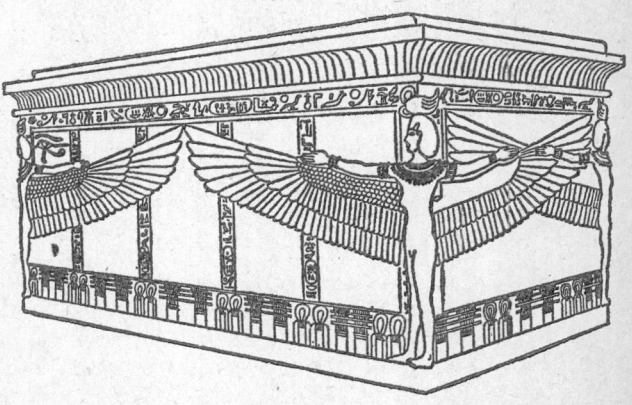

The stone sarcophagus, protected by goddesses with outstretched wings

The sarcophagus itself was an imposing block of the finest quartzite, hewn in one piece and measuring 9 feet in length and 4 feet 10 inches in width and height. The four protective goddesses, Isis, Nephtys, Neith and Selket were placed at the corners and their outstretched wings spanned the whole surface.

The mysterious peace and silence of this great tomb communicated itself to us and we could imagine ourselves present at the funeral ceremony, for nothing seemed to have been touched by the hand of time, and we could still hear the pious prayer that the deceased might pass unscathed through the horrors of the underworld to eternal bliss. But how could the artists of antiquity have created such a masterpeice, which they must have regarded as a prayer in stone? The sarcophagus weighed several tons. Where and how had the quartzite been hewn and worked? How had it been got into the exiguous tomb chamber?

The lid of the sarcophagus was of pink granite, highly polished and covered with inscriptions. It weighed 12 cwts. How had the ancients been able to fix it, having regard to the low roof? It was noticed that it had once been broken across. The two sections had been neatly cemented together and the join concealed by red paint.

On the walls of the tomb chamber were paintings of scenes from the funeral. The king's successor is shown swinging a censer and burning incense to the soul of the deceased and on the north wall he appears in the ceremonial act of opening the dead mouth.

The excavators fixed up some scaffolding and a contraption of chains and pulleys. A crowbar was inserted between the lid and the casket and ropes were passed through.

Carter had invited several guests, including representatives of the Egyptian Government, and archælogists and their wives to be present on this great occasion. On a sign from him the workmen pulled on the chains and the ropes tautened under the weight. In a few minutes the lid was hoisted 18 inches. There was no room to raise it any higher.

The first glance into the sarcophagus was disappointing. Nothing could be seen but a dark mass of linen cloths and burial clothes. Carter lifted the first cover, which had once been white but was now a dirty grey. There were five others below it, all of the finest linen. When they had been removed a miracle was disclosed – a coffin of solid gold.

The dead Pharoah, god and king in one, lay there in calm repose as if time had stood still. One forgot that, having proved a youthful weakling unequal to the task of harnessing the sounder forces of a revolution and continuing that first emancipation of the human mind, he had surrendered to the rapacious and ambitious priests and restored everything they had lost. That was why they had rewarded him with a splendid funeral and lavished gold and treasure on his tomb. Their victory was worth it.

Hardly recovered from their amazement, Carter and his guests left the tomb. When they had ascended the sixteen steps and surveyed the scene by the light of the setting sun they all realized that it had been the greatest day of their lives. The sarcophagus was to be removed next day but a great and unsuspected disappointment was in store. He received a telegram from the Egyptian Minister concerned forbidding him to admit ladies to the tomb. Guards were placed to see that the order was observed.

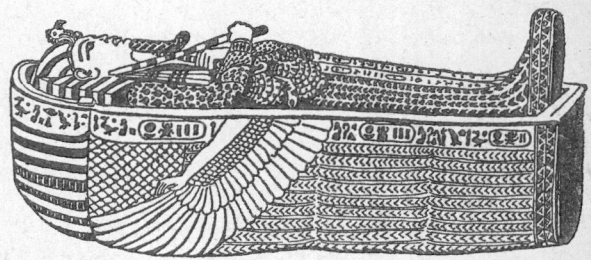

The first sarcophagus open, revealing the second. All the coffins, and the undersides of their lids, were decorated with hieroglyphs referring to scenes from the kingdom of death

He felt that he had done nothing to deserve such autocratic treatment and refused to continue his operations. He even published a protest against the interference and discourtesy of the Minister in the press and announced that after the journalists had inspected the tomb at twelve o'clock it would be closed. He actually carried out his threat, though he did not replace the lid of the sarcophagus, because he thought his dispute with the government would be settled in a few days. But the authorities took up the challenge and forbade him to enter the tomb unless he resumed work on their conditions within forty-eight hours. They even threatened to cancel the concession.

Carter now applied to the Mixed Court to appoint him administrator of the tomb and asked the Minister for permission to visit it to replace the lid. The government refused and not only charged Carter with negligence in failing to leave the sarcophagus as he found it but actually declared the concession forfeited.

The archæologist had spent thirty years in Egypt. He had discovered the tomb of Tuthmosis IV and attained the rank of Chief Inspector of Antiquities. He had lavished time and money without stint on the tomb of Tutankhamun. Now he had found it, and his success had given Egypt world-wide fame and prestige. Visitors were pouring into the country and the tourist industry was flourishing, to the great benefit of Egypt's finances. He had sacrificed his health and personal interests, for he was a most conscientious worker and had conducted every phase of the excavations himself. To crown everything, he had quarrelled with is friend, Lord Carnarvon, in Egypt's interest, having insisted that the whole of the "find" should remain in the country. All this he had done for a land which he loved, and now he was ordered to abandon his work!

While the dispute was still raging a government official appeared one day, accompanied by lawyers and workmen. Carter refused to hand over the keys so the locks were forced. The lid was replaced, the tomb closed and police were placed in charge.

Those were tragic days for him. He found himself forced to employ a lawyer to represent his interests. The American professor, Breasted, did his best to bring about a settlement but his task was not easy. The air was thick with proposals, counter-proposals, refusals and suspicions. Carter had to return to England, a dejected and disappointed man. There was a political background to the dispute. England was occupying Egypt. At the time when the tomb was discovered a nationalist government was elected. It was not prepared to dance to England's tune and there were demonstrations against foreign residents, and particularly against the English and French. Lord Carnarvon and Carter were among the victims of this political development. Egyptian unrest culminated in the assassination of the English governor, Sir Lee Stack, in Cairo. This murder provoked the British to reassert their authority. Carter was restored to his rights and resumed his operations at the tomb. We may return there with him.

What a sight met his eyes! A perfect golden image of the youthful monarch lay before him. A coffin in human form, over 7 feet long, filled the whole sarcophagus. The lid of the coffin displayed the motif of goddesses protecting the king's body with outstretched wings. The figure of the king was astonishingly life-like. The folded arms reminded the spectators of the monuments of dead crusaders in churches. He held a crook in one hand and a whip in the other. His face and the upper surfaces of his hands were of gold, the eyes of aragonite and obsidian and the eyebrows and eyelids of lapis lazuli.

The splendid coffin was of wood and gilded. The young king's brows bore the two symbols of Upper and Lower Egypt – the serpent's and vulture's heads. Even more affecting than the blaze of gold was the little wreath which the young widow had laid on the breast as a token of affection.

It was not easy to remove this coffin which weighed 18 cwts. The excavators were faced with a fresh problem. Why was it so heavy, unless perhaps there was a lead coffin inside? How the ancients could have managed to handle it was a mystery. The lid had four silver handles, however, so that it was comparatively easy to open.

Another thrill of excitement passed through the assembled company when the lid was raised. The first object seen was a shroud strewn with garlands of olive, lotus and cornflowers. It was spread over another coffin, a masterpiece of Egyptian carpentry work. This time the lid represented the king as the god Osiris. In this case the face was of pure gold.

This second coffin was a little shorter than the first, but the incrustations of gold and precious stones were even finer. It had been fitted into the outer coffin so skilfully that it took days to remove it.

Excitement reached fever heat when it was opened, disclosing another pall, red this time and decorated with flowers and pearls. The gleam of gold could be seen through the thin material. Then came the greatest surprise of all, the puzzle of the enormous weight was solved. There was a third coffin, six feel long and weighing over 5 cwts. It was of solid gold and displayed the same decorative features as the first, including the protective goddesses with their outstretched wings.

Two parallel strips on the lower part of the golden sarcophagus bore an inscription, a prayer to the goddess Nut. It ran: "Oh thou great goddess Nut, cover me with thy wings while the stars shall endure."

The three coffins fitting one within the other. The centre coffin is considered the finest. The third is of pure gold, 6 ft. 2 ins. long, 1 ft. 8 ins. across and weighs 4½ cwt. The first and third coffins display the outstretched-wings *motif*

"While the stars shall endure." Such was ancient Egypt's idea of eternity and the ever-repeated *motif* of spreading wings conveyed the notion of protection. The guardian goddesses were winged, just as the guardian angel in the Christian religion is represented as winged.

The splendour of this latest find reduced us all to silence for some time. A few days later, when we were coming down to earth again, I was tapping my ring on the coffin to see how the gold sounded. Carter happened to be standing by and said: "Oh yes, Mr. Neubert, it's all pure gold."

This latest discovery showed that the goldsmiths of those days, even though they had only the most primitive appliances at their disposal, were hardly inferior to the practitioners of today. No trace of any workshop or laboratory has been found. If they used retorts, scales, formulæ or any other mysteries of the art, these have all vanished under the sand.

In view of the wealth of treasure stored in Tutankhamun's tomb, we naturally wonder what must have been the original condition of the many other tombs – found empty – of kings who were far mightier and more famous than this young and comparatively insignificant monarch. It is hardly surprising that peasants, workmen, guards and priests indulged in organized tomb-robbing from the earliest times.

The task of separating the coffins was rendered difficult by the fact that some of the preserving oils had penetrated between them and hardened into a sort of cement. It was necessary to suspend them over a slow fire, a process demanding great skill, care and patience to prevent irreparable damage.

At length it was possible to raise the lid of the third coffin. Another shroud appeared, a red one this time and beneath it the mummy. This precious find was not, however, as the mourners had left it. It was hard and had turned black through the effects of the unguents employed to preserve it. This drab object was in striking contrast to the gold mask, a masterpeice of ancient art, which covered the head and shoulders.

Skilfully sewn into the wrappings were strips of gold leaf on which prayers and praises were inscribed, such as The celestial goddess Nut, great mother of gods, speaks; "I am thy mother who gave thee thy beauty, O Osiris, King, Lord of the Lands, Neb-cheperu-Ra. Thy soul lives, for thou art strong. Thou breathest the air and goest forth like a god to become one with Amun, O Osiris Tutankhamun. Thou goest forth to become one with Ra. How noble thou art, how mighty thy throne. Thy name is in the mouth of thy subjects. Thy immortality is in the mouth of the living, O Osiris, King Tutankhamun, thy heart is immortal in thy body. It is the first of the living and shall endure while Ra reigns in the sky."

More weeks of strenuous work followed. The magnitude and difficulty of the operations can only be appreciated by

Gold mask 22 ins. high and 16 ins. wide

those who have spent long periods in a small subterranean vault in a temperature anywhere between 95° and 113° F.

At length the time arrived for the examination of the mummy, which was first X-rayed. Carter regarded the unwrapping as the highlight of the proceedings and had invited a distinguished company to be present. The results proved a great disappointment.

In 1906 Professor Elliot Smith examined a large number of mummies of kings, priests and priestesses in connection with his investigation into the processes of mummification at various periods. He published his conclusions in a book, *A Contribution to the Study of Mummification*. In his view the preservation of Egyptian mummies is primarily attributable to the dryness of the climate. Most of the bodies he examined had an incision in the stomach wall, showing that the internal organs, the first to putrefy, had been removed. Mummies of the XIth Dynasty, i.e. 600 years before Tutankhamun, showed no incision anywhere, the intestines having been left intact, and yet these specimens were the best preserved of all, if the word can be used in this connection.

Then Elliot Smith examined some mummies of the XXIst Dynasty, approximately 300 years after Tutankhamun. In this case certain substances had been introduced under the skin of the neck, trunk and limbs to give the corpse a life-like appearance. These mummies also were well preserved. With these observations of the Professor in mind, the scientists were naturally curious about the condition of Tutankhamun's mummy.

Professor Douglas E. Derry and Dr. Saleh Bey Hamdi carried out the examination.

Of course voices were again raised in protest, and the procedure was denounced as desecration. The king ought to be left in peace, cried the prophets of woe. But Carter and his friends very properly adhered to their view that posterity had a right to know what was under the coverings. Systematic unwrapping of the mummy proved impossible because the linen bands had perished through the action of the preserving unguents which had generated heat. This development had been observed in previous cases and given rise to a theory that the mummies had been burnt.

But despite all difficulties, the task proceeded. Paraffin was poured over the mass to harden it and the mummy slit open from the breast to the feet. Various gold objects were found wrapped up in the linen bands. The incision in the stomach was also traced – proof that the internal organs had been extracted. No one knows what had been done with them.

There is no doubt that the ancient Egyptians used oils and unguents on the most lavish scale because these were considered to dedicate the dead king on his union with the great god Osiris in the underworld. But although they used the finest linen for the wrappings, their precautions had been in vain. Both the oil in the mummy and that poured over it when it was laid in the coffin had turned to thick sludge, with an effect the reverse of preservation. Semi-carbonization, disintegration, decay and the oxydation of the heart had certainly not been anticipated by the embalmers. It is not surprising. They were not chemists, and the scientific analysis of substances was no doubt beyond them.

By a strange freak of nature the teeth, which give so much trouble to man in his lifetime, cease to decay after death and last much better than the rest of the corpse. Tutankhamun's teeth were well preserved. It was noted that the upper and lower wisdom teeth on the left hand side must have protruded well above the gums while those on the right hand side were barely visible.

The incision in the stomach, $3\frac{1}{2}$ inches long, ran parallel to a line drawn from the navel to the iliac bone. The king's hair had been cut short and the pubic hair shaved. The circumcised penis was drawn forward and wrapped in such a way as to keep it erect away from the body.

The king's skin was grey, brittle and wrinkled. The left kneecap and adhering skin could be detached, revealing the lower end of the thigh bone and the joint. The condition of the remains showed that he was eighteen years old when he died. He was five feet five inches in height, the same as the two statues of him guarding the wall of the antechamber.

The skull had been emptied and filled with some resinous substance. Resin-soaked wadding had been inserted in the nostrils for drainage purposes. The eyes, with long lashes, were half open and had received no special treatment. The upper lip was slightly drawn back, disclosing the great canines. The ears were small and well formed and had been drilled for earrings.

The skull was flat at the top and projected prominently at the back. There was a marked thickening on the left side and the region behind the brain was depressed. The unusual shape of the skull resembled that of his father, who was also his father-in-law, and betrayed the blood-relationship.

The mummy was resplendent with gold and jewels, among which special mention should be made of a three-string gold chain from which hung a scarab engraved with a magic formula and the figure of a phœnix. Of course the inevitable sceptre and whip were not missing. Another outstanding object was the soul-bird on the king's breast, spreading its wings to protect him. On his head was a diadem of gold and cornaline and the headbands were sewn with pearls. Six amulet collars were fashioned from thin gold plates, of which there were no less than 256 on a Nechbet collar.

A dagger of rare beauty was suspended from a belt of beaten gold. The hilt and blade, as well as the sheath, were engraved with beautiful figures. The hilt also bore an inscription referring to Tutankhamun: "The good god, Lord of Courage, Neb-cheperu-Ra."

To the same belt was attached a skirt with seven tiers of gold plates, decorated with coloured glass and fastened at the corners by pearl threads. This skirt extended from the waist to the knees. Close by was another dagger in a golden sheath. Its handle was a bunch of sections, adorned with rows of gold beads and jewels, but its most striking feature was the blade, shining like modern steel. In all probability the iron of which it was made came from the Hittite country in Asia Minor. A hundred years later, in the time of Ramesis II, iron was an ordinary commercial import. Iron replaced bronze as bronze had replaced stone and as steel has replaced iron in modern times.

Alabaster oil vessel representing an ibex

Another notable find was a collar with dark blue porcelain drops falling from the navel to the ground. There was a ring, a blend of gold and glass, in the middle of the breast. Eight others, similar in appearance, were found among the wrappings. A further eight rings encircled each leg and the toes were protected by gold sheaths, painted to look natural. There were eleven splendid bracelets on the arms, fifteen gold rings on the fingers, six pairs of ear-rings which the king had worn in childhood, some superb necklaces and other treasures too numerous to enumerate.

Exception must be made, however, for a small head-rest, if only because it was made of iron. Its inscription is important, though it was falsified by history:

"Awake from the faint in which thou liest. Thou shalt triumph over all that have come against thee. . . . The god Ptah hath vanquished thy foes. They are abased and have ceased to be."

Tutankhamun must have been buried in March or April. The time of year is of no importance in itself but is indicated by the kind of flowers, three small chaplets and a separate bunch, all mainly comprising cornflowers, which were found in the tomb. In Egypt cornflowers bloom in March and April. The fact that there was also a water-lily, which flowers in November, shows that such flowers could be grown out of season in Theban gardens.

Two royal symbols had special significance. The serpent, Buto, stood for Upper Egypt and the vulture, Nechbet, for Lower Egypt. The king's mummy was laid east-west with the head towards the west and Buto was placed to the right and the vulture to the left so that each could face its own region. The Egyptians neglected nothing.

We can be grateful to them for not burning their dead, as the Greeks did after them. The archæologist's task would have been much more difficult.

We must admit that the immortality which they thought they had achieved is still an open question. Death still seems the final answer to everything. How can it be shown that the soul is immortal? The empirical sciences like biology and physiology neither affirm nor deny. Soul and spirit are incorporeal and invisible things which cannot be seen with a telescope or microscope, or treated in a test tube. The continuation of life after death cannot be *proved*, as is shown by the divergences between the views of the great thinkers. Plato, Descartes, Liebnitz and Kant believed in immortality. Aristotle and Spinoza rejected the possibility. Hegel regarded the question as open and his followers are divided into two camps.

But where science cannot supply the answer metaphysics steps in and its strongest weapon is faith. The Egyptians had faith and faith remains one of the greatest human instincts even today. To many it brings comfort and consolation, which is the secret of its power.

It remains to consider the question of the so-called "Curse of Tutankhamun".

I have already said that Lord Carnarvon died suddenly. But why was it announced that his death was caused, not by the bite of a mosquito but the sting of a scorpion, a creature sacred to the Egyptians? Why did no one refer to the inscription at the entrance to the tomb: "The wings of death will surely strike him who disturbs the peace of the dead Pharaoh"?

When Carnarvon was dying, his thoughts turned to Tutankhamun. In a lucid moment he called out: "It is finished. I have heard the call and am prepared." At that moment all the lights in the house went out. Ten minutes later he was dead. He was only fifty-seven.

When Carter was living in England, shortly before the Tutankhamun expedition, he said one day that he had had enough of living alone. His friends wondered whether it meant that he was going to get married and made some enquiries. They learned that he had bought a canary.

A singing bird is a rarity in Egypt and many of the peasants used to congregate outside Carter's modest hut when his Hartz Roller started up. They considered that the bird brought luck. Soon afterwards he made his great discovery, and the natives accordingly christened it "the tomb of the bird".

It will be remembered that in the antechamber of the tomb were two guardian statues of the king with the serpent's head on their brows. The native workers said that the function of the "sacred cobra" was to protect the king and slay his enemies, whether ancient or modern.

A little later, something very odd occurred. One evening, Carter's birdcage was in its usual place on a mound outside his hut and the canary was singing with all its might. No one was about. There was a sudden silence. Carter's servant, wondering what had happened, came out to see a cobra poised in front of the cage and in the act of devouring the bird. A horrid sight! The snake had probably drawn its prey through the bars with its long tongue. This is a true story. Carter himself is our authority. Of course the natives attributed the mishap to the "curse", but the Europeans continued to disregard the warnings, treating them as idle talk.

An important official of the Egyptian Government visited "the Valley" and brought with him the famous snake-charmer, Mussa, who, he thought, might be able to find some explanation for the mysterious rumours. While they were engaged in their experiments, a cobra and a grass snake emerged from the dark vaults. How had they got there? The official went on with his work but soon began to feel ill and before long had to stop. He was converted to the curse theory – but too late. A few days later, he was dead.

Some have wondered whether poison was the true explanation of all these deaths. It is known that the Egyptians were experts in poisons, some of which were even more deadly than those produced by the modern Malays. Might this be the real reason for the warning notices in the entrances to the tomb? Had the priests mixed poison with the mortar in the walls? It is known that some poisons retain their potency practically for ever, particularly in a dry climate like that of Egypt.

We remember that the tombs had been visited by thieves, most of whom seem to have fled in a very great hurry. It is generally assumed that they were surprised by the guards, which explains why so many gold rings concealed in the wrappings of the mummies were left untouched. But may the real reason for their panic flight have been something quite different – some surprising discovery, such as the presence of poison?

The truth is shrouded in mystery. Could it be the mystery of the goddess Isis? Occultism, self-delusion, mystic phrases, superstition, legend, these are no explanation. Where knowledge, with its insistence on proof, ends, mystery begins.

Sailors used to be addicted to superstition but I myself cast off its chains at an early age and have always remained an optimist, despite a feeling of bewilderment when I think of the occasions when I have escaped death by a miracle.

When I was six some heavy scaffolding fell on me. My rescuers thought I had a broken neck or a fractured skull, but three days later I was none the worse. At the age of eleven I went on a frozen pond. The ice was treacherous and I fell in up to the neck. No one was about to answer my calls for help. At the moment of crisis, when I was almost frozen stiff, fate brought along a boy who saved my life.

In Africa I was struck down by a tropical disease. The ship's doctor feared for my life and had me transferred to a hospital on shore. A few days afterwards I had completely recovered. Some years later I met my captain again. He looked at me in amazement and said: "Can it really be you? I thought I had left you for dead in Africa. The ship's doctor said you couldn't possibly live."

In the first war I served on a cruiser which was sunk after a hard fight. Nearly all my comrades were lost and it was pure luck that I survived. On another occasion I fell overboard and had to fight for my life in the very cold water. A boat arrived at the very moment when my strength gave out and death seemed inevitable.

Later I was serving on a minesweeper which struck a mine and sank. Once again death reaped a rich harvest, but I escaped with a fright and a few scratches.

Some years after that war I had occasion to travel to Munich by rail. I was a stickler for punctuality but somehow or other missed the train that day. I was very annoyed with myself. A few hours later the papers announced a terrible railway accident. My expresss had collided head-on with another. The death roll was heavy. It was clear to me that some guiding hand had saved me once again.

A year later I had a crash on a motor cycle and was taken to hospital unconscious. The medical finding was concussion and a broken left kneecap, but four days later I astounded the doctors by leaving at my own request and a month afterwards I joined an expedition to Spitzbergen.

During the second war I was trying to get to an air raid shelter one day. The guns were firing continuously at enemy bombers. A shell splinter as long as a fountain-pen suddenly fell a few inches in front of me and struck sparks from the pavement.

A tomb painting showing representatives of subject races bringing gifts to Tutankhamun

While I was working on this book I frequently suffered severely from stomach trouble. I kept putting off the decision as to whether I should agree to an operation. At length the surgeon decided for me and removed a substantial portion of the stomach. Ten days later I was sitting up and resuming work on the manuscript.

I could mention other occasions on which my life was hanging by a thread. The fact that I have cheated death so often convinces me that I have been destined by fate to finish this book and carry out what I believe to be my duty to warn the world and restore it to its senses.

But back to Egypt. There remains the question why archæologists, savants and officials should be struck down by fate, and not the humble labourers and mechanics employed in the excavations. There is no answer. All we can say is that the discovery of Tutankhamun's tomb was a great triumph, and triumphs must be paid for. If we accept the curse theory we should expect Carter, the hero of the discovery, to be the first to die. As we know, he reached a ripe old age. I might add that I myself have spent a good deal of time in Egyptian tombs and am quite familiar with physical discomfort and emotional stress, yet my health remains excellent and I have nothing but happy memories of the land of the Pharaohs.

Chapter 10

THE GOD SAILS TO THE KINGDOM OF DEATH

In addition to the three vaults described as antechamber, sidechamber and tomb-chamber there was a fourth, measuring 11 feet by 13, which deserves a chapter to itself. It contained a quantity and variety of treasures surpassing anything previously discovered and offered a spectacle that positively astounded the excavators. Carter accordingly named it the treasure-chamber.

The gilded chest with the god Anubis. It was filled with gifts. The sides are decorated with the symbols of life – Djed and Tjet

As the Egyptian Government consider that previous publications do not do justice to this marvellous chamber, they have asked me to make good the omission.

On a litter in the doorway was a gilt chest filled with jewels of every kind and surmounted by a figure of the sacred hound, Anubis, lying at full length. No doubt his function was to guard its treasures. This figure was of wood, lacquered black, and the collar round the neck was embroidered with lotus and cornflowers. This collar and the ears were gilded, the eyes were of gold, alabaster and obsidian and the claws of silver.

The artist had intentionally made the animal sexless so that its canine habits and impulses would not disturb His Majesty's repose. Egyptian dogs were no better behaved than ours! It is to be feared that Anubis failed in his duty to keep thieves away from the tomb.

On the left, Tutankhamun standing in a boat (30 ins. high, 28 ins. long). On the right, the pharaoh on a leopard (34 x 32 ins.)

Distributed about the chamber were twenty-two small cupboards, all closed and sealed with the exception of one which had lost its door. It contained a gold statuette of the king. The other cupboards, which were of cedarwood, also contained statuettes, some of gold and others of wood. The eyes were of obsidian, alabaster and glass. There were thirty-four figures in all, of which seven represented the king and twenty-seven divinities whose names were given on the base.

Ihi, the god of male musicians, was among them. Incidentally, there were female musicians also, with Hathor as their guardian deity. Geshet, to mention another, was the goddess of writing.

Many of these figures had a magic function as guardians to keep enemies away from the tomb. One of the inscriptions ran:

"I am here to prevent the sand from burying this tomb, to

drive away evildoers with the flame of the desert and to keep Osiris Tutankhamun from harm."

The modelling of these figures showed that those who made them possessed an artistic sense and feeling for nature far above the average. Strength, charm, and sentiment are blended in the most expert fashion. One gold statuette of Tutankhamun shows him wearing the crown of Upper Egypt; another with that of Lower Egypt. He is seen in various attitudes such as standing in a boat about to hurl a spear, holding out a sceptre or standing on a leopard and brandishing a whip.

Opinions vary as to the reason for the presence of all these figures in the tomb.

This treasure chamber also contained a large number of chests. Most of them were either gilded or of wood, painted in bright colours. Some of them were of alabaster, painted in the sacred colours, white, green, red and blue, and carved with hieroglyphics. One chest must be signalled out for special mention for its intarsia work of 45,000 separate pieces. Unfortunately, many of these chests had been broken open and rifled, but a few were still intact. At least sixty per cent of the contents of the chamber had been stolen or damaged, but the rest was in reasonably good condition.

One of these chests contained a jewellery casket of filigree work filled with thirty-four objects, small sceptres, mirrors and writing materials, including two ivory palettes and some quills. Some of the chests had been used as containers for herbs or medicaments. There were no locks. The Egyptians used cords with seals instead.

Among the chests and cupboards lay twenty-two models of ships and boats. All these vessels had their bows pointing west. Some were intended for the king's use when he made his pilgrimage to Abydos, others to make him independent of "celestial transport" when he passed through the Fields of the Blessed. Other boats were needed to convey him along the canals of the underworld on his journey to meet the sun.

All these boats were most artistic and yet complete to the last detail. They were painted and gilded. Four of them were designed to accompany the sun on its journey through the firmament. As they were to be carried along by supernatural powers they were not provided with oars or sails. Many of them resembled Venetian gondolas. A light boat made of reeds was for the use of the god Horus on his aerial flights. Finally, mention must be made of four funerary ships, which were all fully rigged.

Model boat (48 x 47 x 6 ins.)

There was a fine model of a barn, divided into compartments filled with different cereals. Close by was a hand mill. Grinding the corn was a job for the women in ancient Egypt but the king had to be his own miller in the kingdom of the dead.

In one chest was a life-size figure rather like a mummy. It had been stuffed with fertile Nile earth, sown with corn and then watered so that the seeds sprouted. This peculiar object was called the "sprouting Osiris". The idea was that the king's body would live on just as Osiris lived on in the growing corn, for Osiris and the dead are one.

I have already referred to the finding of wine in tombs, but it must not be forgotten that beer was considered the drink of the gods. One chest in this treasure chamber was full of materials for making beer.

In one corner was a cow's head, the symbol of the tomb in the afterworld. The horns were of copper, the eyes of gold and there was a gold collar round its neck.

In addition to the four chariots in the antechamber mentioned previously there were two hunting chariots in the treasure-chamber. The coachwork was of gold, upholstered and very ornate. Chariots in daily use were open and light, in contrast to the ceremonial chariots, of which there was only one specimen. Unfortunately, thieves had broken off the gold ends of the shafts.

The construction of these chariots, particularly of the axles, hubs, spokes and shafts, and the way in which strips of wood had been bent, revealed technical skill of the highest order and the same can be said of all the ornaments, lions' heads, statuettes of gods, carvings and so forth scattered about the chamber.

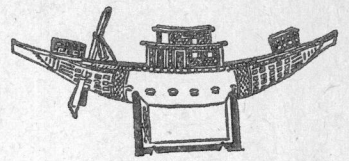

Small boat with a cabin

The thieves had no doubt got away with a great deal of loot but there was much that was missed, and for that we must be grateful.

The examination of finds in such a "warehouse" calls for the greatest patience on the part of the archæologist who is not unmindful of the warnings of the past but appreciates his paramount duty to posterity. Every piece stands for an idea. One of the most eminent savants has written: "It must be admitted that one of the fundamental elements of religious belief in Egypt was that every object, and even the representation of an object, had its own mystical significance. . . ."

It will be remembered that 143 separate objects were found on and in the mummy. Other personal belongings such as gold chains, pearl and jewelled brooches, ear-rings which the king had worn in childhood, a sceptre and whip of ebony encrusted with gold, were found in one of the chests.

The achievements of the royal goldsmiths are certainly astounding. Their technique, invention, artistic sense and skill in engraving, stamping, graining, tarsia and filigree work, and other operations, are most remarkable. Gold, electron, silver, and to a less extent bronze, were the principal metals used. Chalcedony, cornelian, turquoise, serpentine, amethyst, lapis lazuli, green felspar and transparent quartz were mainly employed for decorative purposes. There was also an exquisite olive green stone and gold of a deep orange hue, both unknown in these days. Ivory carving was widely practised.

Among the greatest curiosities was a fine ivory goblet, with sides over six inches thick.

It was from such materials that the Egyptians fashioned objects associated with religious ceremonies, objects such as *cheperu*, the scarab, known to us as the dung-beetle. This is the insect which feeds on horse manure, chewing it into little balls in which it lays its eggs. It was considered very sacred, and figures as such in Tutankhamun's seal. This beetle carefully pushes the "maternal ball" into the hole previously prepared for it. The young beetles emerging from the eggs in this "gloomy cavern" were supposed to symbolize the sun starting on its daily round.

As I have said before, the sceptre and whip were among the most important emblems of royalty. The sceptre, symbol of Osiris, is a sort of shepherd's crook and probably the original of the staff borne by cardinals and bishops in modern times. The whip, or "flagellum", its inseparable companion, stood for royal power or authority.

It is a remarkable fact that not a single papyrus, nor any written record which could have furnished valuable information, was found in the tomb. There was a rectangular basket made from papyrus which looked as if it might contain documents, but it was empty.

Osiris, lord of the dead, demanded that those who entered his realm should be ready to resume their occupations in life, ploughing, sowing, watering, cultivating and shifting sand from east to west. Hence the agricultural and domestic implements found in the tomb such as picks, spades, panniers, water-jars, sickles and rakes. The excavators found 1,866 small bronze or copper models of these implements in a wooden chest.

Some of the figures of shawabti wood representing the king as Osiris, 413 of which were found in the tomb, showed him holding such implements.

Many of the statues of alabaster, granite, quartz or wood were highly artistic productions and some were obviously designed to show that death could be a thing of joy. Others, on the contrary, were very primitive. From the dedication by high officers of state I will quote one or two:

"Dedicated by the servant who hath rendered good service to his master, Neb-cheperu-Ra, by Mej, guardian of the treasure chamber."

"Dedicated by the king's scribe, the officer Min-echt, to his lord Osiris Neb-cheperu-Ra, the Just."

Such was the tenor of inscriptions by those whose obligations to their master did not end with his death.

Four gold statuettes of gods (20 ins.)

The contents of another chest, some iron tools, made the scholars cudgel their brains. They included a pair of wooden-handled chisels so small that only a modern watchmaker could use them. They may have been minute models of larger tools, but no one knows. These iron implements, two daggers and the head-rest previously mentioned, were something quite different from the other finds and may lead to a revision of opinion about the use of iron in those days.

There was iron ore in Egypt in sufficient quantity, but the natives confined themselves to copper, bronze and gold, although more metallurgical knowledge was required to work them. No one knows when the Egyptians first began to find out about iron or use it. Some think it was in use when the pyramids were built.

In any event, iron was considered impure and therefore unfit to be deposited in any form in a tomb. No iron implement or other object had been found prior to the discovery of Tutankhamun's tomb. Carter records that all the museums in Europe and the Cairo Museum, with its five hundred exhibits of all kinds, cannot produce between them more than a dozen examples of ironwork, including the six he found himself.

It is incredible that the Egyptians, ignorant of the uses of iron and steel, should have produced such durable masterpieces from softer metals.

It is impossible to describe all the finds in the treasure-chamber, but a few others must be mentioned.

One of the chests disclosed a small coffin which might have been the model for the king's. It was in human form, thirteen inches long, lacquered black and adorned with gold strips with inscriptions. The head and foot were swathed in linen bands, the ends of which were fastened with seals. Everyone wondered

Four coffins fitting one into the other. In the small coffin were found the lock of hair and amulet

what it contained. When it was opened it was found that there was an inner coffin, gilded like a royal coffin. Within it lay a third which, when opened, disclosed a mummy, presumably that of an infant. When this mummy was unwrapped it turned out to be a fourth coffin. A mummified coffin was indeed a rarity.

But it was the contents of this fourth coffin which provided the greatest surprise. We were expecting to find the mummy of some small sacred animal, perhaps a rat, but what we saw was a gold amulet which the king had inherited from his deceased grandfather, Amenophis III, and a lock of the hair of his grandmother Teje, who was still living at the time of his death – a touching family memorial, betraying a habit of mind inexplicable to modern ways of thought.

In another chest lay a black coffin in human form about half a yard long with a gilded coffin inside it. The latter contained a small mummy, the head and shoulders covered with a gold mask similar to the one protecting the king's mummy. When the wrappings were removed, the body of a stillborn child of Queen Enchesamun was seen. The experts pronounced that it was a five months child. There was no sign of eyebrows or lashes. The head was covered with white, silky hair. The navel string was less than an inch in length.

Another chest contained a similar double coffin but somewhat larger than those previously described. In this was a mummy but without the gold mask. What appeared to be the missing mask lay in a corner, but it did not fit. Had its maker got his measurements wrong? This mummy was of another stillborn child of the queen, a seven months child, also female.

Two children born dead indicated either accidents or the existence of some physical malformation. Or may the explanation be that some jealous rival staged "accidents" in

In the centre a double coffin with the mummy of a still-born infant wearing a gold mask. To right and left the lids of the two coffins

order to frighten the queen to death? Another alternative is that these two infants were the children of children. It will be remembered that little Tut was only twelve years old when he married Nefertiti's third daughter, who was only nine. These still-births may have been the result of such a union. In hot climates boys usually reached puberty by eleven and girls by ten. Child marriages were no rarity in Egypt. They were necessitated by political considerations. They are still recognized in India and the East, and in such cases the marriage is a formality until the parties grow up. Unfortunately this custom has been attended by great abuses.

Second coffin containing a still-born infant. On the extreme left, its gold mask

Against the west wall of the treasure chamber stood a wooden armoire 6 feet 6 inches high and 4 feet 8 inches in diameter. It had four goddesses, (Isis, Nepthys, Neith and Selket) one on each side, protecting it with outstretched arms. These charming figurines were of pure gold. The cornice was filled with a row of sacred serpents' heads crowned with discs representing the sun.

Inside this armoire was another, very similar, which was opened and disclosed a small alabaster shrine on a gold base, a masterpeice which could challenge comparison with anything made today. At each corner there was the figure of a goddess in relief. The sloping lid was secured with a gold cord.

Gilded wooden armoire (6 ft. 6 ins.) enclosing another. The two gold statuettes of goddesses are 31 ins. high
Alabaster box (34 x 22 x 22 ins.) containing canopic jars for the royal viscera

Inside the shrine four charming portrait-busts of the king in white alabaster served as lids to four round stone jars ("canopic" jars). In each of these jars was a tube and in each tube a small gold casket containing some part of the king's internal organs.

These organs were considered divine beings by the Egyptians, because they quietly continued to perform their functions even during sleep. One papyrus gets quite lyrical about the stomach:

"It has never worried us all our lives. We have drunk to excess every day and had as much fish and game as we liked. We have eaten to repletion yet nothing has ever disturbed our sleep."

The internal organs were classified on certain anatomical principles and distributed in four jars, each of which had its attendant priest occupied in prayer and meditation. The heart and brain were placed in one jar, dedicated to the goddess Imesti, the lungs in another, dedicated to the goddess Lepi,

On the left, four canopic jars. On the right, four portrait heads used as stoppers

the liver in the third, dedicated to the goddess Duamutef, and the stomach and intestines in the fourth, dedicated to the goddess Kebekhsenuf. In the corpse the heart was replaced by the sacred scarab.

This process of preserving and dedicating the internal organs was the occasion of a most impressive ceremony, marked by a series of ritual dances conducted by the priestesses. The embalmers carried out their task of ensuring the immortality of the remains under the aegis of their special divinity. The embalmed contents of the four jars were turned out into the four caskets, dedicated to four other goddesses.

These small caskets are splendid miniature copies of the great King's coffin. The youthful face and laudatory inscriptions are repeated. Other inscriptions on the inner surface refer to funerary ritual and death's long night.

As I have said before, the sarcophagus, coffins, shrines and caskets had all to be made during the seventy days officially prescribed as the embalming period – a requirement which makes the feat all the more extraordinary.

By way of conclusion, one can say that the world had never seen such a spectacle as that presented by the tomb of Tutankhamun. When we think of the great hoard of unique treasures accumulated round a few shrivelled corpses in seven coffins, it is not difficult to believe that there is no spot on earth so rich in evidence of an ancient civilization reaching so far back in time. The world it reveals was the scene of glory and splendour, beauty and order – of bondage and horror also – dominated by a king who was only a tool in the hands of the priests.

Such was the land of Egypt, a land brought up in reverence

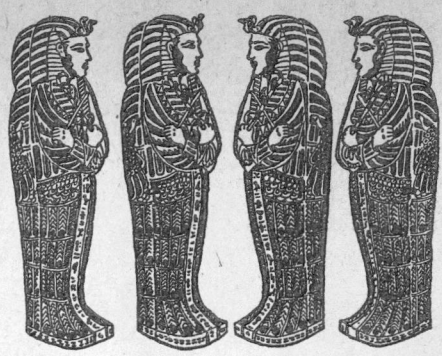

In the four canopic jars were four miniature coffins of pure gold containing the King's intestines. Each coffin is 16 ins. high and weighs over 30 lb.

for the gods and worship of ancestors, and where a fatalistic obedience was the rule of life. Pharaoh, cracking his whip, was lord of all. Thebes was his capital, the cradle of his hopes for salvation in the tomb. It was here that men laid away their dead, secure as they thought against the prying eyes of posterity. How wrong they were! Greedy thieves found them, and the modern humanistic archæologist has followed in their tracks and turned the god-king into a spectacle for tourists.

Tutankhamun died suddenly and his tomb must have been a comparative makeshift because, unlike his ancestors, he was not granted a reasonable life-time in which to prepare it. Yet if this astounding array of treasures was the result of hasty and makeshift arrangements, what must the tombs of the great pharaohs have been like, the tomb of Rameses the Great with its seven chambers, for instance, or that of Cleopatra? What was stored in the tombs with twelve and more chambers, or the tomb of Phiops with its thirty-one chambers or that of Seti I, the builder of the temple at Abydos, a tomb more than a hundred yards in length, dug in the solid rock? Here stone steps and corridors lead to a large chamber from which other steps and passages descend to a great hall, its roof supported by six immense columns, in which the superb alabaster sarcophagus rested. Frescoes and inscriptions quite as fine as those at Abydos adorned its walls. What a sight this tomb must have been in the days of its glory, judging by the modest tomb of Tutankhamun, with only four rooms and a mere 3,500 treasures!

Even primitive cave-dwellers put contemporary weapons and utensils in their graves and many of their descendants followed their examples. The Egyptians observed this custom for 4,700 years, every family enriching the dry earth with such gifts as its means and station in life permitted. In that period about one hundred and fifty million people were buried, so that it is hardly surprising that Egypt is the richest of all cemeteries and a positive paradise to the archæologist. It is a case of "dig and you will find!"

Of the 320 pharaohs, the tombs of between sixty and seven-

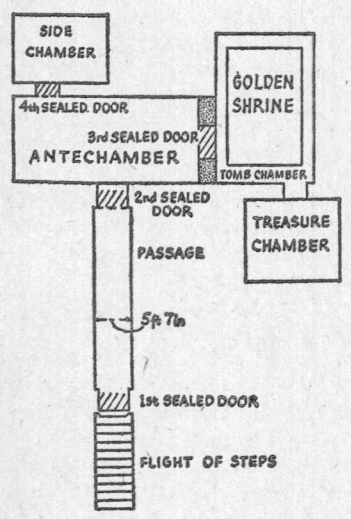

Plan of Tutankhamun's tomb
Dimensions:

Length of entrance passage	24 ft. 2 ins.
Antechamber	26 ft. x 11 ft. 8 ins.
Lateral chamber	13 ft. x 9½ ft.
Tomb chamber	20 ft. 8 ins. x 13 ft.
Treasure chamber	11 ft. 4 ins. x 12 ft. 10 ins.
Roof height	13 ft. 8 ins.
Total area	approximately 100 square yards

ty have been found. Where are the thousands of tombs of queens, princes and princesses, viziers, court officials, nobles and priests? Will they ever be found? Modern man may smile at the ancient Egyptians and their devotion to graves and gods, but it is doubtful whether he is justified in doing so.

Be that as it may, the work of excavation goes on. But nothing has been found comparable to Tutankhamun's tomb, which has contributed so much to historical knowledge and yet leaves so many problems unsolved. Though the ordinary reader may be astounded at the high level of civilization which it reveals, the expert knows that in the arts Egypt was already on the road to decadence.

It might be added that all the objects found in the tomb were handed over to the Cairo museum and have only recently been "on tour" to the great museums of the West. The private collector and the black-marketeer went empty away. The sarcophagus and mummy, however, were left *in situ* as a concession to respect for the dead.

Carter never produced a scientific work about his discovery, though one was planned. Professor Breasted, the great expert in Egyptian history, was to contribute the historical section, Carter and Mace a popular and inadequate account in the three-volume *Tutankhamun, an Egyptian Royal Tomb*.

The clearing of the tomb was complete in 1932. All Carter's notes, sketches and photographs are in England. A full description would fill ten volumes of five hundred pages each. Would anyone less than UNO be prepared to publish it?

Howard Carter was born in 1873 at Swaffham in Norfolk. In 1891 he paid his first visit to Egypt to assist Professor Newberry in surveying the tombs at Beni Hassan. Thereafter he devoted his life to Egypt and archæology. The achievements of this idealist are unique. He died on the 2nd March, 1939. The world owes him, and Lord Carnarvon also, a great debt of gratitude.

THE GOD OF THE LABYRINTH 40p
Colin Wilson

What has the most prolific of England's younger authors got into this time? Book-buyers have been waiting keenly for a new direction from Colin Wilson, and now they have it: "*The score up to page 50 is two sex experiences for the narrator, plus a whipping with a cat-o'-nine-tails which he gives on request to an eccentric colonel, plus several other sex fragments from the forged or genuine papers of Esmond Donelly, eighteenth century rake. This is roughly par for the 300-page course, with passages of Johnsonian pastiche and nutty mystical musing*" breathed the *Sunday Times*, while Janice Elliot of the *Sunday Telegraph* claimed "*the plentiful sex is never prurient: there are some mind-boggling performances (but) he talks a lot of sense*"; meanwhile the Sunday Sun raved on about "*a well-written book with lashings of sex – entertaining and informative.*"

Make up your own mind on this new line for Wilson (in fact an extension of his enquiry into existentialism and murder) by reading *The God of The Labyrinth* yourself. As the narrator says, "I have always been obsessed by the way that sexual experience seems to slip through the fingers like fairy gold."

THE MORNING OF THE MAGICIANS 50p

Louis Pauwels and Jacques Bergier

"Two theories were current in Nazi Germany: the theory of the *frozen world*, and the theory of the *hollow Earth*.

"These constitute two explanations of the world and humanity which link up with tradition: they even affected some of Hitler's military decisions, influenced the course of the war and doubtless contributed to the final catastrophe. It was through his enslavement to these theories, and especially the notion of the sacrificial deluge, that Hitler wished to condemn the entire German race to annihilation."

The incredible yet highly regarded theories of the frozen world and the hollow Earth have never before been expounded in this country. They are two amongst many such theories, including for example man's evolution towards some kind of mutant superman, that have remained secret and hidden in Britain while gaining strong popular support elsewhere. Now a new awareness is growing in our minds, and much of our new understanding we owe to this famous book and its two intrepid authors. Their interpretation of human affairs, very different from that put forward by ordinary historians and commentators on day-to-day events, is much nearer to the unexpressed instincts of the people.

THOSE ABOUT TO DIE 30p
Daniel P. Mannix

"He started forward toward the melee, blood from his wounded side filling up the footprints made by his right foot as he staggered on. The armed *venator* and the spearman exchanged looks. The crowd was shouting, 'No Carpophorus, no!' But Carpophorus paid no attention to them. He was going to get another tiger or die trying."

This infamous but completely factual book tells the story of the Roman Games, where two armies of 5,000 men fought to the death in a show lit at night by human torches. It was the costliest, cruellest spectacle of all time. And hundreds of thousands still crave to satisfy their curiosity about the sport every year – *Those About to Die* is a constantly reprinting bestseller. No other title gives the full facts and paints such a realistic scene: this is an all-the-way book about man's greatest aberration.

TOM BROWN'S SCHOOLDAYS
35p

Thomas Hughes

"As on the one hand it should ever be remembered that we are boys, and boys at school, so on the other hand we must bear in mind that we form a complete social body ... a society in which, by the nature of the case, we must not only learn, but act and live; and act and live not only as boys, but as boys who will be men."

A public school in the nineteenth century was a microcosm of a world that the middle-classes of the twentieth century have embraced as a model of prudent, if prudish, society. Reflected in it is every man's dream of England at the height of her power – confident, sure, brash, brutal and oppressive. Television and film revivals of this famous classic bear witness in their popularity to the atavistic pull that the period and the place of Dr. Arnold's Rugby have for the general public. Thomas Hughes' book is a thrilling, virile and humane evocation of England's greatness and also of the seeds of her decline.